THE AUTO-ETHNOG
TURN IN DESI

CONTRIBUTORS

Anna Aagaard Jensen
Gijs Assmann
Bruno Baietto
Jurgen Bey
Joel Blanco
Théophile Blandet
Jan Boelen
Hsin Min Chan
Chongjin Chen
Meghan Clarke
Adelaide Di Nunzio
Billy Ernst
Hi Kyung Eun
Teresa Fernández-Pello
Andrea Gaspar
Konstantin Grcic
Metincan Güzel
Jing He
Aurelie Hoegy
Michael Kaethler
Hicham Khalidi
Žan Kobal
Lorraine Legrand
Gabriel .A. Maher
Micheline Nahra
Thomas Nathan
Miguel Parrrra
Timo de Rijk
Marie Rime
Sjeng Scheijen
Bianca Schick
Louise Schouwenberg
Carlos Sfeir Vottero
Weixiao Shen/申薇笑
Matilde Stolfa
Irene Stracuzzi
Oli Stratford
Marianne Theunissen
Goda Verikaitė
Erik Viskil
Barbara Visser
Ben Shai van der Wal

THE AUTO-ETHNOGRAPHIC

Louise Schouwenberg
& Michael Kaethler (eds.)

TURN

IN DESIGN

Valiz, Amsterdam

Contents

PROJECTS AND PRACTICES

IDEAS AND DIALOGUES

IDEAS   AND

DIALOGUES

The Auto-Ethnographic Turn in Design

Michael Kaethler and Louise Schouwenberg

The auto-ethnographic turn in design is emerging from a growing recognition of design's capacity to make sense of one's world while at the same time expressing this world in rich, layered, and ultimately meaningful processes or objects. This approach closely tethers research with creative personal expression—forging deeply intimate objects that research *and* communicate personal sentiments, traumas, fears, obsessions, hopes, fascinations, passions, and more. In doing so, auto-ethnographic design resists the temptation of solutionism and the spectre of pragmatism in order to remain at the fusion of research and expression, providing critical commentary, deep insights, and elaborations on particular social material relations.

The practice of auto-ethnography first developed within anthropology and sociology in the nineteen-seventies and has recently gained considerable traction, shifting the orientation of research from distant to personal, from objective to subjective. Ellis and Bochner define it as '...an autobiographical genre of writing that displays multiple layers of consciousness, connecting the personal to the cultural.'[1] This typically entails a radical re-centring: from studying the 'exotic other' and their worlds to studying the world that the researcher themself inhabits—the space or culture which one regularly dwells and knows from the inside out. As such, it deals with revealing deeply personal reflections of our human experiences in the world vis-à-vis the self.

The auto (or 'I'/'self') in auto-ethnographic design situates the designer at the heart of the research—the swarm of subjectivity, memory, intuition, exchange, and so on (this could be reflecting on the past or looking into one's current experiences)—exploring the self through materiality and accepting the vulnerability that comes with the unpredictable. This implies working within the unknown of where the process might lead. The ethno (culture) can be understood as the culture of design and broader cultural realm. Lastly, the 'graphy,' which implies writing or reporting, can be interpreted as the

---

1   Carolyn Ellis and Art Bochner, "Autoethnography, Personal Narrative, Reflexivity: Researcher as Subject," in *Handbook of Qualitative Research* (2nd ed.), eds. Norman K. Denzin and Yvonna S. Lincoln (Thousand Oaks, California: Sage Publications, 2000), p. 739.

materialization or modes of capturing and documenting the friction between the self and culture—committing form to an idea. There is a break here between the auto-ethnographic tradition and how it is taken up in design, where for the 'graphy' the act of reporting and reflection is replaced by creative production; design activates the knowledge component by directly engaging and altering the very world it seeks to make sense of.

The process and objects that emerge from auto-ethnographic design are embedded with new knowledge, perspective, and insight.[2] Auto-ethnography gives an authority to the designer as someone with something to say and a means to say it, rather than as an individual translating their desires towards externalities, which we find in so many design practices (design as an outward act as opposed to a meditative and inward form of creative and expressive research). Such an approach to design fosters aspects that are personal, emotional, and existential rather than merely practical. Personal experiences are not only something in the past to be explored but also the present; one's current self can be made vulnerable through this by accepting the surprises of what can emerge when it foregrounds the designer as the author, speaking about their world and accepting personal responsibility or taking ownership over what is produced—its implicit and explicit meanings, references, and agency.

This book highlights an important turn within design that resists the need for solutionism or the focus on pragmatic externalities and instead operationalizes design practices and traditions to explore deeply personal experiences and translate these into material forms. This we argue offers a sincerity and genuine commitment often missing in design, because it is rooted in one's own fascinations and concerns and is not ensnared by commercial commissions, assumed users' needs, or well-intentioned do-goodism. In this book, we seek to explore and raise awareness of this important contribution to the design tradition: valorizing this approach as a unique form of knowledge production within design as well as in the auto-ethnographic tradition.

2   Allan J. Munro, "Autoethnography as a Research Method in Design Research at Universities," *20/20 Design Vision* no. 156 (2011).

Self-Oriented, Self-Reflexive

Auto-ethnography asks the researcher to interrogate themselves and to deconstruct their own discourse and practices, ultimately bringing their privilege and perspective into question.[3] This results in deeply reflective, subjective, and personal explorations. By accentuating the personal, the body is foregrounded and the self becomes the lens through which to understand the social and cultural realm. Reed-Danahay defines auto-ethnography as 'a form of self-narrative that places the self within a social context.'[4] In doing so, the researcher finds that the self cannot be separated from culture but is a means to understand, participate in, and modify it.

Marie Rime's 'La Désalpe. Traditions as an Ever-Evolving Search for Collective Experience and Transformation' (pp. 164–169), for example, looks at how the tradition of La Désalpe (herding the cows from the Alpine meadows down to the valley) shaped her notion of identity and how this in turn has fed into how she approaches her design work—playing with the liquidity of traditions through re-interpreting visual or material elements. In 'The Not-So-Passive Observer: Occupying the Party Salon' (pp. 230–239), Bruno Baietto shows how his design work emerges out of childhood experiences of being a constant observer of various pageantries occurring in a party salon that occupied the second floor of his family house. His design is embedded in his particular insight as an observer, watching as this space could be radically transformed to suit the desires of a group of people, their hopes, dreams, and wishes mediated through a series of props, sounds, decorations. His design work links back to his childhood, to the spaces that unveiled to him the macabre pageantry that disguises ideology.

Auto-ethnography puts personal experience before methodology and theories, prioritizing the act of articulating experience (intuition and creative

3   Sally Denshire, "On Auto-Ethnography," *Current Sociology* 62, no. 6 (2014), pp. 831–850.
4   Deborah Reed-Danahay, *Auto/ethnography* (New York: Berg, 1997), p. 9.

engagement) in material forms before filtering it through these rational aspects; it is disinterested in impartiality or conventional modes of knowledge production. In this pairing of research and expression, auto-ethnography transcends the objectivizing gaze on 'otherness' that has permeated Western research traditions for centuries. By situating it in the practice of design, auto-ethnography gains additional media and practices of cultural research and self-expression that have hitherto been inaccessible to social science researchers. Additionally, the act of self-interrogation need not only be a theoretical or literary act but one that is tangible, hands-on, and embedded in the deeply tacit relationship between the self and materiality, which forms its own generative language. This turn from research-as-reflection to research-as-creative generation is an important distinction. As Michael Kaethler points out on pp. 48–59 ('Dancing Dirty on the Fringes: The Auto-Ethnographic Turn in Design'), this distinction is a fundamental reason for design to be recognized as a key site for auto-ethnographic research, which doesn't just describe what 'is' but actively alters the present.

Communicating Personal and Intimate Research

Auto-ethnography's emphasis on the personal perspective for knowledge production has stretched how research is communicated, breaking from the dry analytical texts that have populated many academic libraries. We contend that material expressions in the form of design research can parry these dominant modes of representation and their associated narratives, while offering novel and unique viewpoints on matters of concern that were previously ignored or disregarded as excessively subjective. We see the coupling of design research with creative expression as a powerful form of auto-ethnography—one that is highly communicative and engaged with actively altering the world; where research doesn't remain in the plain of the intellect but in physically grappling with the world. A materially-oriented auto-ethnography does not rely on language, with all its cultural baggage, structural limitations, and syntactic restrictions; instead, it uses the same medium that it studies to express itself, unifying what is researched and communicated and bypassing the need for translation. In other words, design auto-ethnography not only looks at our experiences with the material world but also uses that same material world for expression. This is an important distinction. The chapters in Section 2, for instance, are auto-ethnographic in two ways: 1) the design projects are auto-ethnographic material works and 2) the texts accompanying some of the designs are auto-ethnographic. Both are auto-ethnographic, but we are interested in how specific acts of material transformation can be auto-ethnographic and what this means for specific design practices and for understanding and valorizing such intimate, personal, and creative design as a valid and insightful form of research.

Sidestepping the dominant modes of realist representation, the auto-ethnographic turn in design has led to unusual, surreal, fictional, and fantastic forms of expression and researching oneself and one's context. For example, Miguel Parrrra's 'How to Scare an Octopus. Suggestions to Rewrite a Family Recipe' (pp. 142–147) re-designs his grandmother's recipe for octopus, splicing the original recipe with his own family interpretations and sensual desires, and in so doing, concocting a new (quite saucy) relationship with, and interpretation of, his grandmother, as well as a new family narrative. This opens up how we might frame our realities, alter our trajectory, and ultimately complexify received binaries (such as male/female, straight/ gay, young/old, or also within the design field such as maker/user, producer/consumer, designer/artist, writer/ designer)—thereby unlocking categories of thought and action.

Pushing the Boundaries of Knowledge Production

Auto-ethnography is sometimes framed as a fomenting methodology, one that offers up accounts of life that trouble the dominant representations of society but in the process, providing new accounts and creating new forms of knowledge. For instance, auto-ethnography has opened up how we understand such experiences as grief, sexual trauma, inter-generational strife, class, disability, and other such vulnerable and intimate experiences that are both deeply personal and yet also social phenomena. Auto-ethnographic design pushes research to engage in these intimate areas that involve difficult knowledge to access, whether deeply subconscious, tacit, or embodied. To do this means bringing the body into the act of research: the self also becomes the body-self,[5] incorporating the body as a place of research as well as the research vessel itself. For example, Billy Ernst's poetic account of binary thinking on sexuality in conservative Boer South Africa (pp. 222–229, 'Upon a Rusted Fence: Veld, Sexuality, and the Desire to be Touched') looks at the body through the language and realities of fences that separate and divide, quartering our bodies. His design work renders fences that appeal to the body: they are supple, malleable, and flexible, tempting the observer to come closer, to cross through them, folding and twisting their own bodies as well as social or cultural binaries. This work translates personal experiences and knowledge into powerful, communicative, cultural research bounded up in objects.

Challenging the Tendency towards Solutionism

An auto-ethnographic approach to design recognizes the designer's intuition as a creative force that carries with it a far greater potential for meaningful change than conventional approaches, which stay subservient to the logic of the market or pretentious external ideals for 'saving' the world, and which inadvertently contribute to the well-known problems of overconsumption or overproduction. The auto-ethnographic trend forestalls this tendency towards solutionism by inhabiting the space of the

18

5   Denshire, "On Auto-Ethnography.", see note 3.

personal and intimate. As such, there is no need to step beyond communicating the problem such as by installing or feigning pragmatic motivations or justifications within the design process. This does not mean that the projects remain isolated at the personal level, as many so-called design-art projects of the nineties (expensive limited editions for a luxury market), but that the design intention is first and foremost encapsulated at this intimate juncture of the self-in-the-world, a self that is aware of and responsible for how it relates to the world. What may emerge, whether material or otherwise, are powerful reflections, statements, enquiries, concerns, and so forth that can challenge or enlarge views on our social and human condition. It starts at the intimate and works outwards.

This focus on designing *from* and *through* the self opens up the space for a sincere, poetic, sensible, and subtle form of design to emerge and remain sheltered from the self-censorship and violence that occurs when translating objects or outputs for externalities such as the market, critical or political statements, or for social impact.

On one hand, auto-ethnographic design borrows from approaches such as relational, speculative, critical, and social design; on the other hand, it breaks from these by resisting the pragmatic knee-jerk response to focus the act of designing on externalities—be it a design brief, a market niche, or a social or political issue. This challenges some of the fundamentals of certain design practices and questions how we evaluate and assess design projects. For instance, the design process doesn't start with a problem or issue to address but rather a tension to explore—one that may remain deeply personal or be materialized in abstract or symbolic material formulations. The poetic and intuitive as well as the artistic and expressive modes of design are given greater precedence over the functional, pragmatic, or serviceable. This can be seen in designing speculative Chinese bathrooms (pp. 202–209, 'From a White Bathroom to Envisioning an Alternative Modernity' by Weixiao Shen), meditative tableware (pp. 130–135, 'I Am How I Make' by Thomas Nathan) or performing the stickiness of data (pp. 114–123, 'Sticky Data. Looping Streams of My (Datafied) Self' by Bianca Schick).

The Genesis and Justification of the Book

A Very Personal Genesis

This book emerges out of the body of work and educational practices of Louise Schouwenberg. While this form of design is not exclusive to her work, she has been highly instrumental in developing a cadre of students and professionals who have pushed and stretched design in this direction. Many of the chapters in this book, especially in Section 2, are written by authors whose practices have been directly shaped by the guidance of Schouwenberg and her team of tutors at Design Academy Eindhoven's MA programme in Contextual Design. The conversations in the sections 'Ideas and Dialogues' include a wide variety of influential figures in design education and practice, many of whom have been instrumental in Schouwenberg's trajectory—be they interlocutors, co-creators, or intellectual sparring partners. Michael Kaethler's research on the fringes of design led to a growing interest in Schouwenberg's work and in how to understand it as a specific mode of knowledge production.

Drawing from our personal and academic experiences, as well as input from a wide variety of thinkers from both the design and ethnographic world, we developed the notion of the auto-ethnographic turn in design. This taxonomy, we found, was a useful way of engaging with a whole series of projects that often remain in a sort of no-man's land between art and design. In giving shape, form, and a name to this phenomenon, we are interested in re-orienting design away from some simulated notion of 'the other,' which has been a central aspect of design for centuries. Building on this, we explore what this new orientation offers as a critical lens for design practice and knowledge production.

Re-orienting Design away from the Other

As mentioned above, for too long design has served, often unquestioningly, various masters, such as the market, industry, politics, or some notion of social good. In the process, design has been extended as a creative act for serving 'the other.' Design has thus often become an act of materializing 'otherness,' a form of re-affirming a certain cultural class's (the designer class) notion of the 'other.' What this book explores is the shift from this 'other' to the self, where the self becomes worthy of exploration as both the site and vessel for design. In doing so, the designer is not trapped in a formulation of what type of chair or lamp they might desire but rather is able to speak from their own personal experiences; they use design to understand their world, desires, and experiences, and articulate outwards from that world through a vantage point of material and cultural entanglements. This re-orients design away from grand gestures and towards the sensible, modest, personal, and accountable form of making.

Through binding research, expression, and one's own personal exploration, design can play a crucial role of sense making, of interpreting and communicating the worlds that we live. In a world that is increasingly complex, layered, and evolving, design then has a critical role in not only augmenting this (as it currently does) but rather also in unpacking it to explore it and understand what it means for individuals or groups on a very personal level.

21

Structure of the Book

This book is not a theoretical analysis on auto-ethnography but rather an exploration of this turn in design. The text is divided in two main themes, 'Ideas and Dialogues' and 'Projects and Practices'. 'Projects and Practices' combine personal narratives, contexts, ideas, and objects through images and short expressive texts that exemplify different forms of auto-ethnographic design. These are the inspiration for the book and are thus situated in its centre, acting as the pivot point for the Ideas and Dialogues, which attempt to make sense of these practices and projects, untangle them, grapple with them, and reflect on what they might mean for design practice, theory, education, and research.

Ideas and Dialogues

Different essays and conversations are brought together under this theme to triangulate and frame the auto-ethnographic turn in design. The ideas here provide a loose frame, giving the 'turn' space to be what it is without overly defining, flattening, or reducing it to simply an historical formulation or reductive cultural classification. To keep the framing wide, we have established a constellation of essays and conversations that help enunciate different aspects of the auto-ethnographic turn, whether through analysis, conjecture or dialogue. For essays, this includes situating this turn within personal reflections in design education (Louise Schouwenberg), design practice (Gabriel .A. Maher), photography (Adelaide Di Nunzio), anthropology in general, and design anthropology in particular (Andrea Gaspar), Russian avant-garde design (Sjeng Scheijen), cinema studies (Erik Viskil), and generative epistemologies (Michael Kaethler). The dialogues, which are interspersed between the essays, make good use of the exploratory nature of the book, bringing together a wide variety of differing viewpoints on this turn and on what it means for design as a field, as a practice, and as part of design education. Here, important questions are raised addressing dimensions such as: what the intrinsic value of design is, how to foster a self-oriented form of design practice, how one's own personal experiences can be of value to broader portions of the public, how experienced designers grapple with questions of authorship, what designing for the 'other' means for one's understanding of the self... We have included artists (Marianne Theunissen, Barbara Visser, Gijs Assmann), designers (Konstantin Grcic), educators (Jurgen Bey, Jan Boelen), curators (Hicham Khalidi, Timo de Rijk), journalists (Oli Stratford), and philosophers (Ben Shai van der Wal). The dialogues range considerably in size and style, bringing out critical issues about this turn.

Projects and Practices

The central core of the book are the practices that have led this turn in design. It provides a glimpse at a range of practices by up-and-coming designers that we have collaborated with and who fit within the auto-ethnographic turn. The chapters in this section vary in length, style, and focus. In some cases, we wanted the full auto-ethnographic story in both writing and images; in other cases, we asked for images to do the bulk of the story-telling. These chapters are personal, poetic, and thoughtful accounts of how design emerges from the self and helps us respond to and make sense of our contexts. The chapters deal with a range of issues, from big cultural questions of national identity, family histories, the intimacies of landscape, to how one deals with insecurities at social gatherings. It is a rich collection of fascinating and inspiring projects. The projects are not organized according to any logic, presenting the reader with a collection of projects to wander and wade through.

23

Ask for Forgiveness, Not Permission[1]

Louise Schouwenberg

She wore two different socks and couldn't care less whether we noticed. Mind you, in my high school years this was not a fashion statement. Her choice of socks, as well as her habit of resting her feet on another chair, revealed her indifference towards people's opinion of her, and one could easily sense that this was more than simple nonchalance. My Dutch Language and Literature high school teacher exuded a spirit of rejection towards the proper codes of conduct for women in those days, and of the school's rules on how a teacher should teach and behave. She personified the proverbial middle finger to bourgeois conventions. Her pupils were slightly intimidated by her behaviour, but I was most of all fascinated. Mesmerized. Even more so when her air of indifference would suddenly subside as she started to speak about literature. Her eyes sparkling and her tone impassioned, she would elaborate on the beauty of formulations, the sincerity and depth of feelings, the wealth of an author's insights on the idiosyncrasies, fragility, or downright nonsense of human existence.

I can vividly recall her speaking about Cornélie, the female protagonist of *Langs Lijnen van Geleidelijkheid* (1900) by Dutch novelist Louis Couperus.[2] Cornélie is a divorcee who writes a pamphlet against marriage and engages in various affairs with men, unconcerned with how her actions are perceived as scandalous by her early twentieth-century European contemporaries. This posture of female autonomy would also have been considered a disgrace in my times. Many years later, I understood how this strong female character that freely experimented with an emancipated independent life mirrored my high school teacher, and I also started to recognize the author's subtle hints at his homosexuality, which he largely kept hidden. In those high school years, I was fascinated by

1 Sean Fisher, first-year student of Contextual Design, wrote this sentence as his 2021 'Design Manifesto.' He took the sentence from filmmaker Werner Herzog's great list of advice—a list that, by the way, matches what we aimed for at our programme. I use it as the title of this chapter to refer to my continued effort to fight censorship and precooked morality, and to make a plea for freedom and for following one's artistic intuition. One stipulation is in place: I would not ask for permission, but would probably not ask for forgiveness either…

2 A literal translation of *Langs Lijnen van Geleidelijkheid* is 'Along the Lines of Graduality.' In 2005, the English translation of the novel was released as *Inevitable*. Remarkably, from my initial reading of Couperus' novel, I mainly remembered the protagonist's strong character and unconventional lifestyle, not the slightly disappointing ending. When I recently reread the novel, I discovered that financial problems had driven Cornélie back into the arms of her wealthy ex-husband. The liberated woman was tamed after all. It makes one wonder whether Couperus would have written a different ending many decades later.

my teacher (which in all likelihood had some erotic undertones for me), by the novel's protagonist, and by its gay author, but I could not fully explain what I felt. One thing was clear: I was enchanted by what these characters and their behaviours caused in me, which was no less than an opening up of the limited horizon of my lower middle-class milieu. My troubled teenage mind was liberated from the claustrophobic petty conventions of the times, and it felt as if I had received permission to acknowledge the hypocrisy that surrounded us in a school led by Catholic nuns. At least, this is how I recall it; I was thrilled to receive confirmation of my growing doubts about the lives we lived and thrilled about the imaginative wordings that gave an unexpected poetical shine to reality. Literature soothed the pains of existence. The woman who first acquainted me with its power showed me the importance of being true to oneself and she demonstrated how the imagination can offer an excellent way out from suffocating circumstances.

As long as I can recall, I have felt an urge—an obsession even—to escape from claustrophobic situations, regardless of whether these concern surviving an elevator ride, finding the exit in a building, breaking out of an official meeting, leaving a party unnoticed, or fleeing from my family bonds. When I was young, the *real* was not desirable; or to put it more bluntly: life was shit. Escaping from the more serious traps, such as social class and bourgeois conventions, would become my life ambition and I would do so by trusting my gut feelings, conjuring up fantastical worlds, embracing peculiar and dangerous people, and acknowledging and accepting the precariousness of life. I would become the bold protagonist in my life's novel, as well as its reckless author, and fantasy would be my means of escape.

Why would a personal anecdote be of any interest to the readers of a book on the auto-ethnographic turn in design? Why would personal gossip be a good means to clarify the choices I made when setting up an educational design programme that has fostered a certain approach to design? Because personal experiences matter in developing a practice that requires genuine engagement with the world, be it the practice of an artist, for whom the auto-ethnographic approach usually comes natural, the practice of a designer, or that of an educator. In this chapter, I reflect on my twenty years of work as a design educator, recounting some of the influences and stimuli that led me to adopt this approach to design. I want to show how design is not an objectively executed act but a deeply personal one that emerges from an intimate understanding of the world. I argue that a designer must not only research external questions and aim for instrumental answers, however urgent these may seem, but *also* research their own position vis-à-vis the topics they implicitly and explicitly address. Making sense of the world by way of design starts with the designer's self. If there's any place where relying on personal experiences is important, it's in design education. Learning to position oneself at an early age, finding a distinct voice, and daring to formulate personal ideals for the world, is paramount in a field that is haunted by conventions and numerous ways of hiding behind external questions.

From a Trade-off with the Market to Personal Exploration

27

The inextricable, reciprocal relationships of things and humans make design of paramount importance—it gives shape to our world and to ourselves. However, design has struggled to live up to this immense responsibility; a plethora of pointless objects has polluted the world as 'design' in the past decades, simply because there is a market for them, or because a market was created or opened up specifically for them (such as the art market for limited editions in design). The simple question uttered by Tolstoy so long ago, 'How, then, shall we live?' has today been left to the marketeers who usually base their decisions on 'what sells.' The prospect of financial profit has thus become the driving force behind most innovations in design. The rest is history; consumer society has taken its toll on all levels. Already for some decades, the relationships between people and things have been impaired. Once new versions of

ASK FOR FORGIVENESS, NOT PERMISSION

LOUISE SCHOUWENBERG

perfectly functioning items are launched, the old ones disappear in the garbage bin only to end up in the ocean, clustered as a cynically colourful plastic soup. In design schools, it has become a well-known grim joke to exclaim: 'We design for the landfill.' Now in the twenty-first century, we face the devastating environmental consequences of overconsumption and overproduction and are unable to deal with the resulting waste. One day, hardly noticing it, we became accustomed to the idea that 'humans' had become 'users,' and shortly after 'consumers' (maybe we should now define ourselves as 'polluters'?).

Design never had a particular appeal to me. My real interest, and education, was in art and philosophy. I detested design's entanglement with boundless consumerism and overproduction, its superficiality; most of all, I detested the inflated verbiage by which people are so cunningly seduced to want what they don't need. But should the allegations of overconsumption and overproduction be heaped onto the designer's plate? Can we hold designers accountable, given that they are usually merely answering in the best way possible to clear briefs for specific products? I tend to think we can. Whoever engages in a discipline better have an idea of its scope and influence. Therefore, I wholeheartedly embraced the self-reflective, critical responses of designers at the forefront of the field, such as the Italian radicals of the sixties and seventies and the Dutch conceptualists of the eighties and nineties. Both movements questioned design with tongue-in-cheek DIY projects and offered insight into the larger importance of daily objects and the layered messages that hide beneath their surfaces. However, such critical voices could only be heard on the fringes of the design field and within the design programmes of art academies, where students were encouraged to not wait for commercial briefs but initiate their own projects. The big players in design are still the technical inventors and designers of mass-produced consumer products, mostly educated at technical universities that continue to rely on scientific statistics and psychological reports on consumer behaviour and preferences. If one doesn't step out of a system, looking at the larger picture of how design functions and *might* function, a design practice will abide

28

with the market's relentless urge to produce novelty for
novelty's sake and only when forced by consumers will it
reflect on producing things slightly more sustainably.
In their times, the radical and conceptual designs were great, but
they did not change the design discipline itself. Gradually, the
conceptual messages, many of which were simplistically moralistic (harassing the user as in 'you should make an effort before
using this product'), started to suffer from their readability and
from being repeated in many guises. In the past few decades,
they have been overhauled by the more serious efforts of social
design and design to research larger problems, including the
problems that are caused by designers in the first place. Some
of these attempts suffer from being pre-cooked moral precepts,
unwilling to engage in a truly open debate. But there are also
very interesting initiatives, such as those that recognize and
forcefully oppose forms of hostile design that only grant specific
groups access to public space and thereby prevent a truly inclusive society. Or the relatively recent proposal to view, and place,
human beings and all other creatures—living and non-living—
on an equal level by erasing the usual hierarchies. Through these
proposals and initiatives, new insights are gained on the necessity of taking care of the planet and its inhabitants.   29

> By now, many designers have confronted their larger
> responsibilities; many pamphlets, books, and symposia
> on the need for sustainable materials and production
> methods have seen the light of day. What's particularly
> good about these new insights is that they have not
> merely entered the design programmes of art academies
> but also those of technical universities.

Apart from the question of how effective and innovative these
new efforts are, or the observation that many projects remain
merely demonstrations of good intentions, all these initiatives—
on both ends of design's spectrum—are characterized by a per-
vasive and problematic use of inflated and pretentious language.
Regardless of whether slogans reveal a product's purported comfort, beauty, or even its sustainable use of materials, or whether a
text speaks of the high ambition to save the world from a variety
of crises, the pretences fly sky high and evoke a sense of being
fooled by dishonest verbiage. No matter how promising these are,
many seem to suffer from the same pitfall, which resides in designers approaching research questions as outsiders, not as insiders.

When by coincidence I started to teach design students in the early two thousands, I trusted my gut feeling that something massively important was missing in most design practices. This 'something,' I came to conclude, was the lack of responsibility being taken by designers for the whole narrative that hides in each design project. The missing link has nothing to do with legal or financial accountability, but with a tendency of no longer asking questions. Design's impact is way too important to leave to marketeers and too important to settle for preaching to the converted in closed bubbles of likeminded creatives in the vanguards or fringes of the field. Regardless of whether it concerns a dinner service, a couch, signpost, public bench, or a cell phone—all things represent a worldview, a view on humanity, a view on who will profit, who is being welcomed to a specific part of public space, an awareness (or lack of awareness) of a design's meanings and implications. In most design projects, I miss the genuine engagement of designers with the topics they pretend to address. Underneath the smooth veneer of marketing language, good intentions, and unprovable assertions, one can easily suspect different agendas, including the sleazy agenda of striving for profit only. For many, the trade-off with the market, which defines the majority of projects, may seem unavoidable. But if we want to change anything, as I think we should, the change should start from oneself. To support this shift towards the personal, we need to recalibrate design education.

(Re)designing Design Education

'I don't think many designers employ the full potential of their discipline,' says artist Marianne Theunissen (see p. 110). I wholeheartedly agree. In 2015, designer Hella Jongerius and I composed the manifesto *Beyond the New*, in which we critiqued design's never-ending production of novelty for novelty's sake. Apart from the fun (I admit) of stepping on sensitive toes and evoking debate, it was also an effort to rock the foundations of this cultural domain, which probably is the most important one—at least the most influential one. From products to strategies, the potential of design does not merely reside in functional objects solving daily problems or facilitating the comfortable lives we want to lead, nor do designs only mark the cultural, social, and technological reality of their times as passive recorders of the *Zeitgeist*. Things form widely branching networks with each other. Although companies benefit from dealing with separate things, none of them stands in isolation once they find their homes in houses, offices, or even museums. Things and the manner in which they relate to other things define how people act, move, communicate with each other; how they experience and relate to their surrounding contexts; and how they relate to the world at large. Not only is design immensely influential in shaping our material world but also the social and personal. In other words, we shape designs and vice versa—design shapes us.

What does this mean for design education? It is somewhere in the messy dialectical relationship of shaping design or being shaped by design that we begin to see through the facades of aesthetics, functionality, etc., and begin to unpack the various intricacies of design. Most things we use on a daily basis disappear from consciousness, as they humbly fulfil their roles, whereas other things demand attention through their beauty, traces of refined craftsmanship, the explicit moral messages they communicate, their shrieking colours, or their ugliness or brokenness. In fact, in all designs, references, and meanings hide that exude their effects on how we experience the world. In all designs and clusters of designs, directives for behaviour hide, even if we fail to notice them. Design is thus always unavoidably characterized by an inherent friction of being there and *not* being there, whereas its effects will be sensed no matter what. It's this friction that makes this field such a challenging and interesting one.

When setting up the Master's programme Contextual Design at Design Academy Eindhoven, my team of tutors and I worked with the tension of what is 'there' and what is 'not there' by pointing out the various implicit meanings and references that hide in functional objects, including their materiality and the

31

techniques by which they are produced. We placed emphasis on students' ability to work with such references rather than simply producing nice things. Furthermore, we asked questions on how meanings related to the assumed functionality of objects and the contexts for which they were intended. I soon discovered that having a love-hate relationship with a field is an excellent starting point for trying to redefine what design education can do. We did not merely step into a field and accept its conventions, but questioned everything from the very start. To be sure, I would never have accepted the role of head of a Master's programme in design had I not first discovered the true importance of design and acquired a deep love for excellent, beautiful, and thought-provoking specimens of innovative design projects.

Identifying Auto-Ethnography, Allocating the Self

I consider the true potential of design to reside in its possibility to make sense of the world and to understand and cope with life's challenges and demanding circumstances, all of which foreground the designer. To underscore the designer's personal positioning, my team of tutors and I spoke of authorship, which was not taken in its narrow interpretation of personal 'stardom' or 'signature design' (both of which are mere marketing strategies) but in the truer conception of authorship as accepting 'ownership' for the whole story, down to the product's afterlife. As such, we considered design a practice of cultural critique, which for design education implied that we encouraged students to step out of the system, time and again, and look at the larger picture of how design functions and how it might function ideally, and where they were positioned accordingly. We stressed the importance of designers formulating their own agendas and ideals, and of basing these on personal interests and artistic talents. As a result, the programme became known for its relatedness with autonomous art, viewing the designer not as the professional who merely works in the service of some external commissioner and answering briefs. I considered the autonomy and freedom of the artist an excellent means for designers to rethink the true potential of their field. Mind you, I was well aware that many designers borrow from the art field when it comes to beauty and the sculptural qualities of objects, and aware that many strive for a similar recognition for their creations (aiming for presentations in museums, attention from the art media, and acquisitions by art collectors). But that's scratching the surface and is not what I mean when I propose designers taking lessons from art. By embracing an autonomous approach to design, designers will better understand their personal agenda and positioning. Also important in this context: good art is by necessity subversive, going against the grain of conventions, whereas conventional design tends to affirm deeply ingrained societal conventions. If designers dare to also create subversive designs as self reflective, critical conversation pieces or speculative scenarios, this will open up many unexploited possibilities.

To challenge students' critical and autonomous reflections on design, we exposed students throughout the programme to that which seems obvious but easily forgotten: how each manmade thing, and each designed strategy, is a node in a network of relationships with other people, things, contexts. Questions were asked such as: Which experiences are invited by this particular design? Which views on people's vulnerability, craziness, or spiritual and intellectual power are mirrored by this intervention? Which conventional morality hides in its aesthetics? What larger narrative is implied by this design's purported functionality? We asked students to make their research questions very personal, since we expected deep commitment, well-informed, and surprising knowledge in the projects; we also encouraged them to make the answers both personal and artistic, to add imagination, poetry and beauty to their projects. We challenged them to let their imagination fly high beyond the familiar and conventional. I can recall one of the tutors saying time and again: 'While working on this research question, try to give both a 'normal' answer *and* a hysterical one, in which you test the limits of your guts and imagination.'

As can be expected, the hysterical outcomes became the more compelling ones.

The programme attracted many original minds, people who were already authors before starting the programme. One example is the French student Théophile Blandet. Upon entering the programme, his portfolio contained a wealth of fantastic ideas and expressive designs that merely needed deepening and further development. Throughout his studies, he searched for the extremities of his talents while embracing his personal obsessions, one of which was the simultaneous experience of the volatile endless World Wide Web producing copious amounts of both knowledge and nonsense, and the here and now of how we experience the world via our bodies. In 'Fountain of Knowledge' (see images), thick smears of paint, painted in the well-known amateur Bob Ross style, cover the window to the digital world, thus freezing the screen, just as we become frozen in the face of the sheer volume of the Internet's omniscience spilling out of our screens.

At the end of my time in Design Academy Eindhoven, looking back at what we did, I now consider both authorship and auto-ethnography valuable terms to define what we aimed for. Both terms agree with the aim of educating designers to have their own agendas and being able to use their artistic talents to make expressive translations of their ideas and wild imaginations. Auto-ethnography adds to the notion of authorship the idea that putting all trust on personal experiences and gut feelings will encourage an even more genuine engagement as well as a more specific and informed knowledge from within. Whereas authorship is included in auto-ethnography, it's not always the other way round: not all authorship is characterized by an auto-ethnographic research into personal experiences.

Personally, I make a plea for all designers to embrace authorship, as I think it's paramount to take a distinct and outspoken personal position. I agree with Konstantin Grcic (pp. 80–87), who thinks that *not* taking a position is problematic in design. Even collaborations benefit from strong dialogues, and thus strong individual

1–4　Théophile Blandet, *Fountain of Knowledge*, 2017.
Théophile Blandet has always been fascinated by the simultaneous experience of the volatile and endless World Wide Web (producing copious amounts of both knowledge and nonsense) and the here and now of how we experience the world via our bodies. The theme informed his graduation research which he called *Fountain of Knowledge*. In a variety of projects (each with their own title), thick smears of paint are applied in the well-known amateur Bob Ross style and cover the window to the digital world. The painted images freeze the screen just as the sheer volume of the Internet's omniscience freezes us (as it spills from our screens).

34

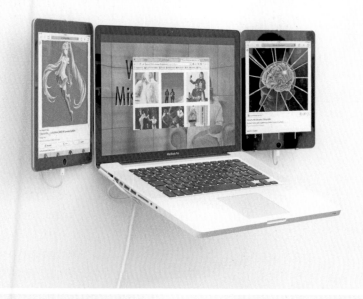

1–2

3–4

voices, each of which is willing to not shy away from taking personal responsibility.

Whereas taking an author's position in design has no pitfalls I can think of, provided the true meaning of authorship is taken (as in 'owning' the full narrative of a design), I do see a possible pitfall of an auto-ethnographic approach to design that is worthwhile mentioning, as we warned students of it many times. If professional designers rely solely on personal experiences, and are not able to widen their projects' meaning and scope beyond the very personal, they may risk creating self-expressions that have little impact in the real world.

Education that Supports Intuition

5–8

Better ask for forgiveness afterwards, than ask for permission in advance. Postponing morality is very important, as I'm convinced that morality, including precepts for the right topics, and for how to correctly approach them, block the imagination. A school is the one free zone where, possibly for the last time, one can investigate one's full creative potential and ideals for the world and students should be able to do just that, uninhibited. In the Master's programme Contextual Design, we enhanced students in following their gut feelings. We considered the intuitions and personal experiences of students, who came from all corners of the world, as the fertile starting points for design projects;

5–8 Metincan Güzel, *Mnemosyne Cabinet*, 2021.
Mnemosyne started as an exploration of taking various author positions; it deals with memories and distortions of memories from Metincan Güzel's childhood home. 'By way of a range of performances, I attempt to rebuild the house with my body, thus exploring immaterial ways of (re)constructing a space that evokes so many feelings. In each performance, I have become another space and another author.'

12–13

12–13 Matilde Stolfa, *Cena Perpetua
(Perpetual Supper)*, 2021.
Perpetual Dinner started with a written
narrative of family dinners and the feelings
that accompanied them. In Matilde Stolfa's
still life, utensils such as cutlery have
become fossils; the table is soaked in
several layers of wine spilled from glasses
during infinite dinners, both of the past
and from the future. A timeless artefact, a
battleground of words, actions, feelings,
'a story of family dynamics repeating
themselves, changing, but never actually
evolving.'

time and again we challenged them to try to redefine
design's potential. Naturally, we also asked the question
'Why?,' and invited students to consider for instance
the social and political relevance of their work for the
world, but we did so at a very late stage in the process.
Instead of imposing our own ideas on what we, the
tutors, considered relevant in today's world, we
mainly trusted what the students came up with
themselves, and tried to give that more grounding
and depth. We did so by confronting the students
with a vast variety of research approaches, by
offering abstract philosophical themes, and inviting
them to reformulate assignments and transform
them into their own questions.

As I was aware that the world for which we prepared our students stays in constant flux, our choices were informed by an attitude of 'not knowing:' not knowing what tomorrow has in store for us, not knowing how designers can play a role within an unpredictable future, not knowing which bonds with other disciplines should be forged, not knowing which skills tomorrow's professional designers need. Design is a multidisciplinary and hybrid practice in which many fields intertwine, including technology, aesthetics, ethics, culture, and politics. The only constant in educating future designers for this complex practice is the student.

9

The older one gets, the more one gets trapped into conventions that are no longer questioned. In all likelihood, young people are not yet capable of fully understanding what they sense, but in general they have better antennae for the times and excellent personal knowledge of the topics that matter in the world. Young people sense fairness and dishonesty; they sense when their personal growth is halted and are not fooled by nice words claiming the opposite. Therefore, as educators, we focused on the attitude, the drive, and artistic talent of the individual student, and not on a precisely defined area of cultural production, or a fixed set of skills.

9–10 Teresa Fernández-Pello, *Hyperlung*, 2021.
The *Hyperlung* was the result of a research into daily 'systems'. The artificial lung, decorated by scanned microscope images of a real lung, regulates the breathing by way of the mobile phone, which tracks through an app one's daily carbon footprint. Consuming patterns can thus be tracked and grouped in population clusters such as cities or even countries. The *Hyperlung* expands our own self perception, making us look at ourselves from a planetary perspective. As Holly Herndon says, 'We are completely outside ourselves, and the world is completely inside us.'

Examples of tutors' assignments that led to very personal answers by the students include: Asking students to create a 'Dekalogue' (showing them the Dekalogues of famous artists as inspiration): ten rules for working in their studios | Asking the students to

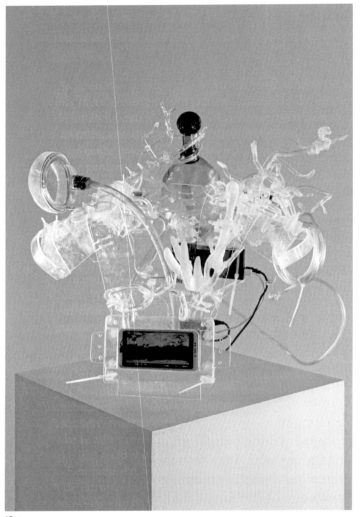

10

create something for a fictive animal and design its 'natural' habitat | Inviting the students to choose an item that influenced their choice to become a designer, to then let them gradually appropriate it and make it their own | Offering students Carl Andre's famous maxim: 'A thing is a hole in a thing it is not' as the starting point for a project | Finding and visualizing the complex systems that define our daily activities, to then find ways of intervening in those systems | Asking students to start research by selecting systems of personal interests that are breaking, slowing down, accelerating, or transforming in this moment of global crisis, and then take a very personal position | Posing the question of whether it's possible to conceive a work or a project with different authors, both human and non-human, and everything or everyone in between, to finally (re)conquer their own author's position (see images of some of the projects that resulted from such assignments).

Research, analyses, and reflection played major roles within our curriculum, and they led to surprisingly well-written research reports and provocative manifestos. But in the end, we were always aware that we would not train scientists and writers, but designers. Knowing this, we focused on how to translate ideas into expressive design proposals and imaginative scenarios. Wild inventiveness and free speculation starting with 'What if…' were considered powerful means to envision alternative modes of living and working. In the second year of the two-year Master's programme, the students were encouraged to choose very personal topics for their graduation projects, which led many to investigate their own cultural backgrounds. See for instance the projects and texts in this book by Jing He (pp. 184–193), Weixiao Shen (pp. 202–209), Žan Kobal (pp. 194–201), and Bruno Baietto (pp. 230–239).

Ample time and attention were devoted to enhancing students' artistic making talents. Many workshops were organized in which the students were invited to freely experiment with techniques and materials and the many references that are embedded in them, thus embracing the unavoidable surprises that result from working with unknown processes. In the course of each school year, Contextual Design's space turned into a messy chaotic landscape, with materials scattered throughout the space—a fantastic sight, as it demonstrated the joy and energy of making. I was always concerned with students staring at length at their screens, waiting for some original idea to pop out of nowhere. The process of a designer is helped by going back and forth between the dirty and

41

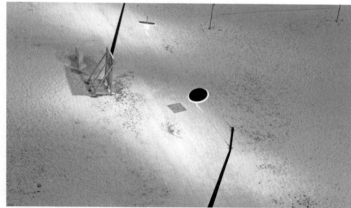

11–12   Chongjin Chen, *Instruction: Apr. 7th Take care of the frustration of the neighborhood*, 2021.
As a Chinese designer living and working in the Netherlands, Chongjin Chen is fascinated by the systems of cultural identity, which force her time and again to rethink culture and adapt to new circumstances. By offering assignments to spectators at the *Pagan Festival*, she invites them to rethink their deeply ingrained cultural habits and value systems.

11–12

ASK FOR FORGIVENESS, NOT PERMISSION   LOUISE SCHOUWENBERG

messy hands-on experimentation with materials and reflecting on how to continue. Such experimentation not only leads to more knowledge and more skills, but also to staying open to the unexpected, welcoming surprise, and constantly adapting and refining a concept.

Situating One's Work in Larger Narratives

Theory and practice hardly ever meet in harmony. It's one thing to agree that students' imaginations and artistic talents should be offered free space for experimentation, but it's another thing to ensure that really happens. We thus did not leave design to the designers, but mainly worked with the experts of imagination, artists, who liberated the students' minds from preconceived ideas on design. Some design schools seek to demarcate design from art, to keep these isolated, and I do see the logic of such a demarcation as it makes no sense to superficially lend strategies from each other's fields without an awareness of how things function in reality. But I definitely see the benefit of letting artists educate design students.[3] For Contextual Design, I intentionally brought many artists into the programme, as they enhanced a much needed, more autonomous positioning of the student vis-à-vis the world, thereby opening up the conventional borders of the discipline. Artists' assignments and advice were often weird, at times troubling, pulling students out of their comfort zones, so as to open up new horizons. In fact, the designers and theorists we engaged (most of them unconventional practitioners within their own fields) became infected by some madness, daring to test the borders of their imaginations. One such unsettling experience was,

3   From 2013–2015, I headed the Master's programme Material Utopias at the Sandberg Institute in Amsterdam, where artists and designers were educated side by side. Here, we did not deny the differences between the disciplines, but stressed the materiality of projects and assumed both artists and designers could benefit from experiencing how each other approached working with various materials.

42

for instance, asking students to hand in their house keys one morning in the middle of winter, to then let them form small groups that would find creative ways of spending the next twenty-four hours. The recordings show clever and hilarious situations; none of the students protested, as it led to fun, to bonding, and to unexpected creativity. Apart from encouraging students to trust their intuition, the tutors helped them contextualize that intuition, offering references and familiarizing students with many research and design methods so that gradually they could find their own. Finally, early on, we decided that our students should have a deep understanding of how things are embedded in larger contexts and larger narratives. To envision the wider context of designs, architects were invited to guide students in creating spatial translations of design projects. Furthermore, film theorists and filmmakers were brought in to familiarize students with options and skills in the narration of their own story through filmmaking.

43

13–15 Lorraine Legrand, *Hern of Pebbles*, 2021, ceramics, part of larger installation (executed at the EKWC/ European Ceramic Work Centre in Oisterwijk, NL).

From a deeply felt connection to the natural world, Lorraine Legrand seeks to restore humans' relation with the world, focusing on their bodily experience of clay—an expressive and flexible material. Her clay objects have solidified into abstract organic forms that bring to mind numerous images, from pebbles on a shore, to the body of an enormous whale, to some unknown living creature. The physical nature of the objects gives the impression of being close to the spectators' bodies, whereas their expressions offer room for multiple interpretations.

13–14

Concluding Thoughts

When I was in my teens, a high school teacher with mismatched socks and a penchant for scandalous literature acquainted me with the power of imagination, the importance of staying true to oneself despite the barrage of cultural and social norms, and the notion that there is great wisdom in one's personal intuitions. She gave me the guts to ignore conventions, which has inspired an approach to education that seeks to do just that—break from institutional models or moulds despite remaining within a broad institution. In setting up a Master's programme, it was paramount to attract people open to their intuition, daring to question the conventions of the discipline, and with the intellectual power and artistic talent for translating wild and clever ideas into imaginative and speculative projects. I wanted to establish a home for students who, like me, desired a creative education and also felt an urge or need to escape from claustrophobic structures. At the heart of this effort is the tension of offering enough support and structure, while not imposing or impinging on the incredible creativity found in young people as they make sense of their world.

15

Coming from a large range of educational backgrounds, including hard-core industrial design, architecture, art, philosophy, neuro-science, in the past decade, a great number of students applied to the Master's of Contextual Design's because of its philosophy and approach to education (as described in this text). We selected the applications in which we detected a free spirit, a tinge of eccentricity, crazy and critical ideas, and a great artistic talent for making. A small part of their projects found their way to this publication, and are representative of the auto-ethnographic turn in design, which I am convinced is an important turn as it lends genuine engagement to a design practice and offers unique insight and perspective on a range of issues, experiences, or material realities.[4] As with many former students who have succeeded in setting up their own design practices and have taken various responsible positions in society (a remarkable number are now leading design programmes throughout the world), without doubt, also the most recent graduates will some day deal with pressing external questions. They will do so from a strong positioning and awareness of what design should be: a genuine engagement by people who truly care for what they claim to care for. Regardless of how we package it, design is always about some aspect of the self, so why not pursue this aspect, foster it, and let the self speak through design.

As for me, I am no longer the fragile schoolgirl and in the process of my many years of experimentations, many studies, fruitful and unusual collaborations, and in following my gut feelings, I like to think that I've become the bold protagonist in my own life's novel (hopefully without the pathetic ending Couperus construed for his protagonist). I suspect some people who know me as a highly critical tutor, would actually call me 'bold', 'typically Dutch' (one could also call it 'honest'; if students deserve anything, it's honesty…why else would they enter a Master's programme?). I'm still living in the factory I squatted with others many year ago, and I'm still not able to imagine myself ever living in a 'normal' house. In love with

---

4   In this publication we stress the projects that were made through an auto-ethnographic approach, and have not included projects that are only based on personal positioning as authors, however excellent they may be.

beautiful things and sensing a fresh contempt for social norms, pre-cooked morality, and keeping up appearances. Sometimes reckless, sometimes dead-serious, sometimes overly passionate, and definitely still battling against conventions. It is with this spirit that I attempt to give shape to education wherever that takes place. In forming an education programme at Design Academy Eindhoven, which was to a great extent inspired by my own personal story and experiences, I hope many designers can continue to explore and make sense of their own stories. The world of design will benefit from it.[5]

46

5   For my reflections on design, and the choices I made for design education, I feel indebted to many inspiring philosophers and authors, whose names I don't explicitly mention in this text, but can easily be guessed by readers …Naturally, at all times, my choices were always informed by the particular needs, questions, and suggestions of the tutors and students I had the pleasure of working with.

47

LOUISE SCHOUWENBERG studied Psychology (Radboud University, Nijmegen, NL), Sculpture (Gerrit Rietveld Academie, Amsterdam, NL), Art Theory (Jan van Eyck Academie, Maastricht, NL), and philosophy (University of Amsterdam, NL). Through her variety of studies and practices, she combines an understanding of the hands-on artistic process with a philosophical curiosity for art and design. These interests have also informed her lecturing practices as head of the MA Contextual Design at Design Academy Eindhoven (2010–2021) and various other schools, including: Politecnico, Milan; Sandberg Instituut, Amsterdam; AdBK, Nuremberg; KABK, The Hague. Schouwenberg has contributed to a wide variety of publications on art and design, including publications on designer Hella Jongerius, photographers Scheltens & Abbenes, and artist Robert Zandvliet. She has (co-)curated exhibitions for presentation institutes, including Die Neue Sammlung/Pinakothek der Moderne in Münich, Museum Boijmans Van Beuningen in Rotterdam, Galerie Fons Welters in Amsterdam, and the TextielMuseum in Tilburg.

Dancing Dirty on the Fringes
The Auto-Ethnographic Turn in Design

Michael Kaethler

In *When We Cease to Understand the World*, Benjamín Labatut gives a fascinating account of the birth of modern physics.[1] He contrasts the great scientists Heisenberg and Schrödinger to demonstrate how very differing accounts of physics, both equally valid, emerged out of contrasting circumstances. Heisenberg's brooding, thorny, and disconcerting account is born out of his nightmarish experience of suffering acute hay fever in isolation on the barren island of Helgoland. While Schrödinger's more poetic account occurs while falling in love at a villa in the Swiss Alps. These two scientific theories materialized out of divergent states of being but both illuminated valid modes for interpreting the very intimate workings of our material realities. Each scientist made sense of the world via their experiences of it—reflecting how the world responded to them. Labatut places their acts of scientific genius in a trialectic between: the context of the research, the thinker himself, and the third unwieldy aspect—the thinker's emotional and physical state. Labatut brings the body and all its fascinating faculties back into the scientific equation, reminding us that knowledge is not abstract, scientific process is not detachment between nature and culture, and that the history of modern physics is not comprised of solely Eureka moments but also of pain, grief, love, madness, and loneliness, all of which reflect back upon how we interpret, make sense of and formalize our understandings of that world. In other words, the knowledge plane does not exist on its own, as Descartes envisioned, elevated above human affairs, but is stuck down here with us in the mud, getting dirty, soiled, and spoiled. We are in an intimate and fetid relationship with knowledge, which oozes and gushes, stinks and secretes, but like all human effluence can, if treated correctly, become wonderful manure for growth.

49

I refer to Benjamín Labatut's book because in putting this edited volume together I came up against several conjectures and critiques from academic colleagues over the nature of research. These can be boiled down to two general themes: 1) that for the sake of research, it is best to avoid anything overtly creative and 2) that research must be reflective and not generative in nature. I found this rather disheartening: it laid bare the conservative

---

1   Benjamín Labatut, *When We Cease to Understand the World* (London: Pushkin Press, 2020).

and reactionary tendencies in how we understand and practice research and therefore also knowledge. Having worked as a researcher in both academic and non-academic settings, I have seen first-hand the limitations and delusions that come with it, such as the view that if you design your research process *correctly*, the world is rendered accessible and knowable. This implies that knowledge is codifiable, communicable, and transferable. I would contend the opposite: that most knowledge is sticky, fuzzy, blurry, and resists being extracted into easily compartmentalized units that can be gathered up, shared, and reconstructed in another context by another person. Moreover, we desperately need more of the most difficult forms of knowledge such as generative and prospective forms of research in order to crack open new media for thinking, raise original questions, and launch alternative lines of inquiry.

In our search for pure methods and crystalline answers, we miss out on a vast array of knowledge or risk flattening it, reducing it to only that which is clean and tidy. As Labatut intimates, the messiness of human affairs, of our physical, emotional and social contexts, and the turbulent winds of our psyche, are inescapable with how we move in and through this world, with how we wield tools, construct language, form communities, develop rules and norms, and divide labour.

Qualifying creative work as research affirms this mode of being in the world not only as a legitimate way of knowing but as important and worthy of pursuit for an individual and collective good. If we accept that our bodies are our knowledge organs, research then becomes an act of letting our bodies go into the world and being sensitive to the myriad reactions that occur. This is an act of sensing and metabolizing our everyday lives and giving it a language (material or otherwise) that is most suited to convey these experiences to others. Design then becomes truly an important part of how we understand, interact with, and shape our world.

It is with this sticky and personal interpretation of knowledge that I emphasize alternative models for knowing and for making sense of the world—forms of research that are enhanced through intuition and inspiration as well as novel forms of communicating This chapter is my personal reflection on design as a knowledge operation; I present several aspects that I feel are critical for situating auto-ethnographic design within a broader framework for research, and ultimately offer an alternative, more messy, and altogether more enjoyable, mode of being a designer-knower.

Nullifying or Acknowledging the Self?

I find Labatut's account of the birth of modern physics particularly challenging as it illustrates just how *much* we are entangled creatures; even our scientific proofs are bound up in the messiness of our personal and physical lives. Indeed, we do not work within a vacuum, but rather within our bodies and within specific contexts. So it is bewildering how much we deny our own personal experiences and contexts when we conduct research. For example, ethnographic research has historically focused on investigating 'the other': this 'other' tends to be from exotic cultures or different socio-economic, sexual, or gender identities. By focusing on the exotic or 'interesting' other, we deny our own exoticness, ourselves as being a site of interest, which goes to re-affirm a hyper normative perspective from which to look out at the world—the position of the researcher is the normative one, all others fall into the exotic. This focus on outwardness sterilizes the bodies and contexts of the researcher as a blank vantage point that is void of conflict, complex dynamics, and experiences. While this may be the intention, the reality is never so black and white; in our objective notations creeps in the personal… Instead of trying to fight this, I suggest embracing it because this is often where research becomes truly remarkable.

For example, the ethnographic diary of Michel Leiris *L'Afrique fantôme* (1934) begins in a traditional observational manner:

soon, the author finds his own fantasies, dreams, and doubts intermingling with his notations on colonialism and local cultures.[2] The diary is as much about the region's masks, fetishes, or language, as it is about Leiris's own cultural questionings and erotic shortcomings—held together as if in a collage of disparities. We see how his ethnographic work begins to slide towards an auto-ethnographic position, where the world he studies is no longer solely the other's but also his own—he iterates between both subject and object. It gets messy and in that blurring of self and other, his reflections are enriched, made powerful and communicative, bringing the reader into the world of both the African tribes and the colonial researcher.

    The personal has an uncomfortable relationship in design. In the design world we find either ego-worship such as with star designers (which is less about one's own personal exploration as it is about self-aggrandisement) or the absent designer, where the designer is rendered invisible by a prevailing view of design as technical function that requires know-how without the know-who—this view posits that if it's a matter of solving a problem, the subjectivity of the designer is of little to no importance. This enables design to carry out practices like ethnography, which normatizes and sterilizes the designer's self and context in order to create an 'other' to design for. Designing for the other enables us to avoid the stench of our own shit.

When design becomes too messy and personal, it is quietly nudged towards the arts. But where is the Michel Leiris figure in this? When is the self a site for design research? Design is an essential part of lives, from the products we use, the houses we live in, to the technology we employ: we are adept at using these and integrating them into every aspect of our lives. We are shaped by design but rarely do we explicitly use design to explore how we are shaped, seldom do we use design's material language and insight to narrate our materially oriented selves.

    As a design educator, I push my students to remain within themselves as long as possible. What I mean by this is to avoid envisioning the 'other,' allowing for design to emerge out of a personal tension, fascination, or urgency.

52

2   Michel Leiris, *L'Afrique fantôme* (Paris: Editions Gallimard, 1981).

Students struggle with this; they want to control the process. However, I have found that if they *know* where they want to go from the start, it will almost certainly turn out to be a banal project because it is simply a matter of execution and demands little of their personhood—the underlying experiences which form their attitudes and intuitions towards the material world. However, when the student can remain in the ineffable and intimate space of the self, the design that emerges has the potential to go *beyond* the clever projects that incite a reaction of 'huh' or the pursed lips and nodding head, to actually resonate with the audience, trouble them, and reside with them for long periods after the encounter.

I tend to interpret this through the lens of the German philosopher Theodor Adorno, who distinguishes between mimetic and instrumental forms of reasoning in his book *Aesthetic Theory*.[3] For Adorno, the mimetic is a primitive and bodily form of knowing that implies assimilating oneself to the object of interest, thereby losing the boundaries and distinctions between the self and the object. This is a view of knowing that favours intimacy over codification. In contrast to the mimetic, instrumental reasoning occurs when one stands back and takes in the entirety of the object from a distance, thus controlling how it is understood, perceived, communicated, and manipulated without ever having to come up too close to it. My desire is that students remain within the mimetic embrace as long as possible in order to become lost and embedded with what they study to the extent that it changes them: research and design then become transformative (rather than instrumental) acts.

> Too often in design, I see an instrumental approach to knowing whereby designers wield the material realm as if it is theirs to control. This approach positions design closer to engineering than the arts, rendering design a matter of technical mastery. Solution oriented design plays into this, whereby the act of design is about finding the best possible solution, thereby requiring controlling the playing field, players, ball, arena, and audience. When we break from a solution-oriented approach to design, something quite powerful emerges. Design, with all its

3   Theodor Adorno, *Aesthetic Theory* (London: A & C Black, 1997).

incredible capacity for interpreting and acting upon the material realm, is free to range, explore, narrate, and experiment operating in the unknown and shadowy realms without briefs, assignments, or problems to solve. Design becomes a means through which one makes sense of the world. But whose world? I suggest that designers *begin* with their own worlds, their own contexts—the spaces, places, people, emotions, materials that they know best—rather than focus on others' worlds (as has been the tendency in design).

From Auto-Ethnography to Auto-Ethnographic Design: Designing on the Fringes

Auto-ethnography as practiced by the social sciences is a provocative but ultimately limited pursuit. It is provocative in that it challenges researchers to see their own context as worthy of research and questions the other-obsessed tendencies of ethnography. However, as its medium is writing and reflection, it feels highly inappropriate and decadent that while our world is burning around us, a bunch of researchers are spending their days wrapped up in inner musings and contemplations of their lives. This retrospective aspect mixed with the limits of ethnographic styles of writing (dry and descriptive) impoverish many of the qualities that auto-ethnography may have—rendering it akin to an intellectualized diary for others to study. For this reason, I am not a big fan of this tradition in its current application in the social sciences. However, in the process of putting this book together I came to be convinced that perhaps the true home of auto-ethnography is design or art (and thus could be better named as 'auto-ethno-design,' or 'arto-ethnography' as Andrea Gaspar outlines in 'From Ethnography to *Arto*-Ethnography', see pp. 70–79). An auto-ethnographic component in design or art is a prospective and generative form of self-exploration that tells one's story through creating rich material artefacts that are transformative and communicative to a wider audience. In this sense, the auto-ethnographic element *does something*: it reaches into our material worlds, interprets them, reacts to them, changes them. What I mean by this is that acts of auto-ethnographic design are both communicating an understanding (research) of the world (based on one's experience) and trying to change it at the same time. Additionally, doing this may also nudge one closer to their subconscious, bringing us closer to who we really are (see Ben Shai van der Wal's 'The Self and the Other: A Psychoanalytical Reading of Auto-Ethnographic Design', pp. 242–251).

Where should we place the auto-ethnographic turn within the design tradition? It's hard to discuss 'design' as it's a wide church with many internal schisms that somehow still manages to hold together without central tenets. This makes critiquing design cheap and easy (there is always something to critique about it) while at the same time elusive (it's so damn malleable and porous that there are always exceptions). Because of design's expansiveness, it's important from time to time to put stakes in the ground in order for certain movements or trends to find a footing, to not get blown away by the winds of path dependency or the fervour of tradition. This book is giving language to shifts that emphasize authorship, contextual design, and poetic or subjective materialized research. There is always a danger with nomenclature, covered in the discussion with Oli Stratford (see pp. 60–69, 'A Matter of Terminology'); but we hope that by recognizing this turn in design and by giving it language and a loose form, we can establish an outpost that can stretch some of design's boundaries and ward off design's inherent tendencies towards clean impersonal lines or technical mastery.

Auto-ethnographic design sits on the fringes of design; it overlaps with the arts and also to some degree with sensibilities in anthropology and sociology. The fringe is often where the action happens: and if design is to be transformed to engage with an increasingly unstable world, then this transformation will occur not from design's central practices but from its peripheries. Design is a practice and mode of thinking that has its own discipline—its own norms, systems of valuation, linguistic alignments, and so forth. Disciplines are very good at 'disciplining' and by this, I mean ensuring that those who fall under its rubric adhere to its principles, establishing a sufficient uniformity, stability, and cohesion. When this becomes too stable, it is problematic. As the epistemological anarchist Paul Feyerabend describes in *Against Method*, almost every major breakthrough in thought occurs at the borders and fringes of a discipline, where radical ideas can be developed without being censored or *disciplined*.[4]

Towards Another Model of Knowing: Designer as Songbird

It's rarely comfortable on the fringe. It's a space of junctures, overlaps, glaring cracks in logic, and uneven surfaces to traverse; intellectual confluences smash together, conceptual tides are fast and high. To survive or thrive in such a space requires a different mode of thinking or being. Here at the juncture between art, design, and to a lesser extent anthropology, we need to find new ways of thinking about knowledge. The reductionist dichotomies such as 'science vs. arts' or 'body vs. mind' render 'design knowing' as either an act for technical specialists (scientists etc.) or cultural specialists (artists). Design knowing is both of these, and more.

Creating knowledge models based on distinction are not the answer but conceivably the problem. When we look to a model of knowledge for design, it's hard to imagine how the typical analytical (scientific) one might fit. Analysis is based on subjecting the object of study to dissection, a violence of opening it up and quartering it into ever smaller pieces until it yields its intrinsic knowledge to the researcher. It's an interrogation that demands answers and will apply a variety of forms of violence until answers are found—from engineering to ethnography and beyond. It's not easy to think outside of the analytical paradigm, as analysis is how our epoch understands knowledge—if

4   Paul Feyerabend, *Against Method* (London: Verso, 1993).

you can't understand something, you break it down into small enough pieces that it becomes comprehensible—decomplexify through reduction. Yet, looking at the world today, the crises we face are defined by their complex adaptivity, non-linearity, and multi-scalarity; we need knowledge systems that have in-built complexity, not ones that must tame complexity first by flattening it to its constituent parts.

Instead of distinction, perhaps a model of similitudes or synthesis is the way forward, showing how design can absorb other models of thinking and practice and how it straddles these to create the uncanny, strange, and troubling modes of thinking that can produce objects that appeal to both the scientific and the artistic—as this book demonstrates—merging ethnographic sensibilities, design's language and traditions, and artistic inspiration. For instance, take the knowledge approach of French philosopher Michel Serres, which is based on synthesis in place of analysis. He looks to the harmonies or divergences that are created through acts of combination. This is a generative form of knowledge creation, one that is more interested in experimentation to see what 'could' be than what 'is' or 'was.' Serres further compares these two models using an avian example: the crotchety wise old owl of Minerva guards the gates of knowledge, sleepy, unimpressed, and stern; whereas the morning songbird flutters from branch to branch in search of discovery, beauty, and newness—it lives in the present, vulnerable but vivacious.[5] Serres argues that we need the lightness of the songbird so that we keep mobile, interacting with as many elements as possible, soaring over the whirlpools of circular thinking, not getting caught up in the brambles of substantives like 'being, justice, or God' and instead providing a way of thinking that is more interested in how things are related to each other than what they are on their own. This is the knowledge model that I see in Section 2 of this book.

I take refuge in Serres' model for knowing; it renewed my passion for research as in it the knower is not the technician

5   Michel Serres, *The Troubadour of Knowledge* (Ann Arbor, Michigan: University of Michigan Press, 1997).

in the white tunic but rather the explorer and wanderer in the patchwork cloak trying to combine as many elements together as possible, in the hopes of both creating something new and understanding the individual pieces through the process of their combination (not their dissection). I view this as a generative dance, a way of *being* in the world that perceives knowledge and research not as a specific intentional act but rather as a manner in which we move through a world composed of objects, ideas, senses, and so forth, suturing them through each movement. I see this in the auto-ethnographic turn in design, a form of research based on combinations and creations vis-à-vis our lived experience, which taps into our everyday life. Instead of the 'decomplexify through reduction' model of analysis, this model is 'complexify through addition.' This model comes to terms with how we interact with the myriad objects that constitute our lives, learning about how things respond to each other so that research becomes an act of novelty and the unexpected—a dance floor of moving parts jostling, embracing, coalescing, copulating. This also implies becoming accustomed to complexity, embracing the messiness of not standing above the world but standing and moving *in* the world.

The auto-ethnographic turn in design, as explored in this book, is about how we move through this world responding to it through shaping its materiality, telling our stories by giving form to material, narrating the sensible via the physical. It is really quite simple. In our multiple entanglements, it is impossible not to recognize how much we are personally, physically, and psychologically embedded in our research—because research is simply trying to make sense of our place in the world and we cannot study the world without being in (and moving in) it. For some, the story of Heisenberg and Schrödinger's scientific theories being markedly affected by their physical and emotional states is difficult to digest—we cherish the idea of pure reason. But life is far too messy for that. As Aristotle supposedly quipped, 'Nothing comes to the mind without first coming to the body,' and our bodies are dancing and moving through a world of interactions, being impressed upon, squeezed, pierced, pinched, and penetrated, giving rise to dreams and desires, despair and desolation. When we allow our bodies to move freely to the beat and rhythms of these interactions, when we embrace a mimetic and deeply personal form of research such as the auto-ethnographic approach to design, we open new possibilities for knowing, and thus being in, the world.

59

MICHAEL KAETHLER is a sociologist of design whose work focuses on the transmission, production, and embodiment of knowledge in art and design-oriented practices. He has held a range of diverse positions, from human rights researcher in conflict and post-conflict contexts, curator, design educator, and writer, resulting in a broad range of publications across both scientific and practice-oriented literature. Kaethler is currently a post-doc researcher in the Planning and Development (P&D) unit of the Department of Architecture, KU Leuven (BE). He holds a PhD in Architecture, an M.Eng in Human Settlements, and an MA in Slavonic Studies. He is based in Italy where he experiments with agricultural projects and plays with his three wild children.

A Matter of Terminology
The Self as a Site for Research

Conversation with Oli Stratford

Michael Kaethler

OS   How do you see the auto-ethnographic turn in design: is it a description of something, a framework that could be useful for designers to employ, or something else? What is it and how do you position it?

MK   This is something that we're trying to grapple with. It describes a pattern that we have witnessed in design over the last decade, a type of design that rises out of poeticism, out of an exploration of the self and its particular context. We want to describe it, give it a name, recognize it as something more than an outlying exception to design—something that is worthy of its own category. As a researcher, I must admit to being keen on applying taxonomies and categories, even if I accept that these are inherently fuzzy, as practice does not adhere to theory, but rather the other way round. In giving it a name, we can engage with it on a deeper level, seek to understand what it means for practice, how it has evolved, whence it came, and perhaps also where it is going and how this will affect other practices within design.

OS   You frame the book in contrast to certain tendencies in design such as solutionism, which in focusing on the idea of a solution can somewhat remove the designer from the equation. It frames the work as being the designer designing for others, for the many, but not necessarily for themselves. Do you think that putting more of the designer into the work, and acknowledging that at least an aspect of design is a personal response to the world, is liberating for designers?

61

MK   Absolutely. There is a recognition here of the designer. For too long, the designer has either been the 'star' (with a focus on ego and grand or fashionable projects) or all too absent (with a focus on design as a kind of science which understands the designer as fulfilling a more technical role of addressing problems). We are looking at acknowledging a different aspect of the designer and foregrounding them within the design process, recognizing that design research is deeply personal and that design need not only be for others but also for the self (coming from a deep personal need or desire, and addressing one's own specific world).

OS   What I find interesting is the move to classify these types of projects under auto-ethnographic design. A lot of the designers I speak to say that they want to escape labels, particularly given that whole discussion around how design sits next to art, and what the difference between the two is. I find the most interesting answers to that come from the practitioners who don't really care, and who are not particularly concerned with disciplinary boundaries because they don't do anything helpful for their work.

MK   I would suggest that there are many who are struggling to understand what it is that they're doing, who would benefit from these distinctions in order to position their work for themselves and to a wider audience. I would also suggest that a taxonomy around a practice can embolden the constitutive characteristics, providing a permissiveness to emerge. There is a concern amongst designers that their work might be too 'artsy,' too much about extravagant expression. A taxonomical *space* can provide safety to develop these practices, valorizing them, and encouraging the further pushing of boundaries.

OS   That does make me question what the terminology of auto-ethnography offers that others don't, however, such as authorship. One idea that immediately comes to mind is that while auto-ethnography is intensely personal, it also suggests a sense of cultural critique and a connection to broader social issues. Even though it acknowledges the subjectivity in design, the positioning also suggests that you can still latch onto things outside of yourself. Perhaps auto-ethnographic design, with its history in the social sciences, emphasizes that outwardness in a way that authorship doesn't make quite so explicit—that this form of design may be personal and expressive, but it's also research and critique. In contrast, perhaps there's a risk that authorship could be misunderstood as emphasizing expressiveness for expressiveness's sake, without the same inclination towards research.

MK   Yes, I agree with much of what you're saying. Authorship is an integral part of auto-ethnography but it is not its entirety. Auto-ethnography is about the position we take in trying to understand and change the world, recognizing the position of the self as an essential starting point for that understanding. Perhaps you could say that it's a form of applied authorship as a method for exploring the self and one's context.

62

OS I think there may be something important that stems from talking about authorship or auto-ethnographic design, and presenting the self as a site for research. The self is always present in design, just to differing extents. For this reason, I find it exciting how authorship and auto-ethnography could influence how the self is articulated in other forms of design, such as product design or industrial design. These types of design are not as far removed from authorship as we might assume, and re-centring those practices through an auto-ethnographic lens could potentially nudge these fields towards more explicitly personal forms of practice.

MK What danger do you see in giving this term life?

OS I find that you get these increasingly baroque descriptions of what designers are doing. The more you try to pin it down, the more it wriggles free. I am more a fan of just saying 'designer' without further elaboration. Artists do that, for instance, and there doesn't seem to be quite the same anxiety about not being specific in that field. Perhaps there is an insecurity about doing it in design 63 because the field has been so hooked with commerce and lifestyle, and with so many elements that are seen as being shallow or unsavoury in society, that designers want to strategically distance themselves from all that. So descriptions of a specific type of design sometimes seem to be as much about rejecting other forms of design as they are saying anything positive: it's almost like saying 'I'm not that kind of designer' as a form of identity. I think it's possible that terms like auto-ethnographic design could give some strength and support for certain design practices to grow, which will in the end also help reshape the broader understanding of design. In this sense, it could perhaps be seen as a useful ladder that we climb up, but which ultimately becomes redundant when its specific qualities become integrated within design at large. Often when we need a new piece of terminology, it's to bring attention to something that is otherwise neglected. Authorship does some good work in doing this because the degree of subjectivity that goes into design is not widely appreciated. However, in doing so it may miss out on other things, such as the element of research that you cover in auto-ethnographic design. But ultimately these terms hopefully fade away to the point of 'of course designers do this,' and thus are no longer necessary. Which is itself a kind of vindication of the terminology that it becomes absorbed into the general language of design.

MK   Indeed, hopefully the auto-ethnographic turn in design is just that, a turn, and these practices will over time be fully integrated and accepted within the wider design practice. I see this turn as potentially being able to expand design, pushing its boundaries (uncomfortably sometimes) and perhaps also building closer bridges or dissolving distinctions between the arts, design, and anthropology. Designers are becoming increasingly aware that their practices offer a nuanced interpretation of the material realm and that this is highly useful for not only expression, cultural critique, serving some function or utility, but also research in academia or in various policy settings. Today when you speak of design research it's often about the types of design that are easily transformed or captured by academia (accessible practices and outputs), or perhaps about the type of design being carried out by academics themselves. This type of design is open to analysis, either through how the practice is conceived or the direction and intention of its outputs. However, other forms of design, the more poetic or 'artistic' forms of design, tend to be relegated to expression and not considered as valid forms of research in and of themselves, or only to be the site of research by someone other than the designer. This book hopes to shift this dynamic by emphasizing the important knowledge and research that can emerge from a materially oriented self-exploration.

OS   When I hear the term 'research' I tend to think about large research projects. But there's something very healthy and helpful about seeing design objects as research and not just as frippery or pretty objects. Not that there's anything wrong with frippery or prettiness, but anything that can point out that these things can be serious pieces of research too is useful and valuable. I guess it's worth remembering that terminologies are not totally neutral and that they have value judgements baked in. The term object is reasonably neutral, I suppose, although of course there are still presuppositions, but something like 'research' implies a huge value judgement. We all love research, and it's perceived as having considerable value. So when we use that term—when we decide what we'll allow to be deemed research and what we won't—we're making a whole series of judgments. Design is often undervalued as a method for research, so I like that auto-ethnography flags that aspect of it up quite clearly.

MK   Indeed. And the term 'research' also has its hidden agendas, which do not always play so well for design. On one hand, it legitimizes design in a new way, seeing it as a way of understanding things and not just making them. But it has also led to an increasing academicization of design, which has included new rules, formulations, and actors that are constraining some of the more artistic oriented forms of design. I am hoping that the auto-ethnographic angle can both enable recognition of a more creative and expressive form of research while at the same time remain too abstract and materially oriented for the mainstream academic gaze.

OS   I am interested in how this may prompt reflection from a wider design audience (non-academics) and if it will help designers theorize or make sense of their work in a different way. Do you think that by putting this terminology out there that it will shape the way people design? To what extent does a new category shape design practice?

MK   An awareness of what one does certainly can help refine and crystalize practices, it also celebrates it. We're not bringing this practice into life; it's been around for decades. However, this book is about acknowledging it as a unique and important mode of practice within design. Giving it some recognition is the least we can do but I suspect that in recognizing it, we are also giving these types of practices a louder voice and conceptual support. I don't see auto-ethnography as an identity, as in 'I'm an auto-ethnographic designer,' but rather as a way of describing a practice and in some cases also the objects that emerge from this practice.

OS   I suppose one important thing about terminology is that it shows a different way to carve something up. It challenges the tendencies to constantly analyze things in the same way. The ways in which we currently frame design are not set in stone and there are other ways to think about these things. It may be time to think of design as a serious mode of research.

MK   Putting the 'auto' in front of ethnography raises questions on whether we need more self-description. I wonder if auto-ethnographic design will be a controversial term, loved by outliers and resented by more established factions within design.

OS   I would be surprised if it isn't divisive. New terminologies usually are because they bring different aspects of the field to light that haven't been well appreciated before. It's easy to bristle at change or to interpret a new term as a critique of what has come before. Equally, new terminologies often come into criticism for pomposity, or navel gazing, or emptiness—which is sometimes fair.

66   MK   Perhaps auto-ethnographic design provides a framework that values navel gazing, understanding the intrinsic value in design.

OS   We see art as producing all kinds of values—aesthetic, commercial, even ethical to an extent. We accept that art can provide a range of values, but when it comes to design, we don't seem to see such a range. I don't think design is always perceived as a legitimate vehicle for cultural expression, or else as providing a sense of therapy for the practitioner in the way that, for example, literature is—the idea that somebody just has to write and that's good for them. But there is nothing intrinsic about design that means that it couldn't have these kinds of values. I suppose these tendencies are just hallmarks of the past and of how we conceived of design when it was very clearly linked to industry, despite there being a number of examples across the last century of it doing a whole range of different things. I think design still seems to provoke a faint sense of bafflement if it's not being deployed for problem solving or to generate commercial value. That is strange, because there are not many disciplines that are quite so hemmed in as that. For example, within writing you can have beautiful, literary writing that isn't practical or doesn't provide clear answers, and that's wonderful; similarly, you can have text which is as dull as dishwater, but which is worth persevering through because there's much to be gained by struggling through it. It's the same with art: we have no problem admitting that it's very catholic as a field, and can be all sorts of things. But I never get the sense that everybody feels that they can legitimately talk about design as a way of creating an assortment of values.

MK Using new language to describe design, such as this book does, might be a method for pushing design's boundaries—in the case of this book, towards the arts. It expands what design can be or mean.

OS Yes, exactly. There's a certain ballsy-ness about it—saying something deliberately strong to shake a preconception.

MK Yes, and to do so by not talking about design vis-à-vis the arts. Art has long made claims to meaning making; making space for meaning making in design is a worthy pursuit.

67

OS I think that design doesn't necessarily have the language to justify that kind of work at present. We tend to talk about 'art-design,' because the type of value that this form of design brings us is recognized in art, but not so much in design. We tack on the 'art' in order to provide that indication. There is nothing necessarily wrong with that—and I'm a fan of not worrying too much about the boundaries between the two—but it's a shame that design doesn't have a terminology of its own, because it risks leaving it trapped in something of a parasitic relationship. It ends up feeling like design needs to tap into the arts to justify itself, because there is not an internal means to recognize those values. It leaves design as something of a country cousin to art: someone who is a little less urbane, a little less open to so many things, and whose concerns are all rather functional and rough and ready. Maybe that is a good way of looking at it: if a terminology is going to be useful, how were people describing that practice beforehand? If they had to rely on the vocabulary from another discipline, maybe that is a good reason to define it in its own right. It is, of course, fine to borrow vocabulary from other areas, but it feels much healthier to do so when those areas are in a mutual relationship with influences that go back and forth. In this case, I don't know if that is always the case. The people involved in the type of work that is described in this book often have to go to the arts to talk about their practices. But why is that, and what does it suggest is missing in design? Who knows. Maybe similar problems will arrive with using auto-ethnography—particularly as it's a term you're borrowing from anthropology.

68

OLI STRATFORD is a writer and editor working in design, technology, and cultural journalism. He has been the editor-in-chief of *Disegno*, the Quarterly Journal of Design, since September 2016. Examples of his essays, journalism, and interviews may be read in books published, among others, by Koenig Books, Gestalten, and the V&A.

69

From Ethnography to *Arto*-Ethnography

Andrea Gaspar

Some years ago, one of the main informants in my ethnographic fieldwork (or companions in the field, as we now say in anthropology) told me that if he were an anthropologist, he would prefer inventing the worlds he would be describing. This provocation has stuck with me ever since. What a fascinating idea for anthropologists to not only describe what they find/experience but to take a step forward and actually design these worlds.

Design Anthropologists[1] claim to be practicing a different kind of knowledge, proposing a way of doing anthropology by means of design and design by means of anthropology. Doing design by means of anthropology and the reverse is not as symmetrical as it sounds, as design anthropologists turn out to be more anthropologists than designers, and are indeed more faithful to an anthropology disciplinary tradition than a design one. One could say that Design Anthropology is a sort of 'good' version of design from an anthropologist's point of view. For anthropologists, design should not be a process whereby experts, say for example urbanists, impose their design plans on inhabitants, but rather one by which experts engage with the social contexts and the communities they design for, rendering the design process as democratic as possible. These anthropologically informed forms of design usually imply that they are participatory and co-produced, which leaves out vast swathes of design practices that do not easily fit within the filters or categories of anthropology—particularly those that are artistically oriented, centred on the designers' individuality, and on creativity.

Despite being an important breakthrough to the discipline of anthropology (because it is an attempt to do anthropology through and *with* design, as well as the reverse, going beyond the distanced anthropology as a cultural critique *of* design), the Design Anthropology debate speaks more to anthropologists than to designers. In practice, Design Anthropology projects tend to be an extension or an improved version of participatory design. It is no coincidence that those involved in Design Anthropology are academics connected to a participatory design

---

1   See the works of Wendy Gunn, Ton Otto, and Rachel Charlotte Smith, eds., *Design Anthropology: Theory and Practice* (London: Bloomsbury Publishing, 2013); and eds. Rachel Charlotte Smith et al., *Design Anthropological Futures* (London: Bloomsbury Academic, 2016).

tradition (especially a Scandinavian one),[2] which actually do not engage with design epistemic cultures and the diversity of different traditions within design itself. One thing is interaction design, another completely different one is graphic design, or product design, or architecture, or speculative design: all of these are very different practices that cannot be easily conflated under one taxonomy. In other words, Design Anthropology would be more effective as a truly collaborative practice if anthropologists engaged with the richness and diversity of design cultures of practice. Design subdisciplines have their own specific practices and discourses, but most anthropologists such as the ones defining themselves as Design Anthropologists do not always engage with these specificities.[3] It requires an epistemic openness to be transformed by these practices and epistemic cultures,[4] and anthropologists, though professionals at studying other 'cultures,' appear to be unwilling to engage with other epistemic cultures than their own, and are often closed to the possibility of transforming their own discipline through encounters with other ways of knowing. Despite the promising proposals and the good intentions of Design Anthropology, it is an approach that unfortunately remains epistemo-centric and normative (in the sense that it promotes what it perceives as a 'good' version of design as being more democratic, participatory, and engaged with communities—a design that is supposedly more anthropological). Ironically, this reveals the difficulties of anthropology to engage with other knowledge cultures.

It is crucial for social scientists, especially anthropologists, to develop improved modes of collaboration, cross-pollination, and engagement with other epistemic cultures in order to respond to many of the global problems we are currently facing. Design Anthropologists recognize that this is a time when simplistic problem-solving approaches do not work anymore.[5] However, despite their recent claims to more interventionist ways of knowing,[6] anthropologists (including some design anthropologists) remain attached to an epistemic culture of observation and textual modes of (ethnographic) description that are unable to respond to the complexities of these problems and their need for urgent intervention, which demand more inventive and creative practices of knowing. Invention and creativity are still, for the most part, a taboo for anthropologists and sociologists, despite debates developed in the last decades of these disciplines, such as the ones around inventive methods, live methods, speculative research and post-representational methods.[7] I contend anthropology will soon become an obsolete science if it does not open itself to learning other ways of doing anthropology and if it remains attached to representational methods (such as ethnography-as-it-is) that perpetuate the figure of the participant observer (a fiction among many possible other fictions). Anthropology risks being absorbed by designers for their own purposes, colonized by them or other disciplines, and being instrumentally reduced as an applied methodology for other purposes, rather than being a science with a contribution for society in its own right. If we anthropologists do not learn how to reinvent ourselves together with other disciplines, such as design (which is also undergoing its own crisis),[8] we are condemned to death, simply because 'Problems don't care about disciplinary boundaries.'[9]

The key, I think, is in reaching beyond ethnography and practicing another kind of anthropology-design (or the reverse, the order is not important), through other epistemic figures. Why not the designer as an

5   For further elaboration, see the work of Alison J. Clark, "The New Design Ethnographers 1968–1974: Towards a Critical Historiography of Design Anthropology," in *Design Anthropological Futures*, eds. Smith et al., pp. 71–85.

6   See Rachel Charlotte Smith and Ton Otto, "Cultures of the Future: Emergence and Intervention in Design Anthropology," in *Design Anthropological Futures*, eds. Smith et al., pp. 19–36.

7   See the following works: Celia Lury and Nina Wakeford, *Inventive Methods: The Happening of the Social* (London: Routledge, 2012); Les Back and Nirmal Puwar, "A Manifesto for Live Methods: Provocations and Capacities," *Sociological Review* 60, no. S1 (2012); Alex Wilkie, Martin Savransky and Marsha Rosengarten, *Speculative Research: The Lure of Possible Futures* (London and New York: Routledge, 2017); and Philip Vannini, ed., *Non-Representational Methodologies: Re-Envisioning Research* (New York and London: Routledge, 2015).

8   See for example the work of Anthony Dunne and Fiona Raby, *Speculative Everything: Design, Fiction, and Social Dreaming* (Cambridge, MA: MIT Press, 2013).

9   See the article by Regina F. Bendix, "Problems Don't Care about Disciplinary Boundaries," *Anthropological Journal of European Cultures* 29, no. 2 (2020), pp. 97–102.

epistemic figure practicing anthropology, rather than the ethnographer as a participant-observer? What kind of epistemic imagination do we need to cultivate in order to respond to problems of being human in this epoch or in the future? It is for this reason that I hope anthropology will leave its comfort zone for and engage more deeply with design (in search of an encounter and true engagement with other ways of knowing that are hitherto unfamiliar to us), despite the considerable frictions that such an enterprise entails.[10]

Anthropologists do not seem to be interested in the fact that designers are now prone to use, appropriate, or reinvent anthropology's method for design—in the case of this book, auto-ethnography. Anthropologists rather tend to be suspicious about the (mis?)use of ethnographic methods. To some anthropologists, auto-ethnography is not ethnography because ethnography is supposed to be an engagement with the world, produced from a phenomenological encounter with 'the other' rather than exclusively from the self. Can auto-ethnography also work as a mode of engagement, though perhaps departing from the self and the personal as vehicles for the staging of an encounter with the world?

Towards an Arto-Ethnography as a Research Device for Art & Design and Social Sciences Alike

In researching for this chapter, I read a selection of this book's chapters to grasp what the auto-ethnographic turn in design entails, what it means, and what it does for designers. In my understanding, it is based on a

---

10   For further elaboration, see Andrea Gaspar, "Idiotic Encounters: Experimenting with Collaborations between Ethnography in Design," in *Experimental Collaborations: Ethnography through Fieldwork Devices*, eds. Adolfo Estalella and Tomás Sánchez Criado (New York: Berhghan, 2018), pp. 94–113.

narrative that is produced by the self (the designer) approaching the creative process: it asks how and why that creative process emerged as it is, and also where from. In all the texts I read, there is clearly a relationship between the 'self' and its material environment as well as the social-political context: the narrative, and most of the time also the object that results from this process, is about how those aspects are intimately connected. Auto-ethnographic design, I learnt from reading the examples, is a way of making the creative process explicit in a very personal way.

This making explicit plays a similar role to the one that Actor-Network-Theory (ANT) plays for the social studies of science and technology (STS). ANT is an empirical analysis based on the mapping of relations that are simultaneously material and semiotic, technical and social, non-human and human; it is used in STS to describe controversies around facts or technologies while they are still open, or before their stabilization—before something actually comes into being. This is actually more an approach than a theory, and it is used to describe the process that lies behind the emergence of any new technical object or a new scientific fact.[11] Anthropologists consider ANT a specific mode of doing ethnography (among many other possibilities), albeit one that is particularly suited to account for the emergence of technical objects or scientific 'facts.' It is a method that allows us to show how these entities are 'produced,' with the particularity that the 'produced' does not have the exclusively humanistic connotation that it usually has. ANT constantly shows how 'hard' matters always come enmeshed with the 'soft' ones, to the point that it is impossible to conceive the soft (human, social) and the hard (objective, material, facts, etc.) as separate realms. This approach, however, would clearly not be fit to describe the emergence of art and design objects because art and design objects are ontologically different from technical and scientific objects: art objects are not meant to be stabilized or 'black-boxed' (closed) into a certain function. An auto-ethnographic approach, however, perhaps plays for art

75

11   For further elaboration see the work of Bruno Latour, especially the following publications: Bruno Latour, *Reassembling the Social: An Introduction to Actor-Network-Theory* (Oxford: Oxford University Press, 2005); Bruno Latour, *Pandora's Hope: Essays on the Reality of Science Studies* (Cambridge, MA: Harvard University Press, 1999).

and design the role that ANT plays for science and technology studies: for example, Thomas Nathan writes (see p. 131): 'I began by attempting to reconstruct my design process by deconstructing it to its smallest and simplest form.' ANT also deconstructs or decomposes into smaller parts, in retrospect (opening the 'black box'), the process whereby heterogeneous entities were assembled and disassembled in the process of bringing an object into being. Once an object is stabilized (a technical, functional one), the messy process that gave it origin becomes invisible. ANT is deconstructive in that sense. It is a method for decomposing anything into its smaller parts, making the process that gave its origin visible, revealing the backstages of science and technology in-the-making—but it does so from an observer's (external) point of view, not the self.

The chapters in this book offer a similar view, like ANT, to the backstage of creative production—the messy, personal engagement with one's world. Design objects always have a context (a social, cultural, political and personal one). Auto-ethnographic design as both a writing and a material genre (this is an important detail, the fact that the material is itself auto-ethnographic and not just an illustration of it) may serve as a means for making that context visible through a personal lens, in the way that ANT does for technical objects and scientific facts. In contrast to ANT accounts, which are very dry and impersonal kind of accounts, auto-ethnography affords a situated, embodied, and reflexive account. This style has much in common with post-modern ethnographic writing as a genre,[12] though the aim of auto-ethnography in design is clearly not theoretical analysis: it plays a different role, a different function, than what ethnography does for anthropology and social science—it is a research process that may generate new *material* concepts rather than new *theoretical* concepts.

[12] One of the main references on post-modern ethnographic writing is the "Writing Culture," a publication that is considered an experimental moment in the social sciences: James Clifford and George Marcus, eds., *Writing Culture: The Poetics and Politics of Ethnography* (Berkeley: University of California Press, 1986). This book showed that the authority of cultural representation in ethnographic texts is something constructed by certain literary tricks of the narrator; the act of writing about culture has since then assumed its constructive character, which turned the ethnographic text reflexive (based on the ethnographers' own subjective experience), making its constructed character visible and always situating the ethnographer in their own contingent circumstances. See also George Marcus and Michael J. Fisher, *Anthropology as Cultural Critique: An Experimental Moment in the Human Sciences* (Chicago: The University of Chicago Press, 1986).

The more I read, the more I realize that comparing auto-ethnographic design with ethnography is a mistake (an epistemo-centric one). Ethnography cannot be the measure for auto-ethnographic design as they serve very different purposes. Before knowing this, I found myself drawing an epistemic line between research and art—a fence of some sorts, as Billy Ernst (pp. 222–229) explains in his auto-ethnographic description of being gay in rural South Africa, a country of many fences. I was erecting an epistemic fence between ethnography and auto-ethnographic design, between research and creativity, between reality and fiction, between subjectivity and objectivity, between creative work and social science. But fences, as Ernst reminds us with his auto-ethnographic designs, can be soft. Auto-ethnographic design probably disturbs that line, that fence, making us uncomfortable with it. I felt a softness that made me see those boundaries blurred. In fact, I was transformed by reading these pieces: they made me travel; they made me see the world through different lenses, which is also one of the reasons anthropological research exists. They are impressionistic in style, evocative of social and cultural questions and problems, and offer a sort of entry point, a way of opening up conversations (as the curator Hicham Khalidi puts it in his interview, pp. 314–319) about social and cultural questions without exhausting them. These texts obviously do not seek for theorization. They do not aim to provide a realist description of the world or to analyze it theoretically (as ethnographic texts do), but rather to *feel* it. What does it feel like to be gay in South Africa? Each of these texts and respective works are a box of surprises: they are gripping, hard to put down. The rewriting exercise of a Spanish family recipe called 'To scare an octopus,' by Spanish artist Miguel Guevara is an amazing example of this. In his text Guevara refers to the octopus' preparation in the kitchen as 'a sudden black cloud,' because

77

> An octopus will release ink from its siphon when scared. The jet of black liquid is suddenly dispersed through water in a voluptuous cloud to provide the cephalopod with an escape mechanism against predatory attacks. Intended to function as a smoke screen, the instant of darkness affords seconds of vital importance. An opportunity to change scenario.

In this case, the octopus preparation was for him an opportunity to change scenario because the transformation of the recipe is able to change the perception of women's traditional roles as housewives, as victims of patriarchal oppression, into a fantastic sensorial eroticization of preparing the octopus, which is another possible side of victimization. This amazing 'trick,' this change of scenario/recipe, shows us that being a housewife in patriarchal Spanish society is a rather more ambiguous one than we are used to believing. The octopus's sudden black cloud defence mechanism as 'an opportunity to change scenario' speaks to me. It leads me again to social sciences, which desperately need devices for changing scenario in regards to research: social sciences need ways (mechanisms, devices) to foster the emergence of new research questions, questions that may change the way we see things, but also change (redesign) the world that we study. Social sciences need more inventive methods, live methods, which is a debate that has been going on since 2012,[13] and ways of not just intervening but being inventive of the world.[14]

So I wondered if auto-ethnographic design could also work for social scientists as a device to be used very pragmatically for creating 'opportunities for changing scenarios' such as when we need to introduce techniques during our fieldwork to make research events[15] emerge? Or, to return to the informant I mentioned in the beginning of this chapter, to what extent can we design the world as a means to study or make sense of it? I do not mean to suggest using auto-ethnographic design as the product of research, but rather as a means, a device, within an ongoing empirical research. It can be used for example in anthropology within a conventional ethnographic process, as a practice within another practice, among many other devices that, it is claimed,

---

13   See, again, the works of Lury and Wakeford, *Inventive Methods* and also Back and Puwar "A Manifesto for Live Methods."

14   See the work of eds. Noortje Marres, Michael Guggenheim, and Alex Wilkie, *Inventing the Social* (Manchester: Mattering Press, 2018), matteringpress.org/books/inventing-the-social.

15   A research event is a term used in speculative research for referring to the ways in which the research question, the researcher, the researched, and research device are actively involved in a process of becoming-with one another. A research event can also be seen as a 'change of scenario' that involves 'a sensitivity to, and a taking seriously of, the 'idiot' (i.e., that which does not make sense (…),' but 'facilitates this openness to the possibilities of the research event,' Mike Michael and Alex Wilkie, "Speculative Research," in *The Palgrave Encyclopedia of the Possible,* ed. Vlad Petre Glăveanu (London: Palgrave, 2020).

make research more inventive; among these devices can be found, for example, epistemic love letters,[16] games and game design as ethnographic research,[17] idiotic objects;[18] and idiotic frictions.[19] Science may still be science and art may still be art (and design is always caught up somewhere in between)—we can let them be. But their (epistemic) boundaries are soft, which means we can borrow things (practices, concepts) from one another and that is fine, fun, and conducive to new ideas and interpretations. In doing so, we appropriate what we borrow, transforming boundaries to our own purposes, and making our practices more rich on each side of the newly softened fence, sometimes crossing them and often provoking them. In order to avoid confusions about auto-ethnographic design and unnecessary epistemic misinterpretations, including the rejection of it from anthropologists as not-quite ethnographic, I propose calling it *arto*-ethnography, rather than auto-ethnography, also rendering another boundary soft: that between design and art.[20]

79

16   See the example provided by Andrea Gaspar, with her special format of 'epistemic love letters': Andrea Gaspar, "In the Mood for Epistemic Love," text written as part of a collaboratory for ethnographic experimentation (online: Colleex, 2018), colleex.files.wordpress.com/2018/08/gaspar-epistemic-love-letters-open-format1.pdf.

17   For an exploration of social/ethnographic research through games, see Tomás Sánchez Criado, "Playing with Method: Game Design as Ethnographic Research," presented at a series of live-streamed events hosted by the Stadtlabor for Multimodal Anthropology, Institut für Europäische Ethnologie (HU Berlin, 14 and 28 January and 2 February 2021), tscriado.org/category/objects-of-care-and-care-practices/participatory-collaborative-design-of-care-infrastructures/experimen-tal-collaborations/games/; and Gerard Samuel Collins and Joseph Dumit, *Gaming Anthropology: A Sourcebook from #Anthropologycon* (Booklet available at anthropologycon.org, 2017).

18   For further elaboration, see Andrea Gaspar, "Teaching Anthropology Speculatively," *Cadernos de Arte e Antropologia* 7, no. 2 (2018), pp. 75–90.

19   For an example of idiotic frictions as a mode of experimental ethnographic research, see again the work of Gaspar, "Idiotic encounters," pp. 94–113.

20   As a special acknowledgement, I would like to dedicate this text to my former epistemic companion in the field (albeit an unfriendly, unpleasant one), the Italian designer Stefano Mirti, from whom I learnt certain things and had many productive frictions. They still have an effect on me. This text resulted from the interesting dialogues I had with the editor of this book, Michael Kaethler, to whom I am immensely thankful. I also want to especially thank my colleague Tomás Sánchez Criado for reminding me that what I have been trying to do since my fieldwork with designers, as I do here, is (in his words) 'trying to unravel the kind of anthropology designers taught me to practice.'

ANDREA GASPAR, anthropologist, is an integrated researcher at the Centre for Research in Anthropology (CRIA), Portugal. Her research is focused at the intersection of Anthropology, Design and Social Studies of Science and Technology (STS). She holds a PhD in Social Anthropology, awarded by the University of Manchester (2013), and a Master's in Sociology from the University of Coimbra (2006). She worked as an assistant lecturer in Social Anthropology at the University of Coimbra (2015–2019), as a postdoctoral researcher at the Centre for Social Studies (CES), University of Coimbra (2014–2015), and as a visiting postdoctoral fellow at the Madeira Interactive Technologies Institute, Portugal (2013).

We Don't Design by Majority Vote
Taking a Personal Position in Design

Conversation with Konstantin Grcic

Louise Schouwenberg

LS   We had regular talks in your Munich studio, preparing my essay for the upcoming publication *Konstantin Grcic – Panorama* (2014). Two hours, five days in a row—I cannot recall having had such clearly defined timeslots with anyone else I have ever interviewed. But it worked excellently, each day we tentatively zoomed in on another part of your practice. As I was punctual, being aware I would speak with a punctual person, I became a witness of the daily routine of eating Pretzels (Brezel in German) with your team members, eleven am sharp. I can remember eating this heavily salted knot-shaped pastry on the terrace outside your studio, no matter what, also in the pouring rain. You seem to be a person of rituals and routines, a person of the clock.

KG   Absolutely. And indeed, no matter what, we would eat Pretzels on the terrace. In hindsight, it was a quite romantic ritual, which allowed for the team to talk about things outside of the work context. The terrace was crucial, stepping out of the office into a different environment. Our Berlin studio has no terrace and it is not the same doing it indoors. Besides, there are no good Pretzels in Berlin!

LS   Let's resume our 2014 talk on design. At the time, you were adamant about designers having to be authors, especially in working with the industry. How would you now describe authorship? And how would you define the benefit of taking that position in design?

KG   The role of the designer has changed, not only within the industry, but also in general. It's you who confronts me with the term 'authorship.' It hasn't really been in my personal vernacular for years. It does have nice connotations to the other disciplines it derives from, literature and filmmaking, but within design discourse the idea of the designer as author reeks of the past, the nineties. I come from that generation, it was my upbringing in design, but I feel a vague sense of discomfort when people still call me an author because the term became synonymous for the star designer who merely focuses on creating stylistic difference. However, while speaking about it, I do see the point of holding on to the idea of authorship. We still need designers to be authors.

LS Authorship—in its true meaning of taking responsibility?

KG Indeed. A designer needs to have a strong voice, make decisions. Designers are not mere mediators, they're not just part of an agency that suggests various options to the client. I consider *not* taking a position a problem of our times. Everything is open: 'It could be this' and 'it could also be that.'

LS Many in the design field say it's no longer about authorship, but about collaborations.

KG That's not a contradiction. An author is the one who takes an outspoken position, and in a team there may be more authors who do so. After all, a good debate requires several strong voices that don't shy away from taking responsibility. In our studio, we design by the stronger argument and also by fighting some fights before reaching a conclusion.

LS Do you organize contrasting voices in your team? Are you for instance good at acknowledging that somebody else has a better view on something?

KG Yes! I'm open to people proving me wrong, both people within my own team and external experts. That's also part of the reason why I've always wanted to work with the industry. In working with companies, I am the author who's called the designer, but in that context, you always collaborate with people who bring in other expertise— with other authors (including engineers, production experts, marketing and sales people). I feel comfortable with these processes and believe good design needs such collaborations between outspoken players. All of them are authors in their own way. Besides, I have a small studio, how could we be anything else but authors?

LS Let's move to how it started. You were not born a designer. Was there a specific moment that made you decide to become a designer?

KG There's not one key moment that I recall. Many things led up to it. Possibly, it was the catalogue my sister gave me in 1984 on my nineteenth birthday, about an exhibition of Achille Castiglioni's work at the MAK in Vienna.[1] An intriguing red seat, Mezzadro, was on the cover and I liked it. The book included texts and many pictures of Castiglioni in his daily contexts, and I felt I could read and follow what he did and why he did it. It kind of put things together, the man and the product. Reading the book made me understand that design is not just a profession, it's a life.

At the time, I was doing an apprenticeship with a craftsman and intended to either study art or architecture (two fields I knew something about). I never thought of doing design, as it seemed a kind of discipline in between other disciplines. I didn't become a designer because of the Castiglioni catalogue, nor did I aspire to becoming Castiglioni. But it was definitely a moment that made a huge impression. I started to realize I could become someone who would spend my life doing, developing, making things. I still have that book. I know every page. I studied it over and over again.

83

LS Could you imagine such a book be now produced about you, and would you know which images of your life you would include?

KG In fact, I made a very personal book in 2006, *KGID*, published by Phaidon. At the time, I wanted to tell my personal story. Now, I would definitely refrain from doing so. I'm now happy to talk with you about personal things related to my work. Normally I don't like it. We're living in a time in which every project becomes a kind of campaign on social media, focusing on behind-the-scenes, the making-of. I don't think the current interest in personal data, which I see in all fields, adds anything valuable to a project and what it intends to convey.

LS You despise the superficial human-interest stories that accompany projects. However, the person Konstantin Grcic by necessity hides

1 MAK-Museum für Angewandte Kunst/Museum of Applied Arts. The catalogue Grcic refers to was edited by Paolo Ferrari, and published by Electa in 1984.

in what he does. You gained recognition worldwide for both your sober product designs, many of which have become iconic pieces, for your remarkable exhibition designs by which you communicate your larger views on the discipline, and for your collaborations with architects. Your work stands out for the precision and the vast research into materials and technology. What does your work reveal about you? Would you for instance say that your lived experiences, your social class, your cultural background, and the countries you could call your home for a while,[2] have an impact on your design decisions?

KG   It would be hard for my lived experiences to *not* be part of my work. This is who I am. My biography, my experiences, my socializations, are all part of my work process. But if we speak of the work itself, it's not so much about my personal background, but all about the thirty years of my career in design and the training it provided. Part of that training entailed that I learned how to deliberately step outside of myself. Almost like an actor becoming somebody else. That stepping out of oneself is still subjective, it's still about me controlling it. But it's not only about me. I'm also able to take on different personalities. Like a form of 'method acting,' which is a theatrical technique in which the *actor* experiences sincere emotions by fully embracing the role of the character they play. So the actor doesn't merely act like the other, but actually becomes the other, starts living that other life. I'm not sure whether this metaphor is a good one, but it does tell something of how I work. In a project, it's not only me, but also me trying to put on other glasses, or even me getting into another head to truly understand other points of view. In the end, it's me doing that, it's me trying to find out how far I can go—understanding the filters I use, understanding my readings and reflections on specific experiences.

LS   So it's always you vis-à-vis the world, at times by taking on different roles. Wouldn't you say that in design this stepping out of oneself is actually the normal way of working? Designers pretending to be able

2   Konstantin Grcic was born to a Serbian father and a German mother. He studied in the UK, and currently lives and works in Germany.

to understand and give answers to users' needs, regardless of whether this concerns small practical questions or global problems? Isn't this the pitfall of the discipline: designers not owning the responsibility for all implications and consequences of their work, as they hide behind assumed external needs?

KG The other perspectives feed back to me. It's me who draws conclusions. So it's never only about stepping outside. It's always about how I personally relate to the world, being someone with some skills and not other skills, being a person who has their own experiences as well as one who has stepped into the footsteps of others, for a moment. Based on all these experiences, I take a clear position. At times I do see the limitations of this approach, of relying on my outspoken personal outlook, which, one could say, represents a limitation in itself. But it's always embedded in the complexities of having had many experiences. My contribution to design is better if I accept this way of working rather than try to be more objective or neutral. Others are better in that.

If I had strived for an objective position, my office would have become a large agency organized in teams, all of which would be working on something different. It was my conscious choice to stay small. This authorship is not a formula I found and applied; it's a continuous confrontation with issues and principles that I want to understand. You never just move straight ahead. By necessity, each designer's work life is full of contradictions and changes.

LS When do you decide a change is needed? And is there an authority you would then try to get answers from? Or is there someone you call?

KG In the end: I decide. I'm reflective enough to feel and hear the alarms within myself—for instance, when I sense a growing insecurity or I experience people don't understand what I'm saying. Then obviously something's unclear in how I say it. Then something needs to change. There are different ways of dealing with these kinds of (I wouldn't per se call them 'crises') moments in which you need to step out, go sideways, go back. I tend to become a real introvert. I start reading, looking; I try to find out what has disturbed my balance, and give in to introspection and reflection.

Is such brooding mainly triggered by larger issues or practical problems you encounter?

KG It's about the bigger things in design, but very likely it's a particular project that triggers questions. Some people have the idea that designers are supposed to save the world, change the world, make it a better place. This form of expectation gives me the shivers really. I definitely see a responsibility we have for larger issues concerning the world, but we are not the ones who can save the world! I enjoy it most of the time: what we do will end up being a physical thing, a product. But more importantly, as a designer I want to ask the right questions, try to get to the essence of something. I try to make sense of things, make sense of a situation. Sometimes that produces a solution; sometimes it's more of an offering, a possibility that evokes something, makes people think. As such, design becomes part of something slower, an evolution.

The position of a designer as author is an artistic interpretation of the role of the designer, but the context in which we work is always different, as we are always working with different clients. The difference between art and design is that the latter is embedded in a reality context. Art is fantastic when it's completely free, self-indulgent even. Art doesn't have to serve anyone, but design does.

LS How about the COVID-19 situation, did it cause problems for your office?

KG For months I have been working with my team in a remote way. It was a way of getting things done, but I didn't enjoy it much. However, I had one good experience with a particular project in which several partners from different countries were involved. The project could not have happened other than via Zoom. Since last September, we are having two one-hour meetings every week. It's incredible how this has become

86

routine, it's like a clock inside all of us. I have been trying to convince other clients to also set regular meetings. This simple routine ensures an ongoing dialogue and thus enables progress. It's not perfect, by no means, but it works.

LS You're a man of rituals, dialogues, collaborations with many other authors, but you're also a man who has a strong personal voice in setting up such rituals and room for dialogue. In the context of your own studio, you are the one who makes the final decisions.

KG Now I have to be careful not to say something that might be misinterpreted. But I think a democratic process is not a good design process. We don't design by majority vote.

87

KONSTANTIN GRCIC. Since founding his office in Munich in 1991, Konstantin Grcic has been developing furniture, products, and lighting for leading design companies. Today, Konstantin Grcic Design is based in Berlin and works on a range of projects from industrial and furniture design, exhibition design, to collaborations in architecture and fashion. Many of Grcic's products have won international design awards, such as the Compasso d'Oro and the German Design Award. The world's most important design museums (including MoMA, New York; Centre Pompidou, Paris; Die Neue Sammlung, Munich) have included his designs in their permanent collections. Grcic defines function in human terms, combining formal strictness with considerable mental acuity and humour. His work is characterized by a careful research into the history of art, design, and architecture and by a passion for technology and materials.

Honest, Small Scale, Poetic, and Symbolic

Understanding the World by Starting with the Personal

Conversation with Timo de Rijk

Michael Kaethler

MK   What is your gut reaction to the auto-ethnographic turn that we're discussing in this book?

> TDR   My gut reaction is very positive. I see two qualities in what this book describes as the auto-ethnographic: vulnerability and certainty. Both of these resonate with Louise Schouwenberg's work.

MK   This book is about making sense of phenomena in design that we describe as auto-ethnographic. How do you—as a cultural historian—relate this to other design movements or trends in the past?

> TDR   At first glance there appears to be a strong relationship with Bauhaus. Of course, Bauhaus stands for almost everything that is both good and bad in design nowadays. But there is a similarity in that both Bauhaus and this auto-ethnographic phenomena are artistically driven.

With Bauhaus one often misses the symbolism as its works are designed to look as if it's been engineered, like a machine-aged product but in fact it was not part of Fordist production. In this, there's a kind of symbolism, and sometimes this same symbolism resonates with the types of arts-oriented projects that are less about producing an object that serves a specific use than one that is poetic or makes us think. These types of projects are very individually driven, not connected in a *real* way to their objective, and thus symbolic.

MK   You mean, design that is focused on 'raising awareness'?

> TDR   I take issue with design projects that focus on raising awareness; that's a job for journalists, not designers.

Louise Schouwenberg has always been aware of this; she has been devoted to an arts and crafts idea of design, where an artistic influenced design production will communicate key ideas to society. I often accuse her of being too romantic in her thinking. This is not necessarily a criticism. She developed the idea of what you can do as an individual designer. She is aware that symbolic craft-like production isn't going to save the world; she's looking for that middle ground: a design that's a little larger and broader than the individual but not as bold or perhaps as arrogant as some of the save-the-world projects out there.

MK The auto-ethnographic turn in design can be critiqued as being too individualistic, too self-oriented, too local, and perhaps lacking in a broader ambition—especially in light of the fact that as a society or planet we are facing manifold crises. Do you agree: is the auto-ethnographic turn design too insular?

TDR Yes, I understand the critique, but the small, local, and particular can communicate for countless others. Perhaps it's interesting and useful to compare this auto-ethnographic attitude to a long tradition in the field of history: the early twentieth-century French School of the 'Annales.' For them, history was about the smallest pieces and stories, the human experience of one's intimate surroundings (and not only about the big actors that change the world, such as Napoleon). Until recently, many historians would ask, 'What does the detailed history of a small village say about the world?' The Annales School would point to how the experiences of such a village represented countless other villages. In other words, one's individual experience is never quite so individual and therefore represents so much more. In the Netherlands, the book *How God Disappeared from Jorwerd* by Geert Mak tells the story of a small village that is special but not unique; it tells the story of changes that many older generations across the Netherlands can relate to. Designers like to think of themselves as unique individuals. Sure, they may have unique qualities but they are also like many others in the world.

MK Small is good?

TDR Small projects have a significant capacity for change. For example, aesthetics and poetics reach us without needing to solve a specific functional problem. They are not about 'awareness raising,' they don't address an intellectual faculty. They address some other part of us, *touching* us. The world needs poeticism as well as functional remedies. But poeticism needs to be aware of its limitations.

MK Do you see many dangers and/or limitations in this self-oriented and poetically inspired form of design?

90

TDR   Absolutely. The strongest concern I have is that
designers are not honest about what they can do.
I say, 'Be honest, don't try to fool me by saying
you're going to address all the problems in the world.'
There are obvious limitations as to what designers can do,
but this is about being honest with themselves as designers (in terms of what they can do) and subsequently being
honest with how they represent their work to a wider
public. I don't mind if a project is only poetic but don't
sell it as something else. I am a bit moralistic about this.
Too many designers are not solving anything but standing
in front of the problem, potentially blocking others who
might actually be able to start addressing it. The work of a
designer is about integrity, about being honest and clear
with what they do and what purpose their work serves.

MK   Auto-ethnographic design tends to favour the personal exploration, *initially* remaining at one's very specific context in order to
understand the dynamic between the self and the context.

TDR   Design is about changing and understanding
the world in combination, simultaneously;
perhaps this change needs to start first at a very
personal and individual level. Too often designers
are obsessed with trying to fix things without
understanding them. As Rem Koolhaas used to say,
'First try to understand the world and the morality
comes later.'

MK   It appears that engineering-type design is showing its limits to
understand complex contexts; is there a need for more poetics
in design?

TDR   The world is absurd, that's why I think the world
keeps on inspiring us to try to understand what's
happening. What does it all mean? The world is
not rational, and because of this, purely rational or
functional pursuits are severely limited. We need
diversity in design approaches—both the engineering and the artistic—if we are to understand and
possibly change the world.

TIMO DE RIJK is an art historian and is the director of Design Museum Den Bosch (NL), a position he has held since 2016. Previously, he was professor of Design History at Delft University of Technology (NL) and Leiden University (NL), and professor of Design Cultures at Vrije Universiteit University Amsterdam (NL). He has made several exhibitions and has produced many publications in the field of historical and contemporary design. De Rijk was editor-in-chief of the *Dutch Design Yearbook* and chairman of the Association of Dutch Designers (BNO).

91

The Independent Artist

Sjeng Scheijen

'Every work of art, be it a poem or a dome, always is a self-portrait.'

> Joseph Brodsky

'Play a scale in C major metronomically and ask someone else to do the same. The difference in the playing is proof of the presence of personality.'

> Igor Stravinsky

This chapter contemplates the use of auto-ethnography (as term and theory) as a way to understand, or present, a model for self-representation in creative activity, especially in the visual arts and design. It originates from my experiences as both a scholar of Russian avant-garde art and teacher at a design school. To illuminate one particular technique of self-representation in the art and design of the Russian revolutionary avant-garde, I will turn to the work of their most radical representative, Vladimir Tatlin (1885–1953).

> When contemplating a work of art, we firstly have to make one bold assumption: that the artwork exists. I mean, we need to assume that there truly is a distinct category of objects that we call artworks. We all know that there is a powerful group of theorists, sociologists, and philosophers, who would vehemently deny that such a distinct category of objects exists. They would argue that perhaps a typical social function we call art exists, and that function can be closely associated with the historical practice that was or is considered to be art—but the objects produced are in the end no different to any other kind of produced object, and that the labour needed to produce these objects is the same that was needed to produce a toilet in a ceramic factory. In short, they would argue, art is a sociological phenomenon only; it is defined by its reception and not by its creation. This postulation I vehemently oppose, and if you don't, then there is no point in continuing on reading.

[Handwritten margin note: Art is only sociological phenomenon defined by perception/reception not by creation]

We have to be even bolder and must assume that such an 'artwork' is real. And by real, I mean as real as a fist in your face, as your lover's tongue in your mouth, as a bomb at the exact moment of its explosion in a driving train. What I mean is that the artwork at the moment of its reception by me is experienced by the full force of my combined senses, my emotions, and my intellect: it is experienced as one dynamic whole… I experience it as a child who devours a piece of birthday cake and while eating it detects its various layers, trying to define its tastiest bits and imagining an even bigger one. I do not claim to make any philosophically viable statement here; I just mean that the artwork is as real as it gets from an everyday human perspective, whichever philosophical interpretation you would like to give to the concept of reality. Or in more pretentious terms, the real event is the kind of event where sign and signified completely collide and form a perfect union in time and place. When the incoming fist reaches the skin of your face and starts the rare event of smashing your nose out of its place, this is the moment that you know that you're experiencing a real event, not a reproduction, or a representation of the event, not only a sign, but the full experience of reality—whatever your assumption of the nature of reality is.

While the above refers to the reception of art, the same must be said of the artistic practice—the production of art. It is produced as a whole, with the full embodiment of our undifferentiated, unanalyzable, self. That is, of course, ideally speaking. Let's say this wholeness is the great striving which lays at the fundament of the ideal of being an artist. I deliberately use 'wholeness' instead of, for example, 'holistic.' With its status as a simplistic neologism, a tool for the lesser educated, and its origin from the abracadabra of the 'become-spiritual-in-a-week' leaflet, it is exactly what I need. I think, rather subversively I'm afraid, that the world of abracadabra, of goodhearted vulgar spiritualism, of the urban legend, and outright nonsense, is a more stimulating and less hostile environment for artists than the cold-hearted and repressive environment of academic theoretical discourse. But this aside.

While in this range the 'fist in the face,' 'your lover's tongue' etc., represent the ultimate 'realness' of human experience, on

think of other analogies as real as a slap in the face, a tongue in your mouth, an ambulance siren ricocheting 94 through off the empty air

the other side of the spectrum there are phenomena that are far less real, that belong to the kind of experience that, although detected by our senses, are mostly ignored by our brain. They are filtered out, so to say. The rumbling of our bowels, the undifferentiated chatter and soggy munching of other couples in a restaurant, the drawling of a Latin prayer in church—these belong to the lesser real phenomena. While we might assume they exist, their impression on us is so fleeting and redundant that we, at best, notice their existence only when the peripheral whizzing and blabbering suddenly stop.

The theory and terminology with which I try to reflect upon the artwork obviously belong more to the unreal than to the real, more to the rumbling, mumbling, and blabbering than to the 'fist in your face.' Theory is only a means to reflect, and as such will, at its very best, give a fragmentary and distorted hint of what the artwork really is. In a way, one could say that fragmentation and distortion are part of the intention of theory. It can only function by smashing the artwork to pieces and then handing over a few shards to the reader as evidence of its existence and as a starting point for our contemplation. Or maybe even sillier, the theorist is like a palaeontologist who lives among a tribe of Neanderthals but is always looking to the ground until he finds a single tooth and a bone fragment, picks them up and shouts: 'Wow with these findings we now know so much more about Neanderthals!'

This is true of all theoretical reflection on art, but especially when considering the subject of self-representation in art, which is clearly one of the central problems of understanding the nature of creative production we call art. I started this chapter by quoting two rather eminent figureheads of twentieth-century art, Brodsky and Stravinsky, to use their status and knowledge to declare that there is no art without self-representation; that self-representation is an undeniable, intrinsic part of both artistic production and artistic reception.

I make all these rather childish observations because it is my assumption, or my conviction if you like, that the artistic process is not, or does not, need to be self-reflective. When the representation of self in art is intrinsic, inseparable from the process of artistic creation

95

Theory is only a means to reflect [handwritten marginal note]

itself, then reflection on the self is not an inseparable, intrinsic part of the same process. One cannot be the creator of the text and its translator at the same time. This is of course, in theory. Obviously, the artistic creative process is very often an oscillatory process of creation and interpretation by the artist. My point is that the interpretation, being self-reflective or self-reflexive, does not have to be a part of the artistic process. It is the creative impulse that predestines the labour of the maker as a work of art. It is the dominance of the creative impulse that is the sole defining element that determines if a product of labour can be called an artwork. It goes too far here to specify how I would define 'creative impulse,' but I think for this purpose it is enough to say that the creative impulse is the urge to sing under the shower, or the urge of a child to take up a pencil, draw a few unorganized lines, and state that it is a boat. It is a text, irrespective of context.

When I say that a certain quality defines the artwork, I do not mean that this quality constitutes or describes the wholeness of the artwork. I mean instead that it provides a minimum, a certain aspect the artwork cannot do without, otherwise it would be something else, or wouldn't exist at all. So, in my view, the artistic impulse defines the artwork, and self-reflection (although it is presumably a part of almost all kinds of creative activity) in the end does not. To continue with the analogy used earlier, the artwork is defined by its text, not by its context. The artwork is not instigated by demand, be it demand from markets, from governments, or from any other social constellation, but instigated by a psychological, or spiritual if you like, unprompted drive.

All of the above leaves many questions open, but one is of specific interest here. If the biographical is an intrinsic part of artistic creation, and if self-reflectivity is not an intrinsic part of it (and, I think, is often better avoided), then how can a creative producer use autobiographical material or autobiographical information deliberately in his creative process? It seems perfectly clear to me that deliberate, ostentatious, self-conscious use of autobiographical material and information has proven to be a goldmine for artists. But why should an artist do this, if not for self-

96

representation, as this is already implicit in everything they do?

I think it is here that the use of auto-ethnography as a theoretical system can play a role: in order to provide a strategic model for the use and legitimization of autobiography in design and art. There are many reasons why this would be necessary, or at least effective, for the production of design and art. Since the beginning of a professionalized discipline of art history, and art theory, the autobiographical approach was under fire. The emergence of formalist art theory ('Kunstgeschichte ohne Namen' [Art history without names]), and Panofsky's 'iconographic' method led to a consensus in which 'a work of the visual arts [was seen] either as a realization of a supraindividual history of 'form' or as an expression of the 'History of Ideas.'[1]

> The above-described tendency is dominant in all cultural history, although nowadays cultural history focuses not so much on 'a supraindividual history of ideas,' but on a supraindividual exploration of identities or other sociological categories. But this distinction is irrelevant for the current argument. At the same time, an autobiographical approach to artistic creation is still dominant in popular forms of art history, as represented in documentaries, fiction films, children's books, and even wall texts in museums. The artist mythologies constructed upon the life-stories of Van Gogh, Chagall, and Pollock for educational and commercial purposes are well known examples. This paradox of an academic theoretical rejection of autobiography and its simultaneous popular and commercial promotion (often performed by the same institution) is the main reason for the established and maybe growing divide between popular art history and academic or quasi-academic studies (like this piece) of cultural history.

In short, the creative producer treads on a theoretical minefield when trying to use autobiographical material in a deliberate way in their creative production. While, as said, the artist is utterly incapable of not being autobiographical; and while the use of their private history, private social environment, private

---

1   Gerd Blum, "1.9 History of Art," in *Handbook of Autobiography/Autofiction*, ed. Martina Wagner-Egelhaaf (Berlin: Walter de Gruyter, 2019), p. 87.

spaces are very often the only trustworthy material that they have at their disposal, it is very clear to me that the theoretical rejection of autobiography and the educational and commercial vulgarization of autobiography are both societal tools for the repression and ultimately desired ruination of the artist, who understandably is considered an irritant if not a threat for the efficient functioning of modern markets and governments.

Auto-ethnography started as a methodology of 'self-representation by trained anthropologists that includes a critique of privileged points of view from the outside and which incorporates a resistance to structures of knowledge as power.'[2] By trying, instead, to engage fully with the realities of their subject and using ego-documents as an instrument of notation and analysis, they supposedly would be able to fulfil their pretention of professionality, while at the same time become part of the subjective environment of their interest. In short, they tried to become object and subject in one. If this indeed is a viable working method for ethnographers, I cannot judge; but for artists it is, in a way, their natural habitat. The artistic practice always implies being subject and object in one.

For designers though, this typical artistic positioning has always been problematic, as they produce functional entities that are obliged to perform in environments independent from the personality, background, and intentions of the maker. The designed object belongs solely to the context and loses its status as text. In short: in order to function as 'design,' the subject (the maker) needs to be erased. In order to become viable 'designed objects,' and accepted as such by markets and governments, the creative origin of the object needs to be absent. (Of course there exists the typical category of 'art design' but here the artistic aspect is mostly only a representation of artistry, a kind of recognizable artistic script, that only communicates to the owner or user that this object 'talks' artistic, and is therefore a valuable object—without the full unleashed force of the true ambivalent, heterogenic, unanalyzable quality that empowers the artistic object, the artwork, an object that arises from a creative impulse, and not from a political, societal, or capitalist demand). At the

---

2   Neni Panourgia, "Auto/ethnography: Rewriting the Self and the Social by Deborah E. Reed-Danahay," *American Ethnologist* 27, no. 2 (May 2000), p. 552.

same time, we know that many objects that normally would be categorized as design do originate from a creative impulse and are as artistic as an installation or a performance. So, the designed object hides its nature, acts as if there is no subject, no author, no text, and postures as a contextual object. The designer does this willingly and deliberately.

This raises the question of how we can emancipate the designed object and force out its artistic ancestry. In order to emancipate themself, the designer needs to build a theoretical wall between themself and society that will guard them from the nihilating force of demand, but at the same time give them the opportunity to communicate with context. This is the challenge: this is where auto-ethnography comes in. Now, how should this kind of auto-ethnography take shape in the designer's practice? To answer this, I would like to give an example rather than an analysis.

Let's talk about Tatlin.

Tatlin, generally accepted by his peers as the most innovative artist of his generation, was renowned within the art world equally for his life-stories as for his artworks. He never wrote these stories down. In fact, the sparse biographical information he left in official documents is extremely limited and contains important and unexplainable lacunae. His life-stories are exclusively handed down in texts by others. From these rendered stories emerged a fluid, meandering autobiography, which was partly based on real-life events, and partly outright fabrications.

He loved to talk about his days as a young boy when he fled the parental home where he had been abused; about his subsequent wandering years through Russia and Ukraine, where he learned to play the Bandura, a local lire-like instrument used by blind, wandering beggars. To flee poverty, he worked as a sailor on a ship on the black sea. These stories are generally accepted to be truthful, though the rendered details may vary widely. (His claim, for example, that he had been a snake charmer in Egypt, seems less convincing, as was his assertion that he was able to levitate during meditation sessions in the privacy of his studio—although he convinced Daniil Kharms of this, who told it with assured excitement to Samuil Marshak). His stories about working as an extra (a so-called statist) in opera productions (assumably in the role of 'corpse'), or as a wrestler in circuses, seem to have some connection to the truth but are far from sure. Tatlin was certainly not the only avant-garde artist who fictionalized parts of his biography; but it seems fair to say that for him, more than for any other avant-gardist, fictionalizing the self was a central characteristic of his artistic persona. I prefer the term 'fictionalizing' as it seems to indicate an active 'creative' attitude more so than the rather normative term 'mythologizing.' And as I hope to convey in this paper, the fictionalized self, the role-play, and travesty, and the identification of artwork and fictionalized biography, were constant elements in his whole artistic output.

[handwritten margin note: fiction over myth.]

The fictionalization of Tatlin's biography can be seen in his artworks, where a role-play with the self is evident in paintings like his two self-portraits, but also in his installations, which he named after himself. The same occurs in 'Tatlin's Tower,' the unofficial (but employed and maybe instigated by him) name for his *Monument to the Third International*, and the flying device *Letatlin*—a contraction of his last name and the verb *letat* [to fly]. In his illustrations for the children's book *Vo-pervych i vo-vtorych* (*First, Second*) by Daniil Kharms, he emerges as the 'tall man' who travels with a few children, a goat, and a car in an unknown land.

Already in the first artworks that attracted some attention, he started to play a game with these life-stories. His painting *Sailor* from 1911, first exhibited in 1912, is generally considered to be a self-portrait, although Tatlin never presented it as such. The particular shape of the head and the full lips, though, leave no doubt about the identity of the depicted figure and many contemporaries refer to the work plainly as a self-portrait. Still, this is not a biographical 'self-portrait,' but a portrayal of the self in performance, playing a role. As Marian Burleigh first noted, the name on the sailor's cap reads 'Steregushchii': what in this context can refer to nothing but the *Steregushchii*—a ship that fought in the 1905 war against Japan and perished there, apparently because the sailors didn't want to surrender to the Japanese.[3] In 1911 Czar Nicolas, who was eager to publicize

3   Marian Burleigh-Motley, "Tatlin's "Sailor": A New Reading," *Source: Notes in the History of Art* 11, no. 3/4 (1992), p. 48.

the supposed support of the common man for his rule, raised a monument to commemorate the bravery of the sailors, who as a social group were commonly identified as proletarian par excellence and therefore, in the contemporary political debates in the Russian empire, were far from obvious supporters of czarism. In this monument, the sailors were sacralized as martyrs for czarism, and the czarist propagandists tried to appropriate the sailor as a social type as a pillar of czarist rule and orthodoxy. Nicolas publicly emphasized his support for the monument by attending the unveiling ceremony in April 1911.

> In one sense, Tatlin's sailor of the *Steregushchii* is a typical carnavallestic gesture. A bohemian artist, a lowbrow figure by middle-class standards (as Malevich's father once stated to his son: 'Most artists are in jail'), impersonates the elevated figure of the official hero, thereby mocking and de-sacralizing him. As so often in satiric communication it is the mockery of pretension, the mockery of a suddenly heightened status that is partly opportunistic and not fully recognized yet by society, that is easiest and most successfully attacked.

This is one way of using auto-ethnography in artistic production. By taking on the role of the depicted person, Tatlin prevents the 'objectification' of the depicted, and deconstructs the assumed hierarchy between the artist and the depicted 'other.' At the same time, the artist appropriates the context of the canonization of the *Steregushchii* sailor, which certainly could be seen as disingenuous. The result is utterly ambiguous—which is of course the reason why it is such an interesting artwork.

> Before Tatlin could use a partly similar, partly quite different technique in his role as designer, something disquieting happened. Sometime in 1922, the proudly presented *Monument to the Third Internationale*, an artwork that brought Tatlin world fame, was chopped to pieces and used as firewood (of course, without the artist being informed). After this debacle, Tatlin diverted his attention from the utopian and grandiose to the domestic and intimate, a radical repositioning of his artistic aspirations, which he summarized in the slogan that was to be the motto of his studio: 'Not to the old, not to the new, but to the necessary.' Note here that he very deliberately used the extremely ambivalent word 'necessary,' instead of

'functional'—which had come into vogue at the same time, and which haunted twentieth-century design ever since. Tatlin very well understood that succumbing to functionality would mean succumbing to context and demand, and would eliminate the element of unprompted creative drive.

In this new role, he researched the domestic environment as a defence mechanism. The domestic as an instrument for autarkic, self-sufficient living, as a way to defend the self against the sociocultural pressures of the outside world. He employed this certainly not communist, anti-collective positioning, while using the rhetoric and even the visual language of the early Soviet state, thereby commenting on, and ironizing, Soviet policies and the increasing oratory and social pressure with which it was implemented.

The clothes he designed, like his Normal suit and Normal coat, originated from a process of everyday trial and error and self-usage. He and his young family were the test subjects. In that environment, he designed 'a standard suit' that could be expanded or adjusted by adding or detaching layers and pockets. With the same attitude, he designed a stove, pans, and kitchen utensils, the basic outfit for survival in the modern city. They were all made from everyday and easy to obtain, cheap materials. All objects were not 'produced' but presented as a construction scheme, so that every citizen, even the poorest, would be able to make them. Still, although these works were deliberately, and ostentatiously, contextual, they were presented as another life-story, with a sad looking Tatlin who promoted not so much a new and inspiring life-form, but a modus of survival. By presenting his own autobiography so explicitly within a context of socialist functionality, he obviously provoked harsh criticism, and he was indeed fiercely attacked by functionaries and colleagues.

These simple, unassuming designed objects were the first examples of what we now call conceptual design but were also the result of an auto-ethnographic strategy that was implemented to safeguard the creative impulse from the increasingly intrusive demands of a totalitarian state. He understood that in order to be truly critical of the powerful, the artist needs to deny the necessity of demand and of context, because by doing so the artist denies the necessity of their power. He made clear, and paid a heavy price for it, that there is nothing more political than a truly independent artist.

To conclude, I would like to return, very briefly, to my celebration of wholeness. It is the artist's ideal to produce this experience of wholeness for themself and their audience. It seems completely clear to me that this can never exist in a vulgar understanding of 'artistic autonomy.' I say this because I'm certain that the enemies of the artist will certainly rebuff all of the above as another pathetic defence of a (rather mythological) position of privileged autonomy, a defence of an alienated artistry, gloatingly residing in its ivory tower, responsible to no one. No, sillies. The true artist must, in the words of Auden,

> *...among the Just*
> *Be just, among the Filthy filthy too.*
> *And in his own weak person, if he can.*
> *Duly put up with all the wrongs of Man.*[4]

But the artist can do so only if they do not become controlled by outside demand, be it market driven, or driven by societal mandates. The artistic space, artistic lust, artistic taste, is under attack from an unholy coalition of neoliberals and anti-capitalist propagandists of social utilitarianism. In a world ever more subjected to fragmentation, only independent artists are able to produce the sensation of wholeness. Let them sing, and let them take the jump, deep in their selves, in order to find the Just and the Filthy, to represent themselves for all, undemanded and unappraised.

103

SJENG SCHEIJEN is a Russian art specialist, author, and free-lance exhibition curator. He is author of *Diaghilev: A Life* (Oxford University Press, 2009), which was listed best book of the year by *The New Yorker*, *Sunday Times*, *NRC Handelsblad*, and he wrote *De avant-gardisten* (2019), on the demise of the Russian avant-garde, which won the Bookspot Literatuurprijs, 2019. He studied Slavic Studies at Leiden University (NL), where he also obtained his PhD. Apart from his activities as author and curator, he worked as a former cultural attaché at the Royal Netherlands Embassy in Moscow, is a jury member of the Johannes Vermeer Prize, and teaches Cultural Theory, and is a tutor at the Master's programme of Contextual Design at Design Academy Eindhoven (NL).

4   Wystan Hugh Auden, "The Novelist," in *The Complete Works of W. H. Auden: Prose. 1939–1948*, Vol. 2 (Princeton, New Jersey: Princeton University Press, 1996).

Become One with a Chair
Dialoguing with Objects

Conversation with Marianne Theunissen

Louise Schouwenberg

104

LS There's an obvious fascination for things in your artworks. Throughout your drawings, sculptures, installations, performances, and films, things always play major roles. When humans are involved, they engage with things on an equal level, without hierarchy, which often leads to hilarious situations in which furniture appears to be 'sick' and people have transformed into chairs. As you wrote yourself: 'Jane Bennet's vital materialism comes to mind, in which things have an impact on humans and non-humans, affecting their lives and meanings by creating strange, yet strong bonds.' Does this personal interest for material things also influence your teachings?

MT Yes. I try to create situations in which students can experience daily objects in different, non-human ways. It often starts with an impossible assignment, for which there's no practical solution, so students cannot hold on to pre-assumptions of what the goal is. I ask them for instance to create a dangerous bag, or make a bag as a house. First, an existing bag needs to be dismantled by peeling off all layers, not only to discover the construction and fabrics inside, but also to discover the dangerous potential that hides within that bag.

105

LS Turning a banal daily thing into something that seems to contrast the thing's shop-window DNA reveals something about the artist Marianne Theunissen. But it also reveals something about you as a person. I happen to know your house, which is quite extraordinary, as it tells of your peculiar outlook on life in all its detailing, including the display of your vast collection of shoes. From the rather weird new shoe designs, to the worn-out, slightly dirty footwear, all pairs of shoes are draped across the wall of your living room. That's not a usual place for storing one's shoes! Remarkable is also the empty spot on the wall that patiently waits for the return of the shoes you currently wear.

Once I started to notice this obvious fascination for shoes, I started to see evidence of a deeper obsession with things in your house, such as the collection of weird, old, new, expensive, cheap bags; the Chinese paper masks; the great variety of decorated cups and plates in the kitchen area; colourful lampoons dangling from the ceiling; the enormous range of vintage clothes, some of which are proudly displayed on the wall; objects dressed in vintage clothes, like a ball dressed in a stretch ladies-blouse that works its way up and down the

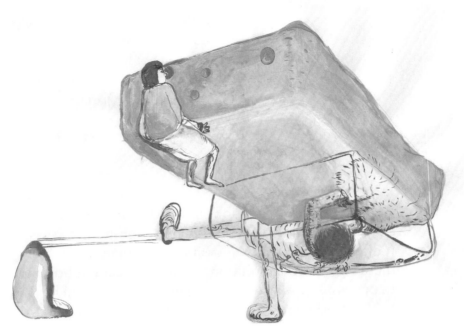

Marianne Theunissen, *Meubilair Ziek* [Furniture ill], 2010.

wall; fragments of decorated Japanese doors, cleverly built into the self-constructed walls. Daily items are interspersed with artworks, either created by you or received from befriended artists. In this house the visitor won't find the usual hierarchy between high and low art, and no preference for throwaway funny gadgets or labour-intensive, carefully crafted artefacts. Would you describe yourself as a fetishist?

MT I'm fascinated by things. They reveal so much about us. Look at the stuff people collect and how much value they attribute to each item. Things seem to incorporate narratives and people want to identify with those stories hiding within. So they keep on buying new things out of fear of loosing a sense of identity and belonging.

I'm not merely fascinated by things themselves, nor am I per se interested in what people project onto them in terms of status. I'm most of all fascinated by how people relate to things. These relationships cause all kinds of mixed feelings. Who's the boss? Who obeys what? People tend to think they are in control, that they define the relationship, but most of the time it's the other way round.

A self assured person leans back and thinks they are in charge of the technical gadgets they own, but in fact their mobile phone completely regulates their life. An insecure person clasps their bag in fear of losing it, or nervously wrings part of their clothes, revealing a totally different kind of relationship with things. Cultural differences also play a role, for instance in how people hold and fold a dishcloth, how a Dutch market vendor plunges vegetables in a plastic bag, whereas a Japanese seller packs each individual item with great care and precision.

One striking example is how you deal with the door key when you return home late at night. It often ends in a battle between you and the key, when you discover the thing has a will of its own. Whether the key slides smoothly into the hole can represent your personal mood, but it can also depend on the state of the key, which may have become rusted and deformed in the course of time. The more you want to control the movement, the harder it gets. But look at a drunk. Having lost an acute awareness of themself, the drunk becomes a friend (who knows what the key wants?), and allows it to guide them in.

How we deal with things always revolves around power relationships. When I'm not drunk, and obsessively try hard to get the damn thing into the hole, it becomes a battle. And mind you, it's not only a battle of getting it in to open the door, but also a battle because I'm aware of me doing this, aware that other people might see me and interpret what they see.

LS   So much brooding on how you get a key into a keyhole!

MT   That's who I am. There's this ongoing questioning of everything, this ongoing dialogue in my head, both with imagined other people and with the things I encounter in daily life. In my work I try to answer such questioning by carefully listening to things and sensing what they want.

A long time ago, I consulted a psychologist to discuss this constant brooding on petty little things of daily life. I gave him the example of going to a bakery and having hundreds of questions in my head before reaching the shop, to then forgetting why I had gone there in the first place. Questions related to how I would cross the street and if people would sense my mood, my thoughts, how the street would affect my way of walking, how perhaps the street would sense the touch of my feet, how I would enter the bakery, what the door would look like, who would be inside, how I would relate to the baker. I thought all people were like me, constantly brooding on things in their heads, but the psychologist said such brooding was exceptional. I was shocked by that answer, which kind of confirmed my idea that something was wrong with me.

LS   The psychologist made you aware something was wrong with you? Seems like the world upside down. Why did you go there in the first place?

MT   (Laughing).
True, this constant brooding was already bothering me. I often sensed a heavy burden, being too open to experiencing everything. I was borderless and often got lost, just like this experience going to the bakery. But gradually I've learned that there's a very good side of such questioning. It merely takes time to reach an acceptance of who you are. How you cope with life can become a valuable part of how you work. That's an insight I also try to convey to my students.
For me, living entails a kind of ongoing phenomenological research, in which my lived experiences constantly inform my making process. These experiences can entail how I deal with daily life issues, but they can also consist of how I absorb the dystopic atmosphere after a rave party, when suddenly the space gets flooded with light, and the audience finds itself in that crazy state in-between loud noise and total silence. It has always been my ultimate challenge to be able to show such an experience by way of objects.
In my work, I try to translate experiences into material forms I can physically relate to. In our contemporary digital world, the relations we have with the physical world are deteriorating. Our bodies are great tools to create real or imaginative relations with things, and thus great tools to create new memories of things.

LS   Could you describe your views on art and design?

Marianne Theunissen & Chris Baaten, *Biosonic Furniture Training*, 2012, video still, photo: Gert Jan van Rooij.

MT   Artists and designers investigate and question the world, which is very good, because questioning makes people aware of the uniqueness of each perspective and the potential of each experience. In contrast to artists, designers tend to simplify things by using an understandable language, which usually leaves no space for questions. Artists often employ functional items as metaphors to tell a story, whereas functional objects don't necessarily aim at being read as metaphors. Designed objects relate in a practical manner to the world of agreements that surrounds us, and apparently that practicality seems to ask for simplification, which comes with the price that it does not always do justice to the reality of things.

LS   With our plea for an auto-ethnographic approach in design, we implicitly comment what you call the 'the world of agreements,' as conventions in design have caused so many problems, including overproduction and overconsumption. Apart from our aim at causing more genuine commitment by the designer, naturally, there's a danger when one starts to focus on the self. Projects can become too private, which is more problematic in design then in art.

110

MT   That's also a problem in art. Art should go beyond mere self-expression. Art can change how we think about things, which is powerful, but design can change both our thinking *and* our behaviour. I don't think many designers employ the full potential of their discipline.

LS   What do you aim at in your tutoring?

MT   I learned from a Buddhist teacher to call out 'Stop' every now and then—to stop thinking about the goal and go back to the moment. While teaching, I reach out to students when I notice them trying to finish something they have thought out in their heads, but have stopped exploring these thoughts on a physical level, not experiencing anything. Projects can become too cerebral, strict, suffocating the imagination. For instance, if students try to execute the drawing of a door, I tell them they should try to remain in the here and now, as every strike of the brush counts and has an effect on all other brush-strokes. Every line matters. If you intensely experience that line, the drawing will always succeed, no matter what you draw. But if the drawing becomes an automatism, you lose it.

LS   What should such experimenting with things bring?

MT   Merging with what you do. Becoming fragmented. Loosing oneself. Trying to abandon the usual hierarchy with things and becoming sensitive to what appears unnoticeable. In normal life, most people don't want to experience everything they might experience, as they want to lead a clear and simple life. They want to choose things they already know, go to the same hotel chains wherever they are in the world, drink the same coffee, eat the same muffin. That's what we could call a 'muf' life in Dutch: a stale, flat life. If you problematize and question things, people may start to enjoy the problematizing act itself. From personal experience, I know how liberating it can be to forget about conventions and enter into an open relationship with things. Become one with a chair, for instance.

111

MARIANNE THEUNISSEN is a visual artist. Starting from a thing-perspective, she probes the non-human world in relation to the so-called human domain. Notions of space and the way she wants the public to experience this space are related to her concern with the question of how a place or thing can change—through movements, emotions, things, or is it only our own perspective that changes? The outcomes consist of installations, performances, films, sculptures, and drawings. Theunissen teaches at theBA Fine Art Department of the Gerrit Rietveld Academie (NL) and at the MA Contextual Design of Design Academy Eindhoven. She also writes for and participates in the performance-group Self Luminous Society as José, The Contagious Condoctor.

PROJECTS AND

PRACTICES

Sticky Data
Looping Streams of My (Datafied) Self

Bianca Schick

Physical bodies stick to our data bodies. Just like our social context frames our physical bodies, data frames us.

When we are born, we do not invent ourselves from scratch. The social context, which is not of our choosing, frames the limits of our self. Data structures are now actively intervening in that social context, providing new input and parameters for how we think of and know ourselves. Our identity is thus entangled in people, objects and also, importantly, our data.

It has been clear to me for most of my life that we are not autonomous beings. I was a shy child: emotional, insecure, entirely eager to please. I did what was in my power to be liked by others. I first began to copy my mother's behaviour. I would replicate her facial expressions. When she was sad, I wanted to feel sad; I imagined her pain to be mine. When I grew older, I did the same with my best friend. If she wore sporty T-shirts with holes, I wore sporty T-shirts with holes. Over time, I learned to observe others carefully—their emotional expressions, gestures, voice tonality—so that I could replicate their way of being as needed. I understood that if I adjusted my behaviour, absorbing every piece of information, I would feel less alone, more likeable, and perhaps even get more attention. I patched together an identity—a sense of self—based on the people around me.

In my desperate effort to find a connection with someone outside myself, it became more and more difficult to neatly trace discernible boundaries between myself and the other, or to create distance from the things that surrounded me. Where does the other stop and where do I begin? When there is no distance between self and other, alienation arises the moment the other disappears. And I often faced this situation. Breaking up with a boyfriend felt like being deleted from the world. Changing friend-circles brought me back to zero. I was utterly entangled with others.

Today I am entangled with my data. Data-driven platforms foster and reinforce my need to be someone. My identity is

```
def action (clicking):
    import <forget your thoughts>
    import <reduce tension>

include <from [left] to [right]; var (random);>
include <from [right] to [left]; var (random);>
```

3–6

1–2   Bianca Schick, *I lick I click I bite I spit*, 2021, installation, video stills.
3–6   Bianca Schick, *Scripting Nervousness*, 2020, video stills.

7–10

defined, confined, and codified. As I dive into a sea of data about myself, I am convinced I discover a stable self. I no longer need to mimic others; now, I have *my* data. Perhaps this is because my data is the product of my bodily actions. It is an extension of the movements of my fingertips; it is something that was, or perhaps still is, stuck to my skin. Like sweat, my data seeps out of my skin,[1] out of my semiconscious movements. Like sweat, it leaves behind a trail. Swimming in my own data, I do not need to mirror someone else to feel accepted. I can look at the scored silhouette of my daily actions that seem to exist outside of time and space. The whole experience becomes a feedback loop, returning to me in the form of custom advertisements and numbers charting my sleeping patterns, footsteps, and the beating of my heart. My phone and computer are personal self-tracking devices. The myriad of colourful apps remark that I ate too much, that I need to drink more water, that today I have not walked ten thousand steps, that if I feel nervous, I should take a deep breath.

Data does not just exist alone. It needs to be generated. Text needs to be typed, images need to be taken, videos need to be recorded, buttons need to be pressed. And with every click, the interface changes my self and vice versa. Perhaps I (and not only my self) entangle my social network within this process—a meshwork of buttons.

In this dialectical exchange can be found an added effect. The data charts not only discrete and countable actions. It can also be used to extrapolate feelings from the way I touch my device or look at the screen: nervousness in my speed of scrolling, boredom in my staring at an image, excitement in my slow and careful reading. Inevitably, this data is decontextualized and treated as something to be improved. Metrics, notifications, new advertisements all incite me to move more, eat less, breathe deeply. I become a data generator while also being influenced by the data,

1   The concept of sweating data is mentioned in Melissa Gregg, "Inside The Data Spectacle," *Television & New Media* 16, no. 1 (2015), p. 45.

12

7–12   Bianca Schick, *I lick I click I bite
        I spit*, 2021, installation, video stills.

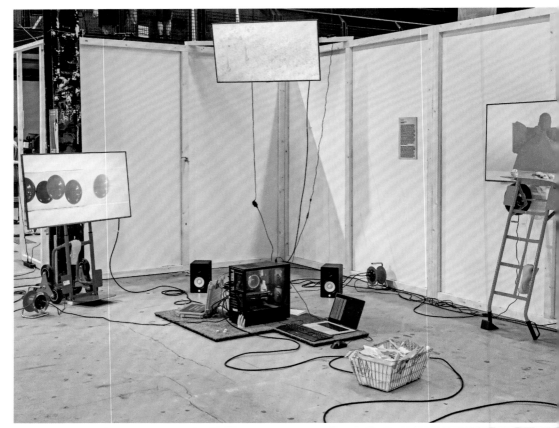

and I lose myself again and again in an act of data-becoming.

My data is not a collection of impersonal data points but rather a record of affective-charged narratives. The data that I produce daily is a repository of what I wonder about, worry over, and an archive of my aimless habits, curiosities, and obsessions. There is an honesty in the accounting; what I fail to do or the ways I hide are laid bare. As such, I genuinely recognize myself in my devices, and so I must contend with understanding myself as data.

While this may come across as negative, I must add that there is a stability in this self-data feedback loop. My data looks back at me without judgement. I can accept it as a means of objectively looking at myself. As the loop tightens, does my identity consolidate? My relentless pursuit of knowing who I am takes place amidst corporate platforms that strive for my attention, maximize my engagement, and sell me the trendiest pair of shoes. Simultaneously, these same platforms model my behaviour and estimate or determine the opportunities and exclusions that should be extended to me. Ultimately, I become a commodity to others and to myself.

This tightening loop of self and data, commodity and consumer, is where I find inspiration for approaching design. Data enables a plurality of performatives: being a subject increasingly means being a data subject (in work and leisure, public and private spaces). My design responds to this vanishing boundary and expresses how emotions, performance, and technology merge in creative practice. As such, my design work combines plenty of introspection with research; it identifies the uncomfortable realities and boundaries of the self and data, such as how feelings and emotions arise from the orienting of our bodies towards digital technologies. How are we performing new data-identities?

To explore these questions, I use a range of media. In particular, I use moving images to give data a shape and a 'body,' in order for it to find a representation closer to the social life as we experience it rather than simply as the numbers, statistics, and graphs that feed it.

15–18

13–14   Bianca Schick, *I lick I click I bite I spit*, 2021, installation.
15–18   Bianca Schick, *I lick I click I bite I spit*, 2021, installation, video stills.

```
def breathing_efficiency (%);
    import <relax>

        pause (3) # Pause for 3 sec
            print ("Breath")
        pause (0.100) # Pause for 100 ms
            print ("Breath")
        pause (0.568) # Pause for 0.568 ms
            print ("Breath")
```

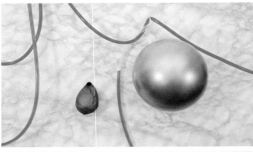

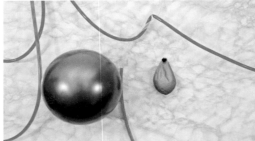

19–22

19–30 Bianca Schick, *Scripting Nervousness*, 2020, video stills.

I work to storify data, to give it colour, to include it in imaginary dialogues giving it sound and specificity beyond zeros and ones. One of my recent research projects, *How I come together*, was an attempt to activate performativity through moving images, sound, and text, with the aim of making claims for my individuality in a multinational and commercial system that fosters categorization and uniformity. The research operates at a small scale: it aims to connect a broad political agenda to the intimate and mundane interactions one makes with oneself in the digital realm.

Another recent project, the video installation *Scripting Nervousness*, responds to the psychometric approaches of the body; it attempts to expose the absurdities of data driven self-improvement and the way in which these create feelings of anxiety and nervousness. To produce and simulate the emotions that arise, I construct different absurd scenes by decontextualizing everyday objects: a desktop screen depicts a dead fish that is slowly dragged by a toy car through a field of dry flowers, revealing the sentence 'continuous self-improvement' underneath; a non-functional code highlights the arbitrary convention of software language (*def. action (clicking): import <forget your thoughts>; import <reduce tension> ; include <from [left] to [right]>; var (random);> include <from [right] to [left]; var (random); >*). The code through which the video scenes are processed determines the final cut, reflecting on the possibilities of generating different combinations of the same scenes. By automating the settings fed to the software, the project offers a generated clip, unique for each viewer. No fixed narrative is sought— only a catalogue of shifting impressions and evocations, similar to browsing through a chronology of fragments of 'reality.' The project both recognizes the datafied self and reacts to it, prompting both curiosity and repulsion.

It is from my sticky interaction with data that these projects emerge and bear witness to the fact that I am a product of my time, using technical and aesthetic choices to express

```
//main function

def nervousness ():
    include <continuous .(self). improvement>

print ("scripting. nervousness")
```

```
def action (insist):
    import time <inf>

print ("continuous improvement")
```

121

23–26

27–30

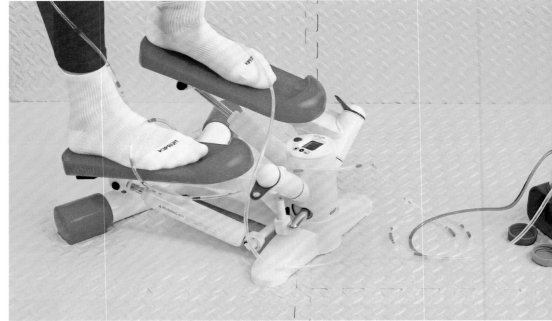

31

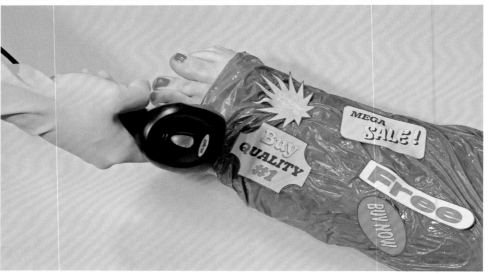

32

31–32 Bianca Schick, *I lick I click I bite I spit*, 2021, installation, video stills.

myself. And in this desire to contextualize data (through sound that extends beyond the sounds of clicks and keyboard taps or the visualization of zeros and ones) there is an underlying desire or fantasy: that within this vast consortium of data, there is a possibility that I can be known entirely. Even though the aim of digital platforms is to continually turn human vastness into stability, there is not a final destination where we find ourselves 'complete.' Thus, I choose to recognize that we exist across wider ranges of frequencies, in complexity, and that we cannot be somehow 'solved' as though logic, as though made up of numbers. Design gives me the freedom to gain a reasonable influence over how I inhabit the technological structures around me; I do this through unusual compositions that illustrate these structures.

Data contributes to shaping our identity. Like us, data excludes. Like us, data has its weaknesses. Like our everyday, data is scattered around. Like us, data can invade, outsource, and colonize. Like us, data is unreliable, but also efficient and entertaining. Ultimately, like us as newborns, data can only know what it sees and can only see what it knows.

I did not choose the identity I got when I was born. Similarly I cannot easily escape my datafied self, which grows daily more and more to be like me, or to be me.

123

BIANCA SCHICK (IT/NL) conducts different experiments to research the nuances of (her) culture. Working across time-based media and graphic design, she engages in questions of identity, affect, and language to unfold the complexity of contemporary social-political constructions. Recently, she has been concerned with how we perform in digital space and how digital technologies perform back. Her multimedia practice constructs jiggly-wiggly imagery, addressing metaphysical mundanity to trigger brainly embodiment. She plays freely with ideas of mediums and materials. In 2021 Bianca graduated from the MA course Contextual Design at Design Academy Eindhoven (NL). She holds a Bachelor's degree in Painting from the Visual Arts Department of the Academy of Fine Arts of Bologna (IT).

Addicted to YouTube Videos

Hi Kyung Eun

I'm addicted to YouTube videos of cute cats moving around within an interior space, far removed from my own home. I'm also fascinated by a multitude of other videos, including V-log, which shows how somebody spends their day to day. Boring as these videos seem at first sight, apparently there's some hidden appeal, as more and more people take part in this global phenomenon of connecting to other people's lives via digital media. Is what they experience real? Or is it a lie? Or is it something else?

It all started many years ago, when I found myself talking to people less and less, and watching my smartphone for many hours each day, roaming around in the digital realm. When I happened to see a video of cats that were combed, trimmed, massaged, I started to feel as if I myself was taking care for the cat, as well as the other way round—as if I was being cared for by someone just like the cat was being cared for. Weird as it seemed at first, this watching of cats being cared for offered a feeling of stability and made me sleep better at night. A habit was born, and the number of cat videos I watched increased, until the online affection for cats started to also turn into an offline liking for cats (which, by the way, never chased away my online habit of watching other people's cats).

Reflecting on the impact of the cat videos on my personal wellbeing led me to investigate a similar phenomenon on the Internet, Mukbang. Here, spectators can watch a video streamer eat a large amount of food in front of the camera. Mukbang started in South Korea and has ever since spread throughout the world; by now millions of people watch eating streamers enjoy their meals, and feel as if they share a dinner party. Why would people want to share such a daily ritual online with others? How is it possible that, in spite of being unreal, the event evokes real feelings of ease and satisfaction? By the time Mukbang became a huge trend in South Korea, more and more people had their meals alone. A new norm developed, the culture of Honbap or 'eating alone,' and eventually it even led to Honbap restaurants in which people are separated by partitions.

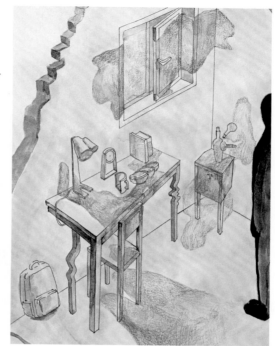

2

125

1   Hi Kyung Eun, *Strange Cohabitation*, 2021, ceramics (executed at the EKWC/ European Ceramic Work Centre in Oisterwijk, NL) and video projections.
2   Hi Kyung Eun, *Strange Cohabitation*, 2021, drawing.

4

126

3–4   Hi Kyung Eun, *Strange Cohabitation*, 2021, ceramics (executed at the EKWC/ European Ceramic Work Centre in Oisterwijk, NL) and video projections.

128

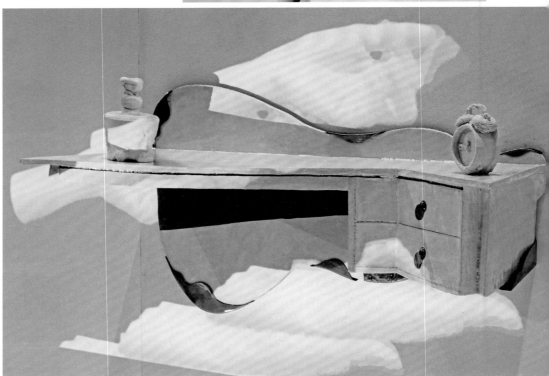

I became fascinated by the simultaneous reduction of relationships in real life versus the growing desire to meet people online. I thus chose this theme as a starting point for a research project in which I investigated my personal online experiences and created various experiments with the threshold between the physical and the digital: the screen.

One of the interesting elements of our online habits, I feel, is how we constantly edit ourselves as objects to be watched by others. We convert ourselves into malleable digital data, and are helped by various digital editing technologies, such as green screen, photoshop, and selfie-applications, to instantly change identity or context. The process of turning on the screen, searching for what to look at while choosing from a great variety of options, putting on the earphones, sitting down or lying on a bed, then pressing the play button—these are all ways of creating a stage for performing a new identity which then relates to others. Through the online interaction with others, my personal deficiencies in the real world are forgotten. And this lasts until that moment in which the screen turns off and all I face is a black mirror, a reflection of my physical being in an empty hole.

The screen is at once a material entity *and* an elusive portal to other worlds, a threshold between the physical and the digital. For my project, the projections of the digital and the physical contexts that catch the projections co-shape one another. The physical and the digital merge and clash, while the both elusive and physical screen takes centre stage.

129

5–6   Hi Kyung Eun, *Strange Cohabitation*, 2021, ceramics (executed at the EKWC/ European Ceramic Work Centre in Oisterwijk, NL) and video projections.

HI KYUNG EUN (Seoul, KR) is an independent designer and artist. Her work investigates how individuals, culture, and objects relate to each other in the contemporary context. In this process, she questions what objects mean to us and explores new perspectives of how to perceive them. She is interested in sensorial, emotional, and implicit languages of different materials. With these languages, she gives reflective and storytelling shapes to her research and interpretation.

I Am How I Make

Thomas Nathan

From a mass of clay, I pluck a small lump. As it rolls between my fingertips, it turns into a sphere. Pressed against a flat surface it's now a dot, flat on one side, embossed with my fingerprint on the other side. I repeat: a second lump. I place it just overlapping the first one. I repeat: a third lump, a fourth lump, a fifth lump. I repeat and repeat and many things begin to make sense from there.

This approach to making—manual, simple, humble, and focussed—is a response to a deep tension I, as a designer, have with the practice of design. The wasteful accumulation of designed objects (be they beautiful, useless, appalling, or inspiring) whether in someone's house or in a landfill, prompts me to ask: Have we not made enough? Making is the fundamental act of my profession. Design, by definition, inheres action: it is a connection between thinking and making. On one hand, I feel an essential urge to make; on the other hand, I am horrified at fuelling the wasteful excess of objects. This deep contradiction sits at the heart of my approach to design.

But is my underlying tension with design misplaced? Perhaps it is not about what we make but rather how? Is the critical element here 'the spirit' with which we make? I used to think that we need to rephrase the axiom 'you are what you consume' with 'you are what you make,' but I've come to believe that it's much more than that. It's actually 'you are how you make.' If no attention is given to the 'how,' then making becomes otherly, detached from the self, and devoid of the intimacy between the act of making and us as emotional beings.

But how was I to change 'how' I made? I began by attempting to reconstruct my design process by deconstructing it to its smallest and simplest form—the material I used. I dug my hands into clay, kneaded, squeezed, and moulded it, until I found a point of departure. I limited myself to small lumps of clay, defying grand gestures of speed, ambition, or ego. These little lumps of clay needed to be plucked, rolled, and pressed; each action required time, energy, and focus. Each act implied me pressing my energy (and

2

131

1–2   Thomas Nathan, *Cup 280*, 2016, ceramics, 5 × 8 × 8 cm.

fingerprint) into the object that would take form, slowly, painstakingly, but satisfyingly.

Instead of overthinking the issue, I let my subconscious travel through my muscles. I turned my internal dilemma and conflict into something productive. I gave in to the urge to make, but with minimal means and minimal physical impact: the how was replacing the what. This was a process embedded in my personhood, foregrounding myself within the design process and situating myself in the material itself. As I made, I found myself increasingly embedded within the design, an interweaving of the material, the object, and myself. Lump by lump, object by object, it rendered my personality, taming my inner conflicts by translating them into a physical form, a tangible form to be dealt with. The ineffable took shape through time, through my fingers, and through the material of clay.

I pluck, roll, press. Pluck, roll, press. Pluck, roll, press.

For each object, I prepare a mould into which the lumps are placed. When the clay is dry enough to take an object out of its mould, the interplay between the object's inside and outside becomes visible for the first time. The outside is precise and smooth, defined by a few distinct curves and edges. Stepping up close, you'll see a fine texture of lines from where the lumps intersect. The inside, on the contrary, subsists on its texture. It is full of nuances and details, traces from the making—my fingerprints. It's well prepared, but never the same. As I feel that a lump sticks well to the mould, I take back my finger and leave it as it is.

The outside is developed in close dialogue with what is happening on the inside. For instance, if a section is too narrow to place a lump with my finger, I'll have to give it a wider angle. Or if it feels good to press a lump into an edge, the mould should respond to that as well. The two sides complement each other—smooth and textured, controlled and intuitive.

The first thing I made was a cup, a basic component of tableware. The banality of these kinds of objects appeals to me. It leaves space for more: more than what is there.

These objects are representatives of our everyday, often not worth an extra mention. But as we question and reformulate these archetypes, we also question the normality with which these objects are associated. My contribution to tableware is modest and calm; it doesn't yell at you, it likes to tell. It's an acknowledgment of my own humanity.

These lumps of clay are no longer just inert material; I have contaminated each piece with myself, adding my specific marking—a fingerprint—to their composition. It's a proof of my presence and interaction, assigning me accountability. I am everywhere in these objects; each cup is a collection of my fingerprints and thus as a maker I cannot hide but am forced to consider each step, each act, and to do so with care. I need to be convinced about what I'm making.

I take my time. I pluck, roll, press.

Each fingerprint is a record of time. It captures the moment of me getting in touch with the world. Ultimately the object itself tells about how it came into being. It presents its technical construction as well as gives a glimpse into the moment and mentality of its creation.

Easily we forget that things don't just appear. There always is a process, a backstory, an idea, someone making a choice.

The process of giving shape to something can be paired with rules and systems, the highest ambition for objectivity or principles of randomness, but at some point someone is making a choice and this bears a certain authority, power, and responsibility. The act of making is to influence the very act of 'creation.' This surely requires regular introspection and self-doubt. Tolstoy asked the question, 'How then shall we live?' In doing so, he fundamentally questioned the 'how' of living (not the why or what, but focusing on the day to day of the 'how'). I want to know, 'How then shall we design?' This is not about the grand questions of morality and ethics related to design, but about the much more localized and intimate question related to the juncture of humans fulfilling a desire to give shape to material.

132

3

4–5

3–5 Thomas Nathan, *Cylindrical*,
2017, ceramics, 10 × 17 × 17 cm,
brown red, courtesy Carpenters
Workshop Gallery, photo: Luke
A. Walker.

6

The how of my approach inevitably gives shape to the what. When you invest so much personal time and energy, what you create becomes intimate, a part of you, a part of the emotions that you were feeling that week, a manifestation of your thoughts. Even if what you create takes the shape of a bowl, it is more than tableware. The bowl has been looked at from every angle, its proportions have been questioned, and its colour has been wrestled with. I want to make sure that the outcome is not a thoughtless gesture but reflects a worthy set of inputs to do justice to the material itself and, of course, to the designer.

What can be done with one lump of clay? What can be done with two, three, or four lumps? What if there are holes in-between, openings? What if I give individual lumps separate colours? Should the use of colour have an influence on the shape? How big can an object be? How much time will it take? What can be made in a day? Can I eat lunch in between? Questions not only circle around the object but also include my whole being. It's a process infused from life, a life that started in its humblest form, a little lump of clay.

The project *Lumps of Clay* has brought a poeticism, thoughtfulness, and consideration to my work, including a sensitivity towards time, space, and energy. These objects are as much about me and my own tensions or struggles as they are about the wider narratives of what it means to be a designer today.

It's a Wednesday of March 2021. I didn't have much sleep. From a mass of clay, I pluck a small lump. I roll it between my fingers and put it into place, just overlapping the two hundred and seventy-ninth lump. The cup is complete.

7

6–7   Thomas Nathan, *Cup 280*, 2016, ceramics, 5 × 8 × 8 cm.

THOMAS NATHAN (DE) is most known for his *Lumps of Clay* works—an ever-growing collection of objects made by connecting small dots of porcelain by hand. His practice is an exploration of thoughts through forms, sensitive to the making-process and driven by the agency of objects. And whatever it is that Nathan is creating it carries tranquillity, consideration, and poetry. Cornerstones of his young career are a collaboration with Rosenthal, exhibiting at the Collect art fair in London's Saatchi Gallery, selling work with Carpenters Workshop Gallery and teaching at the Karlsruhe University of Arts and Design.

135

I AM HOW I MAKE

An Exhausting Pursuit of Exhaustion
One Curtain/One Thread/One Hundred Thousand Knots

Meghan Clarke

1

Nothing Special was a homemade curtain measuring approximately 122.5 by 122 centimetres, with a print depicting lions, tigers, and giraffes peeking out from faded green shrubbery. It hung in the window of a bedroom at number eighteen Dunkeld Court—a house that my parents purchased in 1990 just prior to my birth. As a remnant left behind by old owners, Nothing Special was quietly adopted into the folds of our growing family.

After my youngest sister had swollen our ranks, we had to move and in the process, Nothing Special fell into the hierarchy of things: from bedroom to garage, it became a covering for the tiny window of the back door. But being downgraded once made it easy to be downgraded again. This time, it became a thing to protect other things (from paint, dust, burns, and tears). Its value was derived from the value it maintained in other more precious things. In time, Nothing Special fell so far as to leave the family home entirely, narrowly escaping the landfill thanks to my desire to save unwanted cloth.

From the moment it was abandoned in the bedroom window, Nothing Special was considered a tired cloth; as my family handled it and found use for it, they did so with indifference. The continual shift in use, leading ultimately to landfill, is one which occurs with such regularity that for any not-so-precious cloth it is almost predetermined and is carried out without a second thought. Gilles Deleuze describes this indifference as a state of tiredness, where one no longer seeks possibility, instead focusing on the realization of that which has already been determined.[1] This tiredness is more than heavy eyelids; it is a tiredness of perception and an attitude that we rehearse daily. It is an attitude that encourages us to repeatedly choose the ease of the known and expected, to lean into predetermined narratives rather than open ourselves up to unexpected possibilities. In the case of Nothing Special, we perceived it as a tired cloth that allowed us to easily resign ourselves from considering its possibility or potential. It was a curtain that had been

137

1   Meghan Clarke, *This Work of Body / This Body of Work (Repetition 6, Nothing Special)*, 2020, documentation of textile process, 150 cm × 240 cm, photo: Femke Reijerman, 2020.

1   Gilles Deleuze, "The Exhausted," *SubStance* 24, no. 3 (1995), p. 78.

discarded once, and so was destined to be discarded again.

There are times when the tiredness that Deleuze refers to is innocuous; brushing your teeth, for example, is a ritual requiring little interpretation, which can be carried out in a state of distraction with little consequence. But the tiredness I identify within Nothing Special is one that steps outside of the quotidian, underwriting a larger narrative relating to how we interact with material, attribute value, and engage with time. This tiredness is one that has seeped into our processes and the ways in which we approach making and doing, with the known and expected path being one of result and efficiency. So much so that the first step in a process is often to determine the end result. But what can be learned from a process that is so strictly determined, one that does not value the unexpected?

Through Nothing Special, I seek a process that moves beyond tiredness, one that is less rigid in its possibilities. Instead, a process that lingers in a state of doing so as to allow for layers of meaning to become intertwined— where there is not one goal, or one right answer, but rather a thread of possibilities that are right for right now but subject to change. This state beyond tiredness is one that Deleuze describes as exhaustion. Of exhaustion he writes, 'only the exhausted can exhaust the possible, because he has renounced all need, preference, goal or signification. Only the exhausted is sufficiently disinterested, sufficiently scrupulous.'[2]

So how can one reach this state of exhaustion? Consider the act of saying a word out loud, repeatedly in quick succession. It feels unfamiliar as it rolls off your tongue and there is an acute awareness of the word's momentary lack of meaning. The word is temporarily ambiguous and open to interpretation. In its exhaustion, there is possibility. Repetition then, when engaged with to the level of hyperbole, can move an action, idea, or attitude from the realm of tiredness to the realm of exhaustion.

138

2

3 →

2   Meghan Clarke, *A Dialogue of Knots*, 2020, film still.

3   Meghan Clarke, *This Work of Body / This Body of Work (Repetition 2)*, 2021, textile tapestry, 65 × 23 cm. An additional work in this series that has undergone its own repetitive process of undoing—threads removed from the bottom of the material were embroidered to the top until the two sections became connected.

2   Deleuze, "The Exhausted," see note 1, p. 5.

My repetition begins as one of undoing: pulling Nothing Special apart thread by thread, connecting each thread to the last with a knot. As this devoted undoing stretches over days and as those days become weeks, the expectation of the end result dissolves, allowing me to linger in a protracted interplay of body, cloth, and time.

The first interplay occurs as my body learns the cloth and is trained to respond to its tensions and hazards. To draw threads from the cloth without some breaking is an impossible task, yet I still try. Nothing Special has known a life as more than just a curtain and each stain of paint and varnish tests my patience, threatening to snag and snap the thread. But as I take the time to carefully undo the past, I find that I am simultaneously writing myself into the cloth as each knot serves as a record of my time and my hands. When the tally of knots reaches four thousand and forty nine, Nothing Special takes the final turn from curtain to thread.

And with that final turn, what started as interplay of body and cloth becomes one of body and time, facilitated by cloth. The creation and recording of knots, originally a practical means of building thread, becomes a measure of time and my body's occupation of it. And as Nothing Special is transformed once more, this time from a thread to a tapestry of knots, my repetitions uncover a layer of not-quite-free time. Not-quite-free because in order to access it my body must remain occupied with the production of knots, but in doing so, I am afforded a freedom of mind. I could learn a new language or practice mindfulness, filling this freedom with something productive, or cultured. But when time has come to be so heavily controlled, and ideas of productivity influence not just our work time but also our leisure time, I rail against the idea of filling my not-quite-free time with anything considered productive.

I come to think of my repetitions as non-productive productivity in which I occupy time, so that it cannot be occupied for me. Using this time, which only exists within a process of work, to pursue those things that are considered a waste of time feels subversive.

It is a durational act of sabotage, inspired by the protests of factory workers who would reclaim time from work by throwing parts into the assembly line to halt the machines. As I barrel along at a rate of knots—1,110 per hour, eighteen and a half per minute—each one is another spanner in the works.

At the centre of it all is Nothing Special. A not-so-precious cloth, abandoned by old owners and new owners alike, and never really given a second thought. Stashed away amongst a pile of similarly discarded textiles with their own similarly mundane stories, Nothing Special was forgotten. But after thirty years, and over one thousand kilometres from where we started, Nothing Special is out in the open once more. Not so easily forgotten this time as its traces are carved into *my* body—contoured fingers and strained wrists—reminders of the action of knotting which is now embodied. This is no longer just a not-so-precious cloth. In the pursuit of exhaustion, Nothing Special has been transformed: from curtain, to thread, to over one hundred thousand knots. It is a growing record of my past and my present, of time and hands, and a complicit companion in my durational act of sabotage.

5   Meghan Clarke, *This Work of Body / This Body of Work (Repetition 6, Nothing Special)*, 2020, documentation of textile process, 150 cm × 240 cm.

6   Meghan Clarke, *This Work of Body / This Body of Work (Repetition 7)*, 2020, detail of the reverse of a textile tapestry, 120 × 30 cm. An additional work in this series that has undergone its own repetitive process of undoing: thousands of small stitches can be seen in this small section of the work, representing hundreds of hours of repetitive labour.

5

6

141

MEGHAN CLARKE is a Scottish designer and artist based in Rotterdam (NL). In her expanded textile practice she looks beyond textiles as a commodity, instead approaching them as a method for uncovering the narratives that underwrite and control many aspects of our daily lives. Her work is often materialized through a slow and meticulous process of undoing, handling, and exposing each thread before transforming the material into its new form. Through these highly durational and repetitive processes, she explores themes of time, value, and labour—measuring her body, its output, and time occupied in terms of lines, threads, and knots.

How to Scare an Octopus
Suggestions to Rewrite a Family Recipe

Miguel Parrrra

In this chapter I present a set of annotations to a recipe that I inherited from my grandmother, the involuntary design collaborator with whom I have developed a posthumous creative practice. I do this believing that a recipe, and the rituals that surround it, are as much a text of design culture as, say, a weaving pattern or an assemblage manual. My desire is to rewrite her recipe so that it voices roles different to what history has so diligently prescribed for her to take: the loyal housewife, the dedicated caretaker, the accomplished cook. In other words, my rewriting contests an assigned role in a grey area so lazily described as 'the victim of oppression.' Desperate to imagine the narratives routinely rendered unthinkable by tradition, she and I partake in a joyful misinterpretation of our own bodies. A human/mollusc mix-up in which stretch marks, genitalia, and saliva become interchangeable with suckers, tentacles, or ink. Abuela: the octopus. Shamelessly escaping her tank for all of you to see.

My dear ones,

Oh my God what a lovely party you organized for José's eightieth birthday celebration last night! It was wonderful, my kids! As promised, I hereby put in writing the recipe of the 'octopus à la murciana' for which you gave me so much praise yesterday:

With the help of a paring knife don't *slice* but softly caress *the* contours of your *head to pull the entrails* into a state of tidal relaxedness. One that takes you far, far *away* from your daily duties and worries. *Now,* How does the edge of the knife feel? Is it sharp? Is it chipped? *to* further *extract the* sorrows that tend to concentrate around your *beak, pinch together the flesh around it* and proceed to drawing circles with your paring knife as if loosely wanting *to carve it out. Repeat the same to detach the* tension accumulated around your *eyes.* All these years of looking after others. *You can discard them all.*

Before cooking, you will have to clean the skin of its tendency to blend in with the environment. No more camouflaging into the kitchen. Abuela: *the octopus*! Abuela: *thoroughly* 'capable of mimicking almost any marine species.' Abuela: the abyssal shape-shifter. There you

143

1 Miguel Parrrra, *A recipe to cook pulpo a la murciana*, 1979, letter addressed to my mother.

144

2   Miguel Parrrra, *How to scare an octopus*, 2020, double-faced handwritten text.

guardando 'sa que term...

dijo Ana: "gracias

... do mucho y iba a

lo ; pero no se que pa...

... yo respondí: "me lo

... era mi deseo, y en...

preocupes porque estab...

... a Alicia y se

e dorsito fuerza estampa...

echo una blusa con

bastantes, pero una vez

... no se le notan.

are: fully fleshed *under cold running water. I suggest you* rinse, squeeze, rinse along your skin. Rinse, squeeze, rinse…rinse, squeeze, rinse… Repeat this until you start sensing that uplifting feeling: nothing is curcial/everyone poops. Then *pay* slow and vibrant *attention to the* rinsing, squeeze, *rinsing around the beak (some ink might still ooze).*

Some people like to tenderize the meat by pounding it but I consider you may find *this is a bit* numbing. What is more, *violently* dumb. Because Abuela: 'the smartest invertebrate.' Because your body is constructed by flexible pieces of cartilage and *so* has 'no bones to break,' *I prefer to scare the octopus instead. For this you will have to dip* your eight arms *in boiling* white*water nine consecutive times.* Your smell is deliciously nasty. *Do this quickly and* (if you're still reading this dear readers) *be careful not to burn yourselves!*

Once blanched you can dispose the animal on an oven tray, suckers facing up. Pour half a glass of olive oil, a quarter litre of wine, and a splash of brandy on it. Don't forget to add salt, pepper, and some spoilt breastfeeding milk… see how the cephalopod awakens slowly, very surely from the commandments of the *bay leaves. Keep* your cravings *in the oven at*

220° C and give me one of your saliva kisses, one of those that 'can paralyze a victim *for about forty-five minutes, up to an hour.'* Unbothered to swim with the current *Then* we sink. Once we have reached the seabed at the bottom, Abuela: *turn it upside down, and keep it* ugly, moist, and fuzzy *for another hour.*

As for my suggestions, feel free to *Chop it into pieces once* my need for eroticization has *cooled down.* How foolish of me to think that I was guiding you into territory unseen. You've made it, Abuela, you've led me into your solitary den. It's dark and it's rocky and it's nice and I'm scared and I'm not entirely sure what the hell I've been writing but *As you all know I would always add a dash of lemon juice and call it a dish.*

Y listo, now it is time for you to sit at the table to enjoy it, hopefully together in harmony like we always have done. Many hours have passed since José's birthday party and I must confess that I still feel as if I was floating among clouds (don't laugh at me please!).

Yours truly,

Rosa

Pay attention when you finish reading this, some ink might still ooze.

An octopus will release ink from its siphon when scared. The jet of black liquid is suddenly dispersed through water in a voluptuous cloud to provide the cephalopod with an escape mechanism against predatory attacks. Intended to function as a smoke screen, the instant of darkness affords seconds of vital importance: an opportunity to change scenario.

An octopus can also be scared posthumously. Literally translated from Spanish, 'to scare' an octopus is the traditional way to tenderize its meat before cooking it. For this, one has to dip the mollusc body in and out of boiling water about nine consecutive times. A more culinary-accurate translation of this operation would simply be 'to blanche' an octopus. Used to writing, mostly rewriting, in a language other than my grandmother's tongue, I frequently find myself negotiating meanings. When I translate a family text such as a recipe I can try to follow a professional code of conduct. Blanching an octopus is almost exactly what my grandmother meant to say in the original document. But even in my most canonical translation is, thankfully, a workplace of ambiguity. If my navigation so easily ends up in the department of mistranslation, then why should I pretend I didn't notice an escape route? Why should I continue my task obediently, when it only takes a literal translation for the meaning of 'blanching an octopus' to get blurred?

To scare an octopus: A sudden black cloud. An opportunity to change scenario.

When I rewrite the meaning of words, particularly those that have been intimately inscribed in me, I can access pockets of imagination unthought-of before. If I am able, and daring enough, to feel my way through those darkened places, I can sometimes perceive the contours of deemed-unprofitable meaning: a woman deserting her daily duties? A housewife emerging as an eight-armed marine creature? A grandchild suggesting an eroticization of his grandmother's cephalopod body? The smell of spoiled seafood? Trying to convince you dear reader none of these meanings are scary?

147

MIGUEL PARRRRA (1990) is an architect/designer gone writer born in the Southeast Iberian Peninsula. Parrrra's creative practice involves the study of cultural texts with the ambition of disrupting hegemonic narratives, often by reclaiming rewriting autonomy for those whose story lines have been deemed unworthy. With a sensibility for queer tropes and transgressive plot devices, Parrrra's work is primarily materialized through writing and theatre mediums. He is also one half of the design-critique-turned-design-comedy duo 'The Ironing Board.'

A Dinner for One

Micheline Nahra

3

4

'I was always aware of the fragility of my context, in Lebanon, suffering from an ongoing war. The more matter was destroyed, the more memory we struggled to collect or preserve. *A Dinner for One* testifies to destruction and loss, but also to reconstruction. I destroyed, or deconstructed, a family set, consisting of a big table and four chairs, and then rebuilt it into a one person set.'

1–5   Micheline Nahra, *A Dinner for One*, 2020.

MICHELINE NAHRA is a Lebanese designer and architect based in the Netherlands. She founded her practice after graduating from the MA Contextual Design programme (2019) at Design Academy Eindhoven (NL), as she believed it was essential to bring a different perspective to design than the Western one. Through her work, Nahra explores the narratives of everyday objects and the layering of stories in them. Born and raised in war-torn Lebanon, at the border between south Lebanon and occupied Palestine, she reflects on her personal experiences through objects in an attempt to express the human need to retrace the past and preserve memories.

A DINNER FOR ONE

Border between Normality and Abnormality

Aurelie Hoegy

1

2

3

Border between Normality and Abnormality
deals with acknowledging the hidden life of
real people, including that of the designer,
allowing for design that testifies to human
complexity, craziness and more poetry
in daily life. For Aurelie, this started with
visualizing and materializing slightly neurotic
behaviours in design; it continued with
projects in which she researched various
aspects of the fragile and volatile nature of
human beings and their relationships with
their contexts.

1–2   Aurelie Hoegy, *Border between
Normality and Abnormality*,
Storyboard, 2013, drawings, ink.

3   Aurelie Hoegy, *MacGuffin lamp*,
part of the project *Border between
Normality and Abnormality*, 2013,
700 metres of electric cable, Van
Abbemuseum Eindhoven.

BORDER BETWEEN NORMALITY AND ABNORMALITY   AURELIE HOEGY

5

6

4 Aurelie Hoegy, *MacGuffin lamp*,
part of the project *Border between
Normality and Abnormality*, 2013,
700 metres of electric cable, Van
Abbemuseum Eindhoven.

5–8 Aurelie Hoegy, *Border between
Normality and Abnormality*,
Storyboard, 2013, drawings, ink.

← 4

7

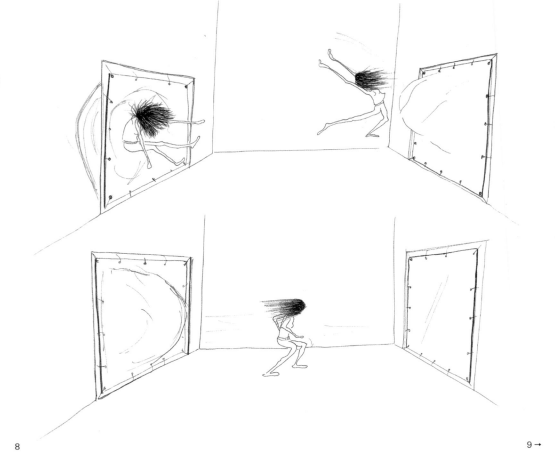

8

9→

10

11

9   Aurelie Hoegy, *Dancers Collection, Dancers First & Second*, 2015, steel, cotton, latex, photo: Daniel Costa, 2017.

10–13   Aurelie Hoegy, *Dancers Collection*, 2015–2016, steel, cotton, latex, photos: Bruno Pellarin, 2015–2016.

12

AURELIE HOEGY is a French artist and designer, recognized and exhibited worldwide. She graduated from Design Academy Eindhoven (NL) in Contextual Design (2013) with *MacGuffin lamp*, a project exploring the border between normality and abnormality in daily life. Hoegy uses movement as a medium and embodies it through her collections of furniture. Her work focuses on questioning and disturbing design archetypes, challenging the borders of what is normal, and connecting us to our primal instincts. She has won a range of awards and prizes and her work has been acquired by major cultural institutions, such as the Centre Pompidou, Paris.

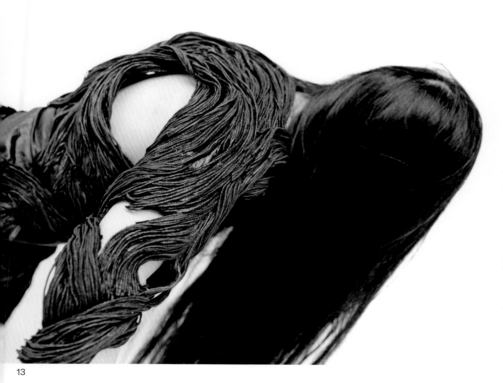

13

BORDER BETWEEN NORMALITY AND ABNORMALITY

Hiding in the Glare of Design

Joel Blanco

Think of all the ways we camouflage our awkwardness. We stare at our phones, checking messages, Instagram, or even answering phantom calls; we suddenly find the art hanging on the wall interesting enough to embark on a detailed study of it; we go outside for a cigarette even when we don't feel like it, or maybe don't even smoke at all. If we weren't able to use techniques to conceal our discomfort such as these, we could end up staring blankly at a wall, visualizing ourselves in the third person.

A few years ago, I found myself in one such situation, and watched myself in the third person. It was summer and I had arrived late to a friend's house party; the guests were in an advanced state of partying. I found it impossible to connect—be it the topics they were talking about, their attitudes, or movements—I felt strange and terribly uncomfortable. What would typically be friendly faces appeared to me as judgmental, or disapproving—grimaces of aggressive happiness, judgmental or disapproving of my sober state. 'I don't belong here; I'm not like them,' I said to myself. However, to leave after barely arriving would have been even more alienating, proving just how little I belonged. I sought shelter in simple ways, such as holding a drink (sometimes full, sometimes empty), snacking, or sitting at a table covering my legs, trying to smile, laughing courteously while counting down the minutes. Even though it was evident that no one was paying attention to me, I felt observed. I couldn't relax—I couldn't be me.

This unremarkable experience of being so hyperaware of the environment to the point of feeling detached from it was not an isolated event. The more I looked deep inside myself, I found that the experience represented a much broader desire to find places to hide (at least, that's what I thought). That is, I sought ways of avoiding the bright glare of social encounters, forms of concealment, spaces of refuge, or means for moderating the level of exposure.

As a designer, I set out to design for this all-too-common experience. I looked for a way to overcome these situations. My initial

2–3

161

<table>
<tr><td>1</td><td>Joel Blanco, Super Lekker Super Mooi Donut, 2017, furniture, 240 × 240 × 45 cm, photo: Yen-An Chen.</td></tr>
<tr><td>2–3</td><td>Joel Blanco, Corner Boy, 2016, intervention, photo: Delany Boutkan.</td></tr>
</table>

design approach was to create pieces of furniture that could go unnoticed and that could shelter and isolate someone from a given context. Essentially, I was creating a social partition: a means of not-so-subtle escapism and a rejection of the tyranny of social participation. To achieve this, I made two design objects. The first was a vase large enough to put over one's head, like a domestic decorated helmet shielding the bearer from the outside world both visually and acoustically (using sound dampening material). The sound effect while having this device on your head was similar to putting your ear inside a shell and 'listening to the sea.' The sound can transport you to another place, a safe space of peace and serenity. This object was about not being present; it transported the user to a safer social space— a false sense of solitude.

The second design object was a plaster-board 'corner.' This corner was designed for ease of transport, to enable it to be mobile and operational in a range of situations. The corner was a literal design object, a corner to hide within. Whereas the vase transported the user to a safe space, the corner created it. I could carry this corner, place it in any spot and become one with the room. In any case, this object required considerable dedication on my part, which, far from abstracting me from the place where I was, made me more aware of it. To use it properly meant that I needed to place it strategically and more and more of my time was spent honing my skills of self-camouflage. But hiding only increases the sensation of danger, the risk of being spotted and outed by others. While inside the corner I felt hyperaware of the exterior, as if my interior was quickly becoming the room itself—an extension of myself. The hollowness of the interior of the corner also started to resonate with my own emptiness—I needed a new approach.

Taking this theme seriously, I continued in my pursuit of using design to help me with these social situations. The vase had attempted to isolate the user's experience from the context; the corner had attempted to blend in with the environment rendering the user completely invisible but present. Both solutions didn't feel right. There was too much invisibility for me, and I wondered how I could balance proximity and privacy.

By drawing a circle to represent myself, and another ring (like a radar) surrounding the other, I got the outline of a doughnut. Of course, there are many objects that are circular with a hole in their middle (I could have called it a toroid, a wheel, a float etc.) but the first thing that came to my mind was a doughnut.

It was perfect: the doughnut hole did not signify the absence of dough, but the presence of doughnut—it's a balance between that which is present and that which is absent. After this reflection, I made the third piece of this series: a giant doughnut made for seating. It was a big, ridiculous piece of furniture that represented the most archetypal idea of a doughnut, but with an advantage: you could sit on it. The obviousness of the work, and the apparent lack of depth of its elaboration, meant that people could approach it to take a seat, to take selfies, and share the space with others. If I was trying to isolate myself at first, now I was doing the opposite. I was generating a common meeting point with enough capacity to divert attention away from me and on to the object—balancing presence and absence. I was hiding in plain sight at a party that was my own.

My work has remained inspired by this trilogy of designs, the pursuit of finding a balance between the unbearable gaze of presence and the lament of absence. The hole is nothing without the doughnut and vice-versa. And therefore, when I design a chair, for example, it is not the chair that I design but rather the chair and the context for sitting or the lamp and the context for reading. In this way, the act of design becomes about the balance between context and object, experience and material, self and other.

162

4

JOEL BLANCO is a designer, artist, and friendly Internet troll based in Madrid. Since 2017, he has been developing artistic research in the fields of popular culture, Internet, and music. In 2017, together with his band Alarido, he created a viral hit in the Netherlands named 'Bitterballen Donder Op,' earning the band hatred from Dumpert's community. He has been working as a freelance designer and has been teaching at several educational institutions including, among others, the Escuela Superior de Diseño (ES) de Madrid (ES), Istituto Europeo di Design (ES), and the IE School of Architecture & Design (ES).

163

5

4–5   Joel Blanco, *Super Lekker Super Mooi Donut*, 2017, furniture, 240 × 240 × 45 cm, photo: Yen-An Chen.

HIDING IN THE GLARE OF DESIGN

La Désalpe
Traditions as an Ever-Evolving Search for Collective Experience and Transformation

Marie Rime

I regularly and knowingly take part in an act of cultural re-enactment. In an era caught up in the search for authenticity, I often prefer to live in a compromise between the world as it is and the world that we narrate through traditions. This is not a default position but one that requires a considerable amount of commitment as well as the suspension of disbelief.

I come from Charmey, a small village in the Swiss Prealps in the region of Gruyère. This region is truly beautiful, suscitating images strongly linked to Switzerland—a postcard of gorgeous clichés—with its medieval castle, the hill of Gruyère, the poya, the armailli, its lush mountain meadows, large wooden farmhouses, and bountiful local traditions.

The images (and objects) that picturesque Gruyère conjure up are part of our vocabulary, anchors in our lives—not in any ordinary way, but as promoted and protected characteristics of our identity. Many aspects of this typical region were part of a Gruyère that existed two centuries ago, when the population was pre-modern and subsisted on agriculture. Today, this is no longer the case and yet we celebrate these traditions in ways that would most likely even surprise our ancestors.

Traditions in the region of Gruyère were kept alive, in part, as a result of the challenges linked to industrialization and the exodus of many of its residents to the city. Celebrating these traditions was a means of holding onto and remembering the values of the countryside. These traditions were re-affirmed when city dwellers returned to the countryside, seeking out what they had lost and looking to quench a nostalgia for something they craved.

I grew up surrounded by this magnification and reinterpretation of the past turned into celebrations and staged rituals. Even though these rituals recall a time that was far-gone, I too have found a strong sense of identity through the performed version of that past reality. I relate to them and enjoy them: they are meaningful to how I think of myself in relation to my geographical location.

2

3

1   Marie Rime, *Sans Titre (Armure 03)*, 2013, photograph, 80 × 65 cm.
2–3   Switzerland.

5

Growing up in Charmey, my yearly calendar was structured around these cultural events. Each season had its celebrations, which I looked forward to and became involved in. *La Désalpe* is one such celebration: it marks the end of the summer season. As the grass disappears from the alpine pastures, the cows come down the mountain to spend the winter in the valley. Originally, each farmer would decide and organize the herds' transition down to the valley. Today, this is celebrated in Charmey as a one-day event on the last Saturday of September, whether the grass has disappeared from the alpine pastures or not. It usually involves eight herds coming down from the mountains and arriving to Charmey at intervals—turning what was once a natural seasonal act into a coordinated and organized parade.

As much as this sounds forced, it doesn't take away from the enjoyment of the celebration; on the contrary, the organized nature of the celebrations amplifies the thrill of the event, as we all come together on that specific day. Locals and tourists gather en masse to applaud the impressive cortege parading through the village back to their winter quarters. It looks glorious: the cows decorated with flowers, carrying heavy bells, proudly surrounded by the farmers wearing traditional costumes. There is a strong feeling of pride within the ranks. A real celebration.

I have seen and lived this 'event' every year, as far as I can remember. Growing up, I participated in in the activities of this one-day event taking on different roles. Whatever I did, I always made a point of being around, as missing it would feel uncomfortable. As a child, I would spend the day strolling through the traditional craftsmen's market looking for treasures. Later on, I became involved as a member of the organizational committee or as a performer in the local wind band. Wearing traditional costumes, we would open the festivities by parading and playing music through the village, much like the cows would do later on that same day. The Désalpe is one specific example of this cultural enactment that spreads out in many other occasions and moments of our daily life

167

4   Marie Rime, *Sans Titre (Armure 05)*,
     2013, photograph, 80 × 65 cm.
5   Switzerland.

as Gruyère inhabitants. On the one hand, I recognize aspects of these traditions that are forced and that do not relate to the actual farming situation. One could say that I grew up in a sort of Disneyland—without a fence or opening hours—which can make it a bit confusing in grasping the line between fiction from fantasy. On the other hand, I sincerely enjoy these events and find purpose and meaning in them: they celebrate 'a past' (i.e. some notion of a desired past), the present, and perhaps project something about a near future. These staged rituals are not only meant for entertainment but also as a way of meeting with others across generations, of collectively imagining a common identity, and as something that can hold us all together, providing a sense of belonging.

Much of my design work has explored themes of staged rituals and the materials involved in sustaining them. My work on masks and magic sticks questions how we can subvert everyday objects, such as paper clips, push pins, drinking straws and so on, to create powerful visual identities that take us out of our present and into either a primitive past or a strange future. By using everyday materials, I play with the liquidity of traditions, the desire to try to encapsulate a past for the present's purpose; in effect, using familiarity as a place for transmitting values and ideas. And yet, just like so many of the traditions that I mention above, regardless of the veracity and historical accuracy, it is not the particulars that are essential for the experience of the tradition but rather the collective sum in its entirety— the cows, flowers, music, people—making it no longer simply about the cows moving down a mountain, but rather about who we are as a community. The masks and magic sticks appear ridiculous, silly, or humorous if you dissect them; but as a single entity, they transcend their materials and speak to some part of us, deep down. They allow us to both recognize the staged characteristics and celebrate them. The staging and experience of the masks and magic sticks bring out the fantastic in the mundane, creating new meaning out of the familiar.

Eventually, the 'origin' of the objects does not matter anymore—they are subsumed by a greater sense, something collective and transformative, bringing individual selves and desires together. In the end, these works show that trying to trace traditions back to their origins might be missing the point, for it is in the evolving cultural assemblages that form through time, energy, and human creativity that we may find real authenticity.

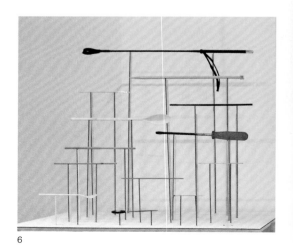

6

MARIE RIME is an artist born in 1989 in Switzerland. She holds a Bachelor's degree in Photography from the École Cantonale d'Art de Lausanne (ECAL, CH) and a Master's degree in Contextual Design from Design Academy Eindhoven (NL). Rime's practice is shaped by various working methodologies and influences, which translates into the use of a mixed range of media and techniques. Routine functions as an operational base. Time and repetition create a framework for thinking, and observation plays a predominant role within the process, which often becomes the work itself.

7

6   Marie Rime, *Magic Sticks*, 2017,
      mixed media, 150 × 80 × 80 cm.
7   Marie Rime, *Sans Titre (Armure 01)*,
      2013, photograph, 80 × 65 cm.

Reflection on Complementary Opposites
The Tinku

Carlos Sfeir Vottero

1

2

I am in conflict, I am the conflict.
I am the Chilean and the Spaniard,
the oppressed and the oppressor.

I come from colonization,
but I celebrate our cultures,
I celebrate our lands.

I embrace within my bodies,
as well as in my souls,
both Magic and Realism.

I am the Tinku.
Andes Mountain Range I am.

black-white make a grey

Tinku in the Inca language of Quechua is a 'meeting,' an 'encounter.' It refers to a confrontation of complementary opposites. It is what the Aymaras, the inhabitants of the Central Andes, observe in a colour called 'Ch'ixi' made of juxtaposed black and white dots that from a distance look vibrant grey. In Spanish, *gris* (grey, drab, sad) is a word of contempt. For the Andean culture, this encounter between contradictions develops energy.[1] The Aymaras know the value of experiencing such tensions, probably because such tensions are distinctive of the landscape we inhabit.

171

The Andes, from the Quechua *Anti* (West), are the materialization of the ongoing collision between two enormous geological forces. The Oceanic Nazca Plate is pushing under the southern shores of *Abya Yala* (America), moulding mountains above six thousand metres high. The frequent earthquakes that we feel in our bodies remind us of the vibrations shaping our landscape. Anti's geology manifests its strength in Atacama. There, where the salty slopes unveil themselves naked as a desert, our cultures and territory have worn the Tinku since their origins.

The Atacama desert is where *Pacha* (Mother Earth) reached the sky with her

3

1   Carlos Sfeir Vottero, *Reflection on Complementary Opposites*, 2021, intervention, 1 × 2 × 8,5 m. *Solar Eclipse*, 10/06/2021, 12:22pm, N 52°25'31" E 04°33'21" ALT 56.96° AZ 144.33°.

2   Carlos Sfeir Vottero, *Reflection on Complementary Opposites*, 2021, intervention, 1 × 2 × 8.5 m. Anamorphism, team at Bloemendaal aan Zee Beach, photo: Clara Gustafsson 2021.

3   Saywas. Incan piles of rocks pointing to Lullaillaco Volcano. Antofagasta, Chile, photo: Carlos Sfeir Vottero, 2020.

1   Silvia Rivera Cusicanqui, 1949, Aymara/Bolivian feminist, sociologist, historian and activist, deepens the Ch'ixi concept in her decolonial thoughts suggesting the emancipatory power of the half-blood dualism in Latin America.

4–5

4　Carlos Sfeir Vottero, *Las lágrimas secas de Andes*, 2021, crystallization on copper, 90 × 90 cm, detail.

5　Carlos Sfeir Vottero, *La Reconstitución de los Andes*, 2021, installation, 3 × 6 m Ø. Copper crystals harvested and left to react with the salty water surrounding the installation, the particles mineralize in a verdant colour, evoking the natural appearance of the copper orebodies.

6　Carlos Sfeir Vottero, *Towards a Reflection on Complementary Opposites*, 2021, intervention, 1 × 2 × 5 m. Sunset, 26/04/2021, The Hague.

7　Carlos Sfeir Vottero, *Towards a Reflection on Complementary Opposites*, 2021, intervention, 1 × 2 × 5 m. Full Pink Moon, 26/04/2021, The Hague.

highest crowns; where the Incas encountered *Chilli* (the end of the world); where the Spaniards' mission baptized Chile; where the last surviving wilderness confronts the extractivism of mining; where even our bodies echo the Tinku. It is the *mestizaje*, the place where half-bloods thrive.

In Atacama's plateau, Tinku is a reflection—a physical state materialized in a mental dimension. Where mineral soil heat touches the mountain's freezing air, the complementary opposites sometimes trigger a mirage. A mirage is an exchange between an observer and a context. A reflection implies a point of view, a subject forging its object. Sky and Earth merge into a mirror on the aridity of the horizon. When I was reflecting on the desert, observing the mirage, people told me that what I was seeing was not an illusion, but the charming City of Quimal—a settlement built with precious stones and silver roads that nobody has ever been able to visit. Quimal's apparitions unfold the encounter of (Anti) theses among Andes, a reality reflected both in our cultures and landscapes.

Up in the desert, the Tears of the Andes, or salt lakes, mirror the highlands' clear skies. They are among the few tangible water reservoirs in Atacama. They host one of the largest deposits of lithium on Earth. The metal, used to produce the majority of the batteries we use, has recently become a symbol of the green energy revolution. In an attempt to save the world from the impact of fossil fuels, intensive extractivism undermines the reflections and mirages in our territory. Lithium concentration pools use Atacama's high solar radiation to evaporate the little water left in the desert. But even where the moisture drains off faster, the remaining drops still seek the sky.

In Atacama, some see the salt flats as an economic chimera, the white gold, while others as a transcendental apparition, the ancestral city of Quimal.

In my journey in Atacama, I at times perceived the surface that appears to form between the layers of warm and cold air, as if there was an engaging liquid body. Once, I tried to grasp the Fata Morgana but it moved with me, until it faded into a lithium mine.

6

7

8

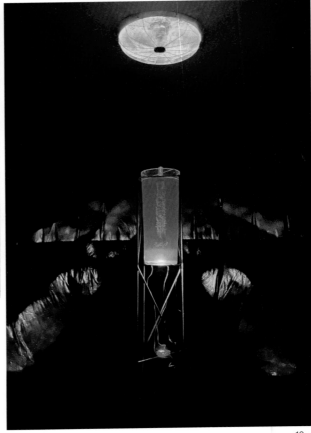

9   10 →

8   Carlos Sfeir Vottero, *La Reconstitución de los Andes*, 2021,
installation, 3 × 6 m Ø.
Two circles of technical fabric sewn
together and inflated by a suspended fan
create a dark and mysterious space.
9   Carlos Sfeir Vottero, *La Reconstitución de los Andes*, 2021,
installation, 3 × 6 m Ø.
A rusted metal structure supports a large
glass vessel filled with copper sulphate.
At the bottom of the container are a few
euro cents that have been thrown in.
A circuit comprising a battery and an
amperemeter pulls the copper particles
covering the coins into an electronic
flow towards a large copper tube, also
immersed in the solution.
10   Carlos Sfeir Vottero, *La Reconstitución de los Andes*, 2021,
installation, 3 × 6 m Ø.
Copper crystal formation materialized
around the tube.

I reflect myself within the diverse forces of the landscape I am from. My personal reflections mirror the tensions shaking the dry mountains. My experiences in this territory have moulded a rooted way of thinking that empathizes with the Andean juxtapositions—this land of Tinkus. My practice has developed into a rediscovery of the value of the complementary opposites, and of those mirages in a world where authentic reflections are being mined. I believe that design and art are tools that allow us humans to reflect with non-human and more-than-human entities, so that we can glimpse the value of the Tinku in this entropic flow.

Instead of gris, can design produce a vibrant Ch'ixi? My work investigates design's role in the human-nature Tinku. I believe that the meeting of these complementary opposites have the power to create mirages, to connect us with a more-than-human dimension in both an emotional and a physical experience.

SUN KITES — BERLIN, 2020

The 2020 spring equinox marked the start of the COVID-19 quarantine. We were forced to stay home right when the sun was inviting us outside. The project sought to reflect this contrast of a *contactless* lockdown with a *contactmore* act. To do this, fifteen kites formed a dance of silvery sunlight reflections, directed and choreographed by the wind. The kites were visual mediators between the sky, sun, and audience.

EMBODIED TOPOGRAPHY — EINDHOVEN, 2019

The Andes mountain range flowing along South America, together with the poncho, the emblematic garment of all its peoples, are the inspirations of this performance. A large cloak made of a plastic textile creates a dynamic performative topography, where participants become living mountains actively forming lakes and flowing rivers through their positioning. The participants embodied an interconnected landscape—human and nature—a Tinku.

ATRAPAVIENTOS/WINDCATCHER — SANTIAGO DE CHILE, 2015

On summer afternoons, Santiago's geological basin is stirred by strong westerly winds that hit the Andes, unveiling the power of contrasting entities: the air of the flat valley, heated by the sun, is pushed up towards the cold peaks. The dense constructions in the capital disrupt the flow of air, but even where the citizens can't feel it, its motion is present. The project *Atrapavientos/Windcatcher* seeks to catch the invisible warm winds in their journey to the cool heights, rendering the invisible tangible. A three by four and a half metre structure composed of plastic bags arranged in a juxtaposed pattern inflate and deflate with the wind, catching it and letting it go, revealing the Andean flows.

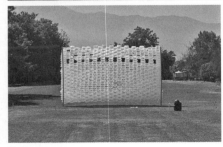

11–13

14–15

CARLOS SFEIR VOTTERO (1990) is a creative working among spaces, designs, and arts, looking for the meeting point between cultures and landscapes. He studied architecture at Pontificia Universidad Católica de Chile (CL) and worked as an architect and teacher at the Design School of the same university in his hometown, Santiago (CL). In 2021 he finished his Master's at the Contextual Design department of Design Academy Eindhoven. His project *La Reconstitución de los Andes* [the Reconstitution of the Andes] investigates Latin American decolonial speech through the materiality of its peoples and the slopes of his country.

11   *Sun Kites.*
12   *Embodied Topography*, Eindhoven.
13   *Atrapavientos/Windcatcher*,
       Santiago the Chile.
14–15   Carlos Sfeir Vottero, *Cathenary v/s*
       Arch, 2021, intervention in the river
       Dommel in Eindhoven, NL (the city
       in which Carlos graduated from DAE).
Four ropes shaped by the flow of the river
mirror the natural shape of the bridge.

REFLECTION ON COMPLEMENTARY OPPOSITES

1

In the Juncture of Ideologies
Reimagining Physical Structures of the Past

Goda Verikaitė

I belong to the first generation of Lithuanian children born after our country underwent radical changes in the wake of its transformation from a Soviet communist system into a democratic and independent State. I share similar memories with people of my generation. We spent our childhood watching and practicing dance moves from MTV's music videos. Computers back then were still very slow. But the first touch of the mouse and the opening of Windows Internet Explorer seemed like magic: without physically crossing borders, we were free to travel anywhere we wanted.

The nineteen-nineties in Lithuania marked a very special moment. It was a decade that still echoed The Singing Revolution, our parents standing forming The Baltic Way, peaceful protests for freedom, *perestroika*, the fall of the Berlin Wall, and finally, the collapse of the Soviet Union. We grew up in times of transformation, but our childhood days were filled with ghosts, fears, and imaginaries of the communist system. Even though we had never experienced the Soviet regime ourselves, we carried its memories through our families. The feeling of belonging to this generation naturally prompted me to think about the future by way of the past.

While living abroad in recent years, I have found myself positioned at a strange juncture between East-and-West, right-and-left. So much of my understanding of my own country is related to making sense of decades of Soviet government. I inherited a 'memory' and was raised on certain collective imaginaries and narratives that demonize all aspects of this previous regime. This creates an unusual setting for self-reflection. On the one hand, while living abroad I don't fear being called a 'communist' (which in Lithuania can often sound like an insult) just because I sympathize with some leftist ideas of communal living and speculative design practices that question the current market-driven system and its propagated ideals. On the other hand, I carry with me all the stories of a corrupt and destructive Soviet regime and how the fictions of equality and 'commoning' were implemented by force and not by free choice.

2

1   Goda Verikaitė, *Recycling Utopia*, 2018, collage in video still.
2   Typical urban area of large-scale prefab housing in Lithuania, photo (photographer unknown).

179

3

The feeling of being between East and West, left and right, raises many questions for me as a person, but also as a designer. How do we treat the uncomfortable past: by erasing it and trying to forget it, or by accepting its outcomes and looking towards its futures? By embracing auto-ethnography as a self-reflective method in my practice, I try to investigate these questions—questions that I believe are relevant not only for me personally, but also for the whole generation born in the former East Bloc after the collapse of the Soviet Union.

This juncture between past and present, socialist and capitalist Lithuania is well captured in the mass-housing projects in Lithuania that, under the communist party, sought to fulfil the promise 'to provide every Soviet family with its own apartment.'[1] Even though the political system that gave birth to these districts collapsed thirty years ago, the Soviet mass-housing neighbourhoods remain, like unchanging physical relics. Too big and bold to adapt easily to contemporary styles, these structures carry the past into the present.

These housing districts have come to define certain physical and political legacies, be it the expectations of the role of the State in providing housing or simply the lasting infrastructure of these estates. And whether we like it or not, they have come to mean very different things for Lithuanians. Having not grown up in one myself, I have long felt a feeling of apprehension towards them. During my childhood and adolescence, they were places that I tended to avoid; they were often associated with 'marozas,' a slang word deriving from *moroz* (frost). Marozas back then referred to local gangster-like teenagers, usually recognizable by their Adidas pants and loud nineties beat music playing from their portable recorders. Later, I started understanding how my attitude was influenced by the collective biases, stereotypes and images of these districts as depressed and unsafe areas. My recent design work has sought to come to terms

1   Marija Drémaité, *Baltic Modernism: Architecture and Housing in Soviet Lithuania* (Berlin: DOM Publishers, 2017), p. 18.

4

3   Goda Verikaitė, *Bolo News
     (Recycling Utopia)*, 2018,
     newspaper, 420 × 297 mm.
4   Goda Verikaitė, *Recycling Utopia*,
     2018, video still.

with these neighbourhoods—the buildings, streets, inhabitants—in order to come to terms with my own identity and those born in my generation, a generation defined by a juncture of ideologies.

As a starting point, I began to document stories, often in the intimate settings of locals' homes, accessing personal spaces in these housing districts. I sought to understand what life was like in these districts both before and after nineteen-ninety, to understand how culture and the built environment developed new relationships through this time of ideological transition. I explored, for example, how a Soviet style apartment block reinvents itself in a post-Soviet era. The highly enriching interviews included one with Tadas (32), who described his life in one of the typical mass-housing buildings, tying together past and present:

> At the moment, I own this apartment. It used to belong to my parents. This particular building was built for electricians, obviously my father used to work as an electrician. I would describe this flat as eclectic-Soviet romanticism and certain nostalgia mixed with artsy installations, weird hipster objects, and Ikea furniture. I used to host many people on Couchsurfing; later, [I] started letting out one of the rooms on Airbnb or for Erasmus students. From time to time, I organize poetry evenings here.

Tadas details both the forms and functions changing in these apartments, how life continues, and how the ideology of the design moves with it. These interviews formed the core of a publication I called *10 Stories How to Inhabit Utopia* (2018). These interviews were later an inspiration for designing the speculative narrative and video *Recycling Utopia* (2018), which used the research as detailed above along with text as a creative medium to re-envision a Soviet housing district as an experimental neighbourhood of micro utopias. The project adopted the theory of bolos (independent and decentralized units of people) that

are assembled according to nima (cultural background, common interest, and time) that they share. The narrative evolved into a video and a speculative newspaper *Bolo News*. By employing different techniques including modelling, mapping, collaging, it envisioned the first socialist mass-housing area in Lithuania, Žirmūnai, as a testing site for thought experiments. In doing so, it provided alternative concepts of luxury, work, leisure, equality, and collectivity.

My work has continued to focus on these districts, seeking to better grasp their role in our collective Lithuanian identity and broader cultural imaginary. In order to bring these locales into a wider debate, I sought to catalyze and provoke imaginative and ludic approaches towards these apartment blocks, seeking to portray them as an important part of both our past and (potentially) our future. In the project called *What Does Eiguliai Say* (2020), I invited locals to share their memories and spontaneous visions for their neighbourhood (Eiguliai) by taking a walk together.

Two months of research, carried out by walking, revealed many invisible aspects, situations, and unheard stories of the neighbourhood, which became a source for the new narratives to be born. These findings were translated into a fictional map and fourteen short speculative stories. This time they found a medium as an audio tour of the neighbourhood, forging a juncture of (im)possible futures, the present, and the ideological physical manifestations of the past. This work has acted as a cathartic gesture to deal with my own uncomfortable relationship with my past and hopefully serves to do the same for many of my compatriots.

182

5

GODA VERIKAITĖ is a spatial designer from Lithuania, currently based in the Netherlands. She holds a Master's degree in interior architecture from the Royal Academy of Arts in The Hague (2018, NL). Besides working in architecture and urban research studios, she has been continually active in several artistic practice fields. In her work, she looks into speculative designs as tools for creating future narratives. Recently she has been exploring walking as a method to research urban environments. Her project *Recycling Utopia* was selected as one of twenty-five ideas for the Future Architecture Platform in 2020.

5   Goda Verikaitė, *What Does Eiguliai Say*, 2020, audio tour documentation, courtesy Kaunas.

Of Laughter and Memory
How to Produce Culture beyond Borders

Jing He

Chinese diaspora

2 →

3–4

186

1   Jing He, *Tulip Pyramid – Copy and Identity*, 2016, ready-mades, acrylic, nylon belts, plastic, 140 x 38 x 38 cm, photo: Femke Reijerman, 2016.

2   Jing He, in collaboration with Rongkai He, Cheng Guo, Weiyi Li, Dangdang Xing and Dawei Yang, *Tulip Pyramid – Copy and Identity*, 2016, mixed media, ready-mades, porcelain, earthenware, acrylic, brass, aluminium, foam, plastic, 140 × 38 × 38 cm, photo: Femke Reijerman, 2016, photo edited by Yoko Wong, 2016.

3   Kai xuan men (Arch of Triumph), Park 1903, Kunming, China, photo: Pengfei Wang, 2018.

4   Night view under the Kai xuan men (Arch of Triumph), Park 1903, Kunming, China, image found on the Internet, 2017.

One evening in the summer of 2015, my dad and I stood in front of a building reminiscent of the Arc de Triomphe. With a façade of mirrored glass, its entire body reflected the dark blue of the sky. The Chinese are used to going for walks after dinner, which is said to help with digestion. That's why we were standing there, a fifteen-minute walk from my dad's house in a newly developed business district whose prime landmark is this building. Neither my father nor I questioned why there was an Arc de Triomphe 8,683 km from Paris.

As the deep blue sky faded to near black, LED lights in the corners of each piece of glass lit up the whole Arc de Triomphe. The colours of the lights changed slowly and regularly. They shone in our faces and my dad and I laughed in unison. I could hear the shouts and laughter of children running around, fascinated and excited by the lights. There were many other families who were also out for a walk.

The next day I went back to the Arc de Triomphe, this time alone. What was behind the laughter that my father and I had shared? It seemed to have been composed of a mix of feelings. There were many layers here to unpack: not only was there a sense of absurdity (indeed there is always some absurdity behind the best punchlines) but also a hint of disdain for the tastelessness of the real estate developers.

There are many replicas of the Arc de Triomphe in China. They are scattered around cities large and small; the one in front of me had a slight connection to France. The French built a railway from Vietnam to my hometown of Kunming in the early twentieth century because of its mineral wealth. Today, this piece of Vietnamese colonial history has become the commercial endorsement for a real estate project to show our city's 'international' side. Another element I detected in our shared laughter, besides absurdity and disdain, was a bit of self-deprecation. 'We pragmatic Chinese have stripped a building of its meaning and replaced it with our own story.' I didn't actually think that the Arc de Triomphe in

5

6–7

5–6   Jing He, *Arches of the Triumph*, 2021, exhibition: 'X is Not a Small Country – Unravelling the Post-Global Era', 2021, MAAT, Museum of Art, Architecture and Technology, Lisbon, Portugal.

7   Jing He, *Arches of the Triumph #4*, 2021, detail, 170 x 80 x 70 cm.

8–9

10

Paris was an inviolable image, I just didn't expect that its meaning would be deconstructed and consumed in such a way in my hometown.

As for my father, his laughter could be attributed to a kind of dark humour; he probably never imagined himself 'meeting' Paris in this way at the age of fifty-eight. In his youth, he would get together with other young local artists to discuss French painters and foreign thinkers—people like Sartre, Nietzsche, and Márquez. It was the end of the ten-year Cultural Revolution in China; the leaders had decided to join the globalized market, and suddenly young people had easy access to a wealth of books and popular culture from the West. My father's generation aspired to the 'free life' of the West. He was the first person to wear bell-bottom jeans— once a symbol of capitalist decadence—at the university. He used to play guitar and paint with his friends beside a river in Kunming they called the Seine, living a kind of imaginary Parisian life. Standing in front of the Arc de Triomphe with its changing lights, he said, 'It's really magic realism.' When he read *One Hundred Years of Solitude* as a young man, he would never have imagined what his hometown would look like at this time. In the forty years since the economic reforms of 1978, China has undergone makeovers that go beyond what anyone could have imagined— perhaps they could be described as a strange concoction of magic and realism.

Should my hometown have an Arc de Triomphe? Or perhaps a better question: What should my hometown look like? I was stuck, unable to answer this. I was born and raised in the nineteen-nineties, during the years of China's rapid development—a development that is constantly overwritten (the new overwriting the old), making it increasingly difficult to trace the past. Everything stays new but is temporary. The romantic 'Seine' of my father's youth has no relation to my youth; it has been transformed into a dark river surrounded by new commercial areas. This constant newness has its effects. Sometimes I imagine myself in the film *Blade Runner* being tested as a

189

8   Jing He, *Attachment – Arch and Tongue*, 2018, stainless steel, aluminum, glass, plastic, paper, 90 × 155 × 10 cm, solo exhibition Jing He 'XiangXie – Elysium', 2019, Gallery Roehrs & Boetsch, Zurich, Switzerland.
9–10 Jing He, *Attachment – Arch and Tongue*, 2018, detail, 90 × 155 × 10 cm.

11

190

Handwritten annotations:

WOULD I PASS AS HUMAN?

temporal aspect of neo-liberal modernity ↓ suspended state of liminality Peter sloterdijk

Anthropotechnic ←

nothing is sacred in the face of the market

11   One of two seventeenth-century
      Delft Blue tulip pyramids,
      collection Rijksmuseum,
      Amsterdam.
12   Jing He, *Tulip Pyramid – Copy and
      Identity*, 2016.
13   Jing He, in collaboration with
      Rongkai He, Cheng Guo, Weiyi
      Li, Dangdang Xing, Dawei Yang,
      Tulip Pyramid – Copy and Identity,
      2016, mixed media, ready-mades,
      porcelain, earthenware, acrylic,
      brass, aluminium, foam, plastic,
      140 × 38 × 38 cm, photo: Femke
      Reijerman, 2016, photo edited by
      Yoko Wong, 2016.

replicant (robot): Would I pass as a human or not? Like the replicants in the film, I can't 'prove' my memories; of all the places in my childhood memories, only a park still barely exists, the rest are gone. These new locations feel like new memories being implanted in my brain in bulk form—all at once, never stopping. Memories are the building blocks of a person's identity. My brain is no longer able to form memories as fast as reality is changing. Laughter catches my attention; children playing near the Arc de Triomphe are enjoying the lights and the fountain. I realize that this triumphal arch will be part of their childhood memories, and that when they grow up they will miss it—replaced no doubt by something else.

Laughter seems to punctuate my experience of the disconnect between memory, place, and identity. Just as I laughed while standing at the foot of the Arc de Triomphe that evening with my father, so too did I give a hefty snort-laugh at a set of two large Delftblauw vases at the Rijksmuseum in Amsterdam. It was 2015 and I was looking at the bottom motif of the vases depicting what appeared to be ancient Chinese people relaxing in a traditional Chinese courtyard, representing ancient Chinese life as imagined by Europeans. I laughed partly because of the unorthodox images and childish brush strokes (feeling that I knew what was 'right') and because of a secret hidden national pride kicking in. Another part of me laughed in delight at 'unorthodoxy' because I like to deviate from authority, even if it is unconscious. You don't see such imperfect and childish brushstrokes in Chinese museums. There, valuable ceramics are near-perfect objects (dead and dull) made for the emperor. Perhaps there is some resemblance between my laughter at the Arc de Triomphe in Kunming and that in the Rijksmuseum in Amsterdam: whether it is a twenty-first-century Chinese Arc de Triomphe or a seventeenth-century Dutch Delftware vase, there is something both amusing and frightening about 'orthodoxy' being dissolved by economic forces—nothing is sacred.

This set of two seventeenth-century tulip tower vases is the result of an imitation of

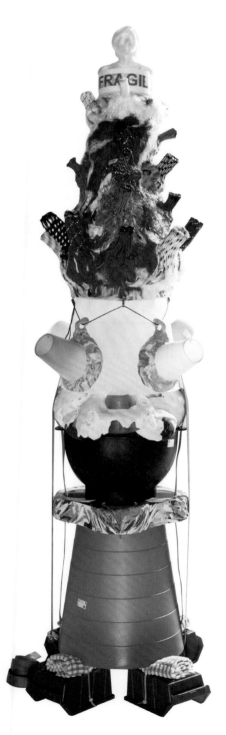

12

13

OF LAUGHTER AND MEMORY

JING HE

Chinese ceramics, keeping in mind not only their aesthetics but also their materials and shapes. The final appearance is so peculiar that it transcends beauty and ugliness. The fact that the two tulip tower vases are considered a national treasure of the Netherlands inspires me greatly: neither the tulip nor the ceramic originated in the Netherlands, but the Dutch themselves mixed them to create an identity that they feel as their own. Can this mixed identity be further blended with something more?

I started researching the history of the Tulip Pyramid. I discovered that a seventeenth-century Dutch explorer went to Nanjing in China and saw the pagoda made of ceramic and recorded the image in a book.[1] At the same time, Dutch merchants started a business of importing porcelain from China. All the ceramics exported from China were made in Jingdezhen in seventeenth-century sweatshops (similar to the factories of East Asia today). European merchants used the silver that slaves dug from South America to buy porcelains in China, which they later sold to customers in the European market. It took a hundred years for Western Europeans to discover the secret of making porcelain, and to meet the demand of poorer classes that coveted blue and white porcelain for their homes. Potters in Delft then invented Delftblauw, the closest thing to porcelain, so they were no longer limited by the material and were freer to create something closer to their own culture in blue and white patterns. It was in this context that the *Tulip Pyramid* was created. Although it is not true porcelain, the firing of a large vase one hundred and forty centimetres high required special skills and was not cheap, so it too entered the upper classes.

The *Tulip Pyramid* and the Arch of Triumph in Kunming have in common that the original cultural meaning was thrown out and the original form was reused in a pragmatic way. This process can and is often considered offensive to the original culture.

I wanted to learn from it, and so developed my own methodology out of it.

As the research for this project grew, I became curious as to what my peers thought. I approached five Chinese designers and artists inviting them to join in the project by replicating vases. I discussed with them my research and ideas, and provided them with the dimensions of the vases. I suggested using any material, but preferably blue and white; in the end, we agreed that each of us would make two layers of the vase to be combined once produced. Because the vases in the Rijksmuseum were presented as a set of two, I produced a second vase: for this one, I replicated elements drawn from the works of five Dutch designers, blending these together in my own way. This second vase is about questioning myself—an inquiry into how I have been changed through six years of education in the Netherlands.

The making of these vases allowed me to understand the Arc de Triomphe in Kunming on a much deeper level. The brightly lit building may still deserve a giggle but perhaps it's not nearly as absurd as it first appears. All cross-cultural exchange includes some strange, fantastical, or just plain incomprehensible elements, as what occurs is no less than two cultures communicating. As such, I have also accepted my hometown as it is, even if it appears outlandish or unfamiliar at times. I now try to weave my memories through time and space, allowing the new and the old to intertwine, allowing past references to become embedded in all the newness that surrounds me.

The vases I created now sit in the Art Institute of Chicago, transported to a new culture, creating new layers of meaning through added cultural crossovers and hopefully inspiring new copies and transmutations of cultural overlaps... and at the least, some layered laughter.

1   Frits Scholten, *Delft 'Tulip Vases,'* transl. Michael Hoyle (Rijksmuseum, 2013).

192

JING HE (1984, Kunming, CN) holds a Master's degree in Contextual Design from Design Academy Eindhoven (NL), and a Bachelor's degree in Jewellery Design from Gerrit Rietveld Academie (NL) and Central Academy of Fine Arts (CN). Her interest in culture, politics, and the history behind various daily objects, leads to imaginative visual representations that include various materials and mediums. Her works are included in the Art Institute of Chicago (US) and the collection in the Françoise van den Bosch Foundation held by the Stedelijk Museum Amsterdam (NL).

14–15   Jing He, in collaboration with
         Shuran Ke, *Arches of the Triumph*,
         2021, still of an animation,
         exhibition 'X is Not a Small Country
         – Unravelling the Post-Global
         Era', 2021, MAAT, Museum of Art,
         Architecture and Technology,
         Lisbon, Portugal.

On Memory and Materiality
From Producing Things to Producing Knowledge

Žan Kobal

2–3

1–3   Žan Kobal, *Nostalgia For a World That Never Existed: Vanitas*, 2020, video stills.

I remember squeezing into its creases. Every time we passed it, I would run around it and hide from my grandparents, trying to see if I could climb higher than last time. It became a family tradition to stop for a few minutes every time we crossed the square. Standing there with its bronze surface glistening in the sunlight, it seemed warm, inviting.

I never questioned what it was; I just knew that I could count on it being there whenever I visited Maribor, a city in northeast Slovenia where I was born. Even though I didn't live there anymore, it still felt like home. Every family walk took us there. And with each visit, we stopped to gaze at it. As I grew older, I started noticing its details. The barely-there faces staring back at me, the transcriptions around its base. I began to wonder about its nature, who put it there, and for what reason.

I later learned that it was the Maribor Liberation Memorial, one of thousands of monument structures built between the nineteen-fifties and nineteen-eighties in the former Yugoslavia commemorating the victims of fascist aggression during World War II. They are the legacy of a bygone era, the embodied ethos of a generation that came before, and the remains of a nationwide network of grand teaching tools for relating to the population, the ethos, history, and narrative of Tito's Yugoslavia.

By the late nineteen-forties, refusing to become a Soviet satellite State within the Eastern Bloc, Yugoslavia distanced itself from the USSR. It searched for legitimization by claiming to pursue emancipation: internally, from class divide and ethnic conflict; externally, by supporting anticolonialism. Pursuing friendly relations, cultural connections, and economic exchange with both rival blocs, it became a country that offered a 'third way,' an alternative to the capitalist West and communist East. Deliberately defying the geopolitics of the East-West divide and its unique presence at the intersection between the two, it enjoyed an outsider's international presence, creating a stage on which to exchange architectural knowledge and ideas across political borders and cultural divisions.

4–5

6

Seeking to emphasize the split from the USSR, the government rejected the traditional 'socialist-realism' style that dominated the region and sought to find its own visual language, looking to the artistic movements of Western Europe and America for inspiration. As architects were freed from the historical mandate of social realism—the singular architectural style of a socialist society until that point—anti-fascist WWII sculptural memorials began to spring up across Yugoslavia in the styles of abstract expressionism, geometric abstraction, and minimalism.

From their drastically different style, to their sheer size and volume, they were a clear statement about the country's shifting alliances and a not-so-subtle nod to the West. The impact of these new structures firmly cemented a new visual language and created a new socialist style, one that was carried through for decades. It defined the architectural landscape of the region for years to come—an architectural landscape I grew up in.

By the time I was born, these monuments took on a different role. Following the disintegration of Yugoslavia in the early nineties and the subsequent Balkan wars, we saw a change in the ideological paradigm that further caused a renewed necessity for creating new memory politics and the rewriting of recent history. These monuments no longer commemorated the struggles experienced during WWII, but became the embodiment of the failed Yugoslav project. As unwelcome symbols of a unified Yugoslavia, they became targets of nationalist aggression and faced neglect and destruction.

This is how my family saw them, as uncomfortable reminders of what they wanted to leave behind; as fragmented sentiments, connecting them to their past life. I was too young to understand. Being born after the dissolution of Yugoslavia, I never experienced them as propaganda, only as benevolent remains of my cultural heritage. I had nothing to resent them for. Existing all around me, like thousands of threads weaving the fabric of my reality, they lay the groundwork for my visual vocabulary, yet I knew very little about their history and politics.

7–8

197

4–6   Žan Kobal, *Nostalgia For a World That Never Existed: Politics of Craft*, 2020, video stills.
7   Slavko Tihec, *Maribor Liberation Monument*, 1975, public sculpture, courtesy UKM.
8   Žan Kobal, *Bamboo Forest in Branica*, 2019, photograph.

It was not till later in my teens and especially once I moved abroad, that I started actively thinking about their nature. In the first few months living abroad, I started noticing more and more of the monuments popping up on social media. Although they shaped a large part of my familiar world, when talked about online they were often described as surreal, foreign, and alien. These sentiments perplexed me as they framed me as an outsider, even though Slovenia was at that point already part of the European Union, not to mention located in Central Europe.

The Western media dubbed them 'Spomeniks,' a bastardization of a Serbo-Croatian word *spomenik* [monument]. Often valued simply for their awe-inspiring form, they were completely decontextualized and stripped away of the necessary tools for understanding them. Presented as incomprehensible objects of a foreign past, they were exoticized, highlighting the Western perception of the Balkans as only peripherally associated with the project of Enlightenment in the Western world.

As a result, these places of remembrance became concrete clickbait. A shared Yugoslav experience of a revolution became only a cultural artefact, somewhat unreadable and vulnerable to commodification. They became silent, exotic backdrops for magazine photoshoots and music videos, exploiting them for their impressive visuals. Their online status as cultural icons becomes apparent when searching the #spomenik on Instagram, with more than twenty-nine thousand results. More interestingly, a large portion of the posts using the hashtag isn't about the monuments at all, but rather about digital self-promotion, implying that they have became an online brand—reduced only to boosting online traffic to personal profiles and events. The disconnect between my very personal understanding and how the world seemed to view the monuments ignited my curiosity to look past their form and rather examine them as vessels for the shifting narratives they experienced. It was a seminal moment in my design practice, re-centring my focus away from solutionist approaches I had been

198

9

9   Žan Kobal, Nostalgia *For a World That Never Existed: Neither Here Nor There*, 2020, installation segments, 120 × 50 × 35 cm, video stills.

10   Žan Kobal, *Nostalgia for a World That Never Existed: Neither Here*, 2020, video still, 3.26'.

11   Žan Kobal, *Nostalgia for a World That Never Existed: Nor There*, 2020, video still, 3.26'.

trained in as an industrial designer (with a concern towards the final product), towards a practice more interested in the production of knowledge and understanding.

When I engaged with them in the project entitled *A Memorial to the Monuments*, I understood that I could not just mine them for their aesthetics or materiality (as references in the production of objects), as this would have perpetuated their narrative of unreadability. Rather, their formal qualities became entry points to start examining and unfolding the complex stories that have nearly been erased, that hide underneath their surface. The project became content driven, delving into several video archives to uncover the shifting narratives around the monuments through the various contexts of their existence.

Taking the form of a video installation, the project includes nine screens that overlap different narratives to recreate a nonlinear tale of otherness and exoticization. These function on two levels. At face value, the installation works as an emotional trigger, mimicking a sense of confusion similar to the one I felt when reading about the monuments in Western media. It is overwhelming and seemingly incomprehensible. Yet when engaged with, individual screens reveal the stories left behind. The stories of a fallen regime, a ten-year war, and nationalist aggression. They reconstruct the monuments' difficult heritage—and mine—by piecing together the region's broken past.

If we start acknowledging the world as a complex and multi-layered system full of opposing narratives and perspectives, and embrace a transition in design towards practices of care and empathy, it becomes clear that practices that merely aesthetically borrow from the past no longer have a place in the contemporary design discourse. Pushing past the sheer fascination of aesthetics and nostalgia, we can examine and unfold the complexities of cultural cannons these artefacts belong to and dig for the denied aspects of the past.

The idea of heritage, as an integral part of my design practice, was further solidified in my Master's project *Nostalgia For a World That Never Existed*. Torn between Slovenia and

10–11

the Netherlands, I was struck at the impact the two vastly different landscapes had in the construction of their respective national cannons. Looking at the vernacular artefacts and art that were the products of, or derived from, rural spaces, I engaged with them as conduits to reveal the hidden mechanism of cultural identity. As part of the project, I travelled back to Slovenia, visiting my grandparents in Branica, a small village in the countryside, where time seems to run slightly slower and change happens at a glacial pace. The ancestral landscape was integral in constructing an image of where I come from, my image of Slovenia. Yet Branica has been transformed in the last couple years by a rapidly expanding bamboo forest, pushing out indigenous plants and subordinating the landscape. The changing material index of the environment disputed the apparent immutable nature of ancestral landscapes and their politics.

In an attempt to mediate the disconnect between the bamboo and its new environment, I crafted a traditional 'Alpine chair' out of bamboo. Its material properties challenged

me as they followed different rules than those passed down to me through the heritage of woodworking in Slovenia. I was required to forget my embodied knowledge and start from scratch, to delve into cultural archives not indigenous or customary to the area in search of skill and understanding. Every cut and bend became an effort towards a practice that was neither native nor *other*. Through time, the final outcome didn't matter anymore; the process revealed a narrative of cross-cultural exchange and put into question notions of heritage existing in isolation.

Just like the monuments or the Alpine chair, our canons are full of similar unseen cultural markers, muddled by revisionist histories and changing power structures. As design turns its attention to critically examine the world, these leftover artefacts can help us better understand not just our present realities, but also our positioning within them. As such, design stops being preoccupied with commodity and becomes part of a larger conversation about material culture. This opens

up the possibilities of trans-disciplinary practices, drifting between anthropology, sociology, and archaeology, with the potential to unravel what is hidden—such as the manifold meanings of the Spomeniks or the ancestral landscape of Branica. Finding a solution is not a priority, as its objective becomes critical engagement with, and the investigation of, our contemporaneity to better understand who we are and how we got there. Design stops being the production of things and rather becomes the production of knowledge.

12   Žan Kobal, *Nostalgia For a World That Never Existed*, 2020, installation view.

201

ŽAN KOBAL (1993) is a Slovenian designer, researcher, and writer based in the Netherlands. After graduating in Industrial Design (cum laude) at the Academy of Fine Arts and Design Ljubljana (SI), he continued his studies at Design Academy Eindhoven (NL) obtaining a Master's degree (cum laude) in Contextual Design. Approaching design as an investigative medium, his work often crosses the traditional boundaries of design by delving into film and installation to frame objects as narration devices, unfolding how material, craft, and discourse co-create reality.

From a White Bathroom to Envisioning an Alternative Modernity

Weixiao Shen / 申薇笑

One day while taking a shower, a thought suddenly struck me. I was staring at my all-white, 'modern' bathroom: white ceramic tiles, white ceramic toilet, white ceramic washing basin, white washing machine, white door. I wondered what a person from the nineteenth century might think if they were to behold this white shiny room. What was once expensive material such as ceramics, usually decorated with ornaments, is now used for excretion and washing. Would they be impressed or disappointed by how we've evolved this space for washing and excretion?

My sensitivity to bathrooms dates back to my childhood experience of the outhouse at my grandparents' house. Despite my deep appreciation and affection for my grandparents, I always struggled to visit them because they didn't have a 'proper' bathroom. My grandparents live in a small village in the Chinese countryside; they farm fish and carry people across the river in a man-powered boat. The village is what most would consider primitive and underdeveloped; only two years ago did it finally install running water. Before then, water was pumped from underground sources.

My grandparents' bathroom isn't a room or separate space. Functions that would 'normally' be conducted in a bathroom are divided up in the house. Bathing happens in a big basin in the kitchen, which is in an adjacent building to the house; brushing teeth happens in the kitchen sink. As for excretion, it is supposed to happen in a hut outside of the main house and next to the plot for growing vegetables used for daily family consumption. There's a big pit inside that hut with lots of firewood and straw piled up next to it. I only ever used the hut once or twice—I remember it as cold, dark, scary, and smelly. Since then, I feared their sanitation system. In fact, every time I was at my grandparents' place, they provided me with a chamber pot in the bedroom.

As a child who had grown up in the city, I was used to 'modern' comforts—an apartment with a bathroom. It was difficult for me to imagine any other way of living. But my grandparents held different values;

2–3

203

1   Weixiao Shen, *Underneath Another Moon* / 别有洞天, 2020, video still.
2–3 Weixiao Shen's grandparents' house and her grandma's chickens on the road.

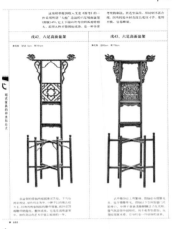

4

5

6

after having lived in the city for nearly a decade, they decided to return to the village and intentionally chose not to 'upgrade' their bathroom. They mainly kept the bathroom as it was. Three years ago, they built an extension room as a 'bathroom' intended for other family members. They saw no advantage of using this addition themselves; it was built for the sole purpose of accommodating other family members who were used to the amenities of the so-called modern lifestyle. But whose modernity was it? It was beginning to feel that modernity was applied unevenly (dominant in cities) and that modernity was not something that reflected many of the values of Chinese domesticity—how space was used and appropriated.

This clash of bathroom culture prompted me to question my assumptions about modernity, or at least how I had previously configured it. My grandparents' rejection of the modern toilet felt like a striking blow against many other aspects of my life, which I began to question. The lifestyle that I was accustomed to, and specifically the one relating to bathrooms, was not perhaps the best or only representation of modernity. Furthermore, in a country with such a rich and vivid history of decorating, why would we just accept a singular visual expression of modernity? What would a more Chinese version of modernity look like, and in particular a Chinese modern bathroom?

The image of a modern bathroom was formed and fixed in Western countries during the second half of the twentieth century. It evolved from a wooden 'toilet' in the church to a 'toilet cabinet/wardrobe' in the houses of wealthy families. The material used in these areas, such as toilets, bathtubs, and washing basins, changed from wood, to enamelled metal, to white ceramics. This process of material change did not occur in China. These modern trends were introduced and imported to China in relatively rapid succession, particularly with the rise of industrialization in the nineteen-fifties, and were further cemented with the opening of China's market in the last several decades.

204

4   Inspiration for *Underneath Another Moon*: Towel rack and basin holder, illustration from Wang Shixiang *Mingdai jiaju yanjiu* 明代家具研究, English translation: Connoisseurship of Chinese Furniture: Ming and Early Qing Dynasties, Volume 1.
5   Inspiration for *Underneath Another Moon*: Chinese Spittoon, late twentieth century style.
6   Inspiration for *Underneath Another Moon*: Gold ingot of Zhenguan Era Tang Dynasty.
7   Weixiao Shen, *Underneath Another Moon* / 别有洞天, 2020, installation view, photo: Femke Reijerman, 2020.

8

9–10

8 Wooden bathtub in bedroom,
 illustration from Jingpingmei Mixitu
 金瓶梅秘戏图, erotic painting by
 Hu Yefo (Chinese, 1908–1980), *The
 Plum in the Golden Vase* [freely
 translated].

9–11 Weixiao Shen, *Underneath Another
 Moon* / 别有洞天, 2020, video still.

12 Weixiao Shen, *Underneath
 Another Moon* / 别有洞天, 2020,
 3D rendering of objects.

Waterworks, sewer systems, and Western sanitary objects first showed up in China because of the European invaders who lived in the concession areas.[1] At that time, China had lost several wars and was at a stage of semi-colonial and semi-feudal society, highly susceptible to the belief that Western culture was more advanced in every aspect; at the time, Western influences in hygiene were beginning to spread slowly through China. However, it wasn't until 1978 that China officially started to accelerate its drive towards modernization, establishing special economic zones in coastal areas for foreign enterprises to open manufacturing plants for the Chinese market; several of these included objects found in Western bathrooms. This began a widespread transition to a new type of thinking about our relationship to cleaning our bodies, to our human waste and its value or taboo. These ideas and values were imported from elsewhere, quickly overriding centuries of local traditions.

 My design research has focused on a speculative notion of a more Chinese form of modernity that frees us from the norms of the Western bathroom. Instead of designing a toilet that represents an alternative modernity, I use design as a periscope for viewing an alternative imaginary of the bathroom. For example, in the project *Underneath Another Moon* / 别有洞天, I propose a 'What if' scenario. What if there was a Third Opium War between China and Great Britain in 1880? And what if this time, China prevailed and set up concession districts in key cities around the world? How would 'modernity' be different? The video I produced shows a domestic household in an imagined Chinese concession district in a European country. It is a metaphorical framework to visualize an alternative modernity. Here, Chinese 'traditional' ideologies are fused with cultural change and product development. I designed the whole house as a system, starting with the bathroom, which sets the tone for the rest of the house.

1 Areas inside key cities of China that became treaty ports that were
 governed and occupied by foreign powers, a form of colonization.

The bathroom balances nature with modernity, whereby the bathroom is not a denial of the body's effluence—it is not scrubbed clean of living organisms or designed as a spartan space of functionality. The bathroom in this household is rather a kind of tribute to my grandparents' experience. It is an outdoor bathroom (not a closed space within a house), comprised of a circular bamboo tent adjacent to a river. The space is multi-purposed as well as sacred: it is used for bathing, human excretion, reflecting, and drinking tea. It is an ornamental and poetic space immersed in nature, enabling the tidal system to bring in fresh water and carry the wastewater out to sea.

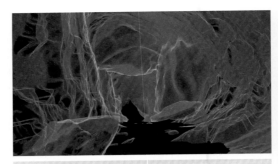

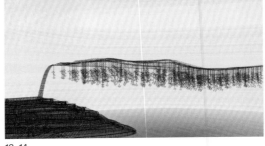

13–14

The toilet itself is a celebration of human excrement and its value as fertilizer for nourishing and giving back to the earth. It is designed not in plastic or porcelain but in jade, and surrounded by gold ingot. Its shape is reminiscent of a 'hulu' vase, which represents health, longevity, and wealth. It allows the user to sit in any direction, with legs perched near the base, enabling it to be situated in the centre of the room—both an object of beauty and function. A towel rack with two spouts is actually a mini water system, which is an adaptation of the shape of the traditional basin rack allowing water to travel through this rack to fill the basin or emerge from another spout for tea. When the rains come, the room itself is flushed out by the six water dragonheads, which cleanse the room both spiritually and physically. The room balances cleanliness, spirituality, and function.

After completing the project it's hard for me to see my grandparents' bathroom in the same light as before: it now feels honest, true, and appealing to something that my generation has chosen to forget in order to embrace the values of other cultures deemed somehow more worthy.

208

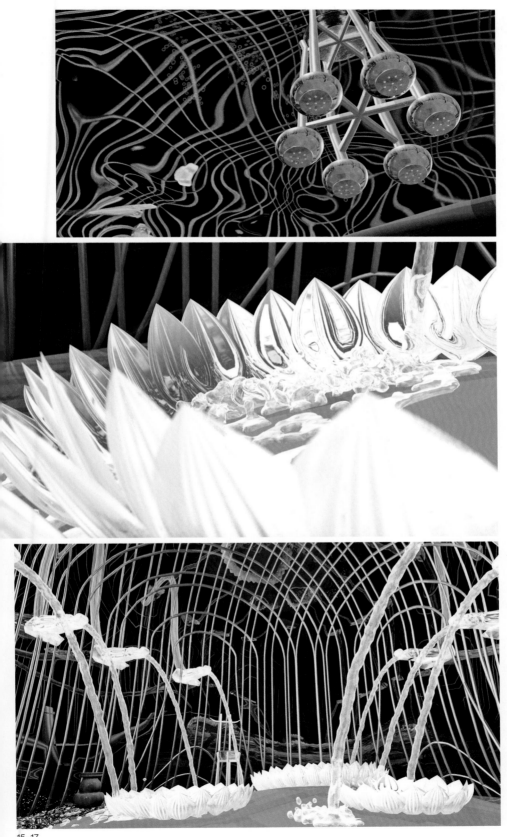

WEIXIAO SHEN/申微笑 is a designer from Wuhan (CN). Her works put the spotlight on mundane objects in people's everyday lives. Diving into the history of what intrigues her, Shen creates a new narrative of these objects with fantasies rich in absurdity and spectacle. Her interpretation magnifies seemingly common details in life, awaking examinations on the rationality and value of ordinary objects, enabling an imagining of an alternative lifestyle. Her works tell the story through a mixture of physical material and digital media in order to create a multi-layered experience.

209

15–17

A Basic Instinct

Anna Aagaard Jensen

2 →

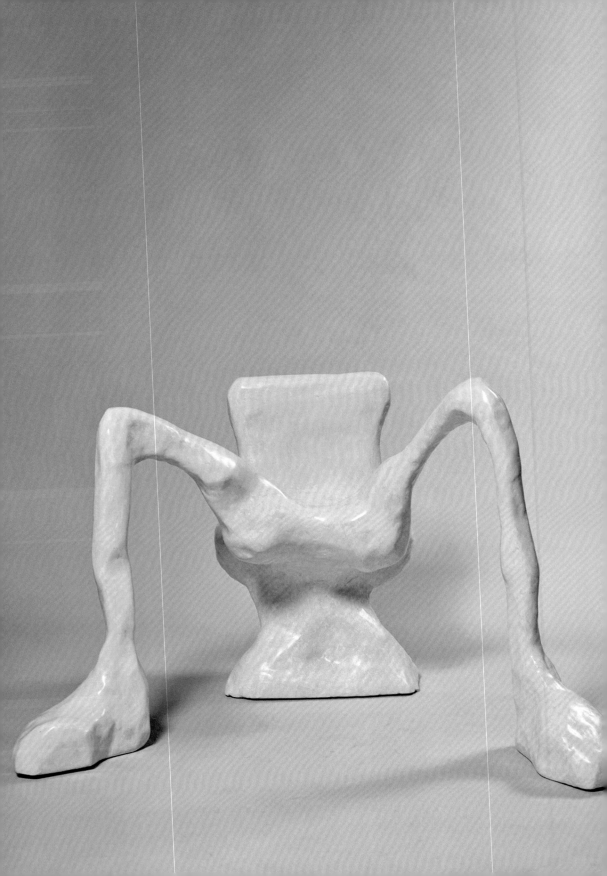

The postures of men and women in public space reveal their unequal positions in society. Anna's project *A Basic Instinct* refers to the famous movie, in which we see actress Sharon Stone taking an unconventional posture with slightly spread legs, confusing her interrogators. 'Men have the tendency of taking as much space in public as they feel or need, whereas women tend to sculpt their bodies and behaviour according to what society allows and deems appropriate.' Jensen's statement chairs allow women to lean back in a relaxed way, spread their legs seductively, and boldly take over space as the most natural thing to do.

ANNA AAGAARD JENSEN (1990) is a designer based in the Netherlands. Her practice interrogates the preconceived dictated behavioural patterns of women and the social factors allowing them to continue existing today. Her objects are alternative representations of the archetypes that surround us, made with a hyperfeminine aesthetic language, using makeup and extracting shapes related to the female body. In creating function, Jensen sculpts form into a story that advocates for a new way of looking at design, and inevitably at our environment.

← 3

4–5

1   Anna Aagaard Jensen, *A Basic Instinct*, 2018, Acrylic One, fibreglass, PU Foam, styrofoam, makeup, installation view: left 100 × 55 × 55 cm; middle: 119 × 136 × 174 cm; right: 75 × 68 × 82 cm, photo: Iris Rijskamp, 2018.
2   Anna Aagaard Jensen, *Laid Back Lure*, 2020, Acrylic One, fibreglass, steel, MAC cosmetics, epoxy resin, 190 × 110 × 96 cm, courtesy Pere Projects & Functional Art Gallery.
3   Anna Aagaard Jensen, *Lady F*, 2019, Acrylic One, fibreglass, styrofoam, PU Foam, MAC cosmetics, 116 × 123 × 80 cm, courtesy Functional Art Gallery.
4   Screenshot from TV show *Jimmy Kimmel Live!*
5   Sharon Stone in the movie *Basic Instinct*, 1992.

De_sign

Gabriel .A. Maher

Gabriel .A. Maher's project *De_sign* aims at deconstructing the conventional gendered meanings inherent in the systems of gender representation.

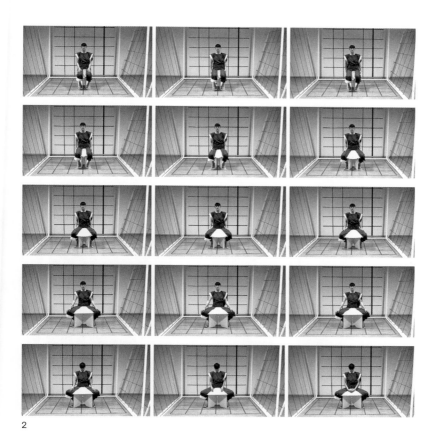

2

3–4

1   Gabriel .A. Maher, *De_sign*, 2014, performance installation, movement by Floriane Misslin, photo: Femke Reijerman.
2   Gabriel .A. Maher, *De_sign, Act of Sitting*, 2014, performance, movement by Floriane Misslin, photo: Gabriel .A. Maher.
3   Gabriel .A. Maher, *De_sign*, 2014, garment #1, movement by Gabriel .A. Maher, photo: Alwin Poiana.
4   Gabriel .A. Maher, *De_sign*, 2014, garment #3, movement by Gabriel .A. Maher, photo: Alwin Poiana.

GABRIEL .A. MAHER (They/Them*) is a designer currently living and working in the Netherlands. With a practice established in Architecture and Social Design, Maher's work centres on critical and analytical approaches to design and design-led research. Within this sphere, they consider the effects of design and the act of designing on our bodies and the shaping of subjectivities and identities. Maher's investigations directly confront the conditions that frame concepts of gender, class privilege, and sexuality from a design as well as a power perspective. They traverse their practice as a queer and gender non-conforming person from a working class background; these intersections inform and frame their attitudes toward design and pedagogic practice. Maher teaches at Design Academy Eindhoven (NL) and at the Royal Academy of Art in The Hague (NL). Most recently, they were the recipient of the iphiGenia Gender Design Award (2019) and were shortlisted for the Hublot Design Prize (2018).
*They/Them/Their: gender-neutral pronoun, third person singular.

How to Use Self-Dehumanization as a Strategy to Empower

Hsin Min Chan

2

In April 2020, I decided to return to Taiwan when Design Academy Eindhoven shut down amidst the first wave of the COVID-19 pandemic. When I arrived in my home country, I was obliged to self-quarantine for fourteen days, during which my whereabouts were constantly tracked through mobile phone data. Besides this tracking, I was placed under the authority of a supervisor who advised me to go to hospital for a COVID-19 test, which I did.

Then the situation started to become grim. The hospital claimed they had to immediately isolate me. I protested and then was arrested; I was placed in an isolation ward that was constantly checked by a 24-hour surveillance camera. Gradually, I started to lose my sense of time; I felt as if I had come to a stand still, as if I had turned into a still life. Every now and then a doctor's voice would check my condition via the ward's intercom, explaining the hospital's 'great' policy. I was told that once somebody like me is trapped into the medical system, they can only be released after sufficient data has been collected, indicating me as COVID-19-free. The endless waiting for test results started. I constantly stared at the surveillance camera, and this waiting and staring was only interrupted by short intervals when food and medicines were brought in (I did not even know why I had to take medicines). Because the nurses were covered by masks and isolation uniforms, I could not distinguish one from the other. This contributed to a growing sense of being reduced to a potential threat, a dangerous body that needed to be controlled. I was deprived of my identity, stripped from my self. French philosopher Foucault has described this phenomenon of absolute authority as 'the eye that knows and decides, the eye that governs,' which he named 'the medical gaze.' The medical gaze dehumanized me, as it separated my body from my identity, fixing me in this inert, frozen cell. I had become an object.

At first I felt powerless and hopeless. All I could do was cry and bury myself in the blanket, turning away from the camera. But suddenly I started to realize that hiding my

217

1   Hsin Min Chan, *To-be-looked-at-ness*, 2021, installation, 250 × 400 × 400 cm, photo: Jian da Huang.
2   Video stills from surveillance camera in Hsin Min Chan's hospital ward, 2020, 92 hours video.

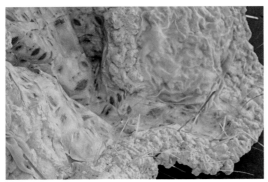

3

4 →

emotions wouldn't change a thing. I thought, 'Why not use my hysteria, my despair, why not turn my emotions into such a spectacle, that they can no longer ignore me.' My hysteria became a weapon for changing the situation. I positioned my body in such a way that the camera and intercom could best record my performance, track all of my erratic movements, my screaming for my mother, and my loud crying. It worked. Suddenly, the voice over the intercom announced that the process of testing would speed up. Both my body and emotions had become instruments that I exploited to give the impression of being a dangerous body as a counterattack. Dehumanization had thus become an empowering tool. Finally, the medical authorities started to treat me like a human being instead of an object; soon after, I was released from hospital.

Upon my return to the Netherlands, I decided to draw from my recent experience in Taiwan for my Master's programme graduation project. At my request, I received the recordings of the surveillance cameras from the hospital. Reflecting on my time in hospital and my experience of losing individuality and a sense of humanity, I started to reflect on how these experiences compared to my 'normal' life. I have always been self-aware and highly conscious of how I look; I never leave the house without make-up. In hindsight, I always test my looks via the imagined male gaze. And I'm not the only woman to experience this. I started to see the similarities between experiencing myself through the eyes of others in public space, and thus experiencing myself as an 'object,' versus being reduced to objecthood via the surveillance cameras in hospital. Foucault also wrote about this phenomenon, describing how the fact of potentially being watched causes people to internalize the surveillance. Prisoners in a Panopticum-shaped prison start to discipline themselves, and the same happens within any situation in which people are constantly watched by surveillance cameras. In hospital, I experienced how I became overly conscious of potentially being watched. Something

Always testing your body through imagined male gaze?

218

3   Hsin Min Chan, *To-be-looked-at-ness*, 2021, detail, installation, 250 × 400 × 400 cm, photo: Jian da Huang.
4   Hsin Min Chan, *To-be-looked-at-ness*, 2021, installation, 250 × 400 × 400 cm, photo: Jian da Huang.

similar happens with women who have become accustomed to the authority of the male gaze, which defines their behaviour. The male gaze not only objectifies the female body, but it is also internalized by women themselves. Women are thus familiar with being seen as 'objects.' They act as if they are beautiful objects.

So why not use my personal experience in hospital, of being able to transform my powerless situation into one of power, into a strategy to battle the male gaze in normal life? How about reversing the power relationships by exploiting being viewed as an object?

To stress the process of objectification in hospital as well as the process of reversing the usual power relationships, I experimented with turning famous women in films, such as Audrey Hepburn who is considered *the* icon of female beauty, into decorative vases. The spectator sees the actress elegantly moving through the interior spaces, closely followed by George Peppard, but because she has turned into a vase with a broad rim, he cannot possibly touch her. Through my intervention, Audrey Hepburn, cum vase, shows off her beauty, but has also become unapproachable.

Then I started to build sculptural dresses, a merging of decorative motives, fabrics, and furniture pieces, which would act as disciplinary devices once I would start to wear them. I solidified the dress's fabric and built a stairway into the expanded skirt, lifting my body high above all other people. As I had done in hospital, I transformed my objectified body into a weapon. I became a performer who fully controls the situation. The final dress, which resulted from a broad range of experiments, serves both as a stage for displaying the to-be-looked-at-ness of the woman who wears it, of me, *and* it serves as an armour, which transforms me into an unapproachable, autonomous creature, no longer owned and disciplined by the male gaze.

220

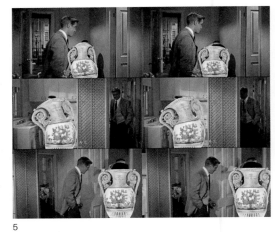

5

5   Hsin Min Chan, *Vase Woman*, 2020, video still, appropriation of the film *Breakfast at Tiffany's*.

6–7   Hsin Min Chan, *To-be-looked-at-ness*, 2021, details, installation, 250 × 400 × 400 cm, photo: Jian da Huang.

6

221

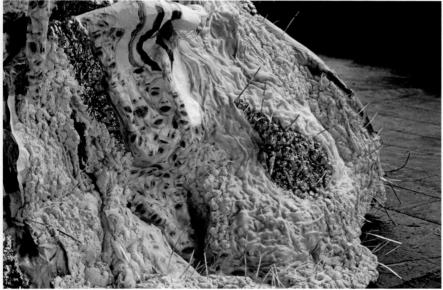

7

HSIN MIN CHAN/詹新敏 is a designer from Taiwan who graduated from the Contextual Design Master's programme at Design Academy Eindhoven (NL) in 2021. Chan's interests in politics, gender, power, culture, and social phenomena are related to her experience and identity. She deconstructs the power dynamics between artefacts, human bodies, and behaviours, to reveal the truth of normal life. Her work is politically engaged and includes critical interpretation; her work can be viewed as a protest, a performative experience.

1

Upon a Rusted Fence
Veld, Sexuality, and the Desire to be Touched

Billy Ernst

2–5

I write from the Highveld where the sun ascends, thirty-two kilometres west of Amsterdam, Mpumalanga.[1] The Highveld holds a place in the Afrikaner cultural imagination as a land of wide-open veld, vast light blue skies, and a sense of belonging, where one can still believe in God. This image is ingrained in my mind by the landscape painting hanging on the wall of my mother's house, an image of pioneer virtue and Afrikaner nationalism—symbolized by the cultivation of land and the absence of indigenous presence. In the faint brushstrokes in the foreground of this expansive landscape, hidden between the upward strokes of thatch grass, runs a fence. The paradisal land is pervaded by a sense of control. My eyes soar free whilst my body paces a line it cannot cross.

My body is the site of my most immediate and intimately felt geography, the farm that I grew up on is the second—its ongas[2] are the folds of skin on my abdomen as I drive home along the twelve kilometre dirt road, my body swaying along the road's water shaped contours. I grew up on Boesmanspruit Farm in South Africa, a seven hundred and fifty hectare fourth generation industrial and residential farm. The farm is separated into industrial tree plantations, rangelands for commercial cattle, rangelands for subsistence cattle, and sections for game. There are also three separately enclosed residential areas occupied by the farm owner (white), managerial employees (white), and labourers (black). The levels of insecurity can be seen in the types of fencing used around each of these housing areas. The farm has been in my family for more than a hundred years and continues as the new generation (both my brothers) asserts its own virtues onto and into the land. The reproduction of new family members and new plantations plays a large role in the ongoing project of legacy and family business. This is especially true for tree farming, where harvesting only happens

223

1   Billy Ernst, *Skin on Skin*, 2019, photo: Morane Grazzini.
2–5 Typologies of fences on the farm, photos: Billy Ernst, 2021.

1   Mpumalanga is a province of South Africa. In Swazi, Xhosa, Ndebele and Zulu, the name means east—literally, 'the place where the sun rises.' Amsterdam is a small town sixteen km from the border of Eswatini.
2   A dry gully, formed by the eroding action of running water.

7

6   Billy Ernst, *Insecurities*, 2019,
film still and Fondle fence, photo:
Johan Pabon.

7   Billy Ernst, *Insecurities*, 2019,
installation, photo: Nicole Marnati.

8–11 Typologies of fences on the farm,
photos: Billy Ernst, 2021.

every twelve to eighteen years, meaning that what you plant today will only be beneficial for the next generation. But in the context of post-apartheid South Africa, the longevity of such a project is threatened by the current redistribution and expropriation of land by the government. Although this sociopolitical policy has the capacity to reduce inequality in South Africa, it shakes the already fragile Afrikaner identity to its core—an identity that is strongly intertwined with the ownership or *baasskap*[3] of land. When I distanced myself from the farm business in order to pursue my own path, I had to reposition myself outside of the inextricable links between family and business, ownership and land. The farm isn't just a home for me but it is the site of a long, ongoing case study through which I can explore myself in relation to my family, the environment, the social climate, and the cultural landscape, all of which mutually shape each other in the present. By looking at the fences on the farm, the relations between culture, natures, objects, and subjects become very apparent.

On the farm there are eight typologies of metal fences that separate different areas into managed, protected, and controlled zones; these prevent interactions between people, domestic animals, farmed animals, wild animals, cultivated plants, and wild plants. These fences vary in height, tension, hole size in the weave, and ability to lacerate. The ones that prevent human passage are the most violent; they are intentionally designed to maim the body. The fences are technical solutions conceived not only to solve social and environmental conflict, but also to control it.

The power that the fence exerts resides in the hands of the landowner, who through demarcation controls the movement of people and animals across the land, the

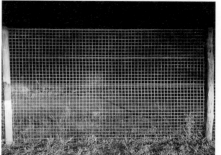

8–11

fencing, borders, control

---

3   *Baasskap* (Boss-ship). This term suggests dominion and control, especially of white South Africans over non-whites. It is a white supremacist ideology. In Fanagalo, an instructive language between Zulu, English and Afrikaans, baas is still used to refer to the white male owner/manager, and kleinbaas to the boys of the male owner. Kleinbaas is still what I am referred to when conversing in Fanagalo. My relation to my father automatically places me in a superior position of control.

management of crops, the allocation of water resources, and access to hunting of small animals. The ideological and spatial demarcation of land is manifested in the fence, a symbolic gesture that supports the actions of separatism and exclusion, a loss of intimacies with other beings, and a clear distinction between what is outside and inside. Even though the fence perpetuates binary thinking in material form, there are more sides to a fence to consider. I follow the path of a jackal that crawls under the fence, the laksman[4] that rests on it, the pompom weed that disperses over it, and the morning glory that twines its hairy stems around its metal wire. The fence line simply becomes a marker whilst being in transit, a place to move through, or falter upon. It is here that I find myself—in the liminality of neither side of the fence.[5] To be a gay *boerseun*[6] is to disrupt the categorically accepted notions of what a *boer* (Afrikaner farmer) and what a *seun* (son or boy) mean. My identity, sexuality, and the land are in a perpetual motion of becoming; identifying as a gay boerseun is a quite recent exploration for me. Growing up

226 in a conservative Afrikaner community, I was exposed from a young age, through the church, school, and patriarchal structure of family, to the makings of a *real* man. Even though in my mind I understood these societal rules, I couldn't get my supple body to move in the same way that men's bodies around me did. Their movements calculated as the cloned eucalyptus plantations on the farm—straight up, uniform reproductions of a heteronormative ideal. Eucalyptus plantations are known for their low bio-diversity, for being devoid of other life forms. It is common knowledge that very little grows under eucalyptus trees. Outdoor farm activities like hunting and fishing is a

---

4   A southern fiscal bird. A bird that is protected and not allowed to be hunted on the farm.

5   I do, however, acknowledge that exploring this liminality comes with the privilege of being able to explore all areas of the farm because of my status as the farm owner's son. There are many forms of life that live here that don't have the same access as I do.

6   An Afrikaner boy or man; a farm-boy, a 'son of the soil.' In present day South Africa, apart from farmers, boer has become a performed masculinity that leans towards the nationalistic and conservative identity of Afrikaners: a boer is considered the embodiment of a masculine idyll. I use the term solely to disrupt (by inserting my sexuality) the link between boer/landowner/man/boss/son.

12   Billy Ernst, *Soft Sensual Fence*, 2020, photo: Billy Ernst.

means through which to affirm men's virility. These sports, with their accompanying clothes and gear, often become performed masculinity (Drag). As a young person, I stayed mostly indoors keeping myself busy with home activities like cooking and laying tables, knowing that if I stepped over the threshold to the outside, I might amplify my deviancy from what was considered as natural and the norm. Modern understandings of sexuality are deeply influenced by historically specific ideas of Nature, and most obviously by the classification of gay, lesbian, bisexual, transgender and queer bodies as 'unnatural.' Over time, I understood that what was keeping me inside was this empirical existence of the nature/against-nature binary—in other words, a fence. I had to cognitively emancipate myself from an assigned aberration and move into spaces that felt natural to me. Walking off track in the field became an act of resistance. The field and I touching each other, the grasses stroking my legs, my hands sensuously brushing their top edges. Like skin on skin.

<u>Fences are physical manifestations of our own insecurities.</u> They suppress the power and information that lies within these sensuous physical and emotional encounters. Overcoming our insecurities involves having the courage to become vulnerable, releasing our control of situations or their outcomes, and showing our true emotions. It means being able to move to the other side of the fence, extending one's self for the purpose of expanding our perceptions, and forming connections. In my project *Insecurities*, the fence is isolated from its intended context, and the clear distinction between object and subject becomes blurred. The installation explores three variations of an archetypical Heras fence, which is commonly seen around building sites in Dutch cities. These modular fences are rentable, quick to install and cheap to manufacture, suggesting functionality; nonetheless, a three millimetre wire with a one and a half centimetre vertical protrusion past the frame endows these objects with a cruelty aimed towards whoever tries to climb over them. As a response, my fences invite this crossing to happen. I use touch as the guiding sense in my practice; by breaking down the metal into small pieces and reconstructing it by hand, I ensure that the metal stays soft and supple to the touch. Turning the overtly masculine straight metal wire into soft pliable materials becomes a meditative gesture of resisting the patriarchal visions of what I should be. The material outcome is metal that appears and feels like waving grasses, the mane of a feline, or an overgrown creeper; a fence made of such material encourages a different type of tactile engagement.

By subverting the material logic through which the mechanism functions, the meaning of the mechanism changes. It is an attempt to dissolve ideological categorization through tactile encounters that champions closeness, fluidity, connection, and care.

These objects were not intended to be practical fences but more embodied experiential objects of provocation. Fences are felt everywhere, not just in South Africa on my childhood farm. They are on the borders, around our farms, in our cities, around our houses, around our bodies, around our hearts, and planted within the imposed categories of how the world has been ordered.

When I walk in the veld I often come across rusted pieces of barbed wire laying on the ground; I used to think that they were animal snares and would vigorously pick them up to protect the animals. It was only after collecting a large heap of wire that I realized I was walking on an old fence line, one my grandfather had possibly erected. These rusted heaps of metal, scattered around the farm, have come to show me that fences are not always hard, rigid, and defiant boundaries. Like our bodies, they break down, shift, and become soft, pliable, and amenable to change.

228

13

BILLY ERNST (1989) is a multi-disciplinary spatial designer. He holds a Bachelor's degree in Interior Design from Inscape Design College Pretoria (SA) and a Master's degree in Social Design from Design Academy Eindhoven (NL). He works across interiors, sculpture, and book making, imbuing everything with vulnerable sensitivity. He uses touch as his guiding sense, which brings him to serendipitous encounters with material. As drawing is deeply connected to the hand, he uses this as his primary source of material inspiration and design practice. He lives and works in Rotterdam (NL).

13   Billy Ernst, *Broken Fences. All that is left are the corner posts cemented into the ground*, 2020, photo: Billy Ernst.
14   Billy Ernst, *Inserting Myself into Dutch Landscape*, 2020, photo: Billy Ernst.

The Not-So-Passive Observer
Occupying the Party Salon

Bruno Baietto

I moved to Brazil when I was seven. My family decided to move for a fresh start to a small city across the border where, compared to the Uruguayan capital city, there was never much to do. But there was *our building*; my father used to joke that it was his temple.

The construction took him several years and resulted in a two-floor building with a bakery production line on the ground floor and a party rental space on the top floor. My father, a construction foreman-turned-baker, designed the party salon with neoclassical elements borrowed from governmental buildings: white walls and angular arches framed the windows. Central columns, granite tabletops, and white marble skirting boards encircled the room. The charm of a temple-like construction, with a high ceiling and noble materials, was his bittersweet ambition to build something to last, which further generations could carry on. However, because of my father's attention to detail, aesthetic commitment, and immense effort, we didn't have another place to live for a while. We inhabited the party salon when it was not occupied by weddings, birthdays, a cleaning supplies pyramid scheme, and the weekly gatherings of a Pentecostal congregation.

Growing up in a party salon was not as exciting as it may seem. One can easily feel misplaced when clients and guests are the ones to set the rules of how to use *your* living room. Meanwhile, the sugar rush quickly reveals people's more authoritarian nature.

Our family's temple could easily be transformed into another's temple by means of decoration. From party supplies and Styrofoam Arks, cheap props defined the use of the space. After the event, I would watch as the space would be transformed, the decorations trashed, and the props, chairs, and other accessories put away. What remained, rather than relief and freedom, was an awkward sense of emptiness. I was subject to these aesthetic regimes; I was an observer who could participate only with my eyes and was excluded from joining in the celebrations or religious revelry. My role as an observer was thus honed from a young age and would come to shape my practices, such as design, later in life.

2

1   Bruno Baietto, *Follow the Crumbs that Fall from your Own*, 2021, detail, porcelain, 2021.
2   Bruno Baietto, *The Higher the Hair the Closer to God*, 2020, chandelier, tape, 105 × 55 × 55 cm.

3   4 →

Besides witnessing feral children's birthdays, the church services were the most exciting to watch. The congregation behaved like a sophisticated lifestyle business. In order to engage their followers, an inventive arrangement of religious objects were sold by the pastor: Holy water in plastic bottles, miraculous soaps that wash the devil away, oil from Moroccan caverns, incense to bring an old love back, and replicas of drachmas used as tokens to buy miracles from the pastor. A new product was presented roughly every week, with the promise of solving spiritual problems and claiming a closer connection with 'God' through its use. However, the exciting part occurred at the services where immediate solutions to financial or health issues were found on stage with cinematic visual effects, miraculous plastic trinkets, and tap water transformed as medicine. This was pure entertainment. Having live magical performances in my own living room while being raised as a Christian atheist placed me as a fascinated and keen spectator rather than a believer. In between staged miracles and exorcisms, my eye for a certain 'camp sensibility' began to develop, honed from the flamboyant pageantry of these services.

After each service, what remained were the trash bins and the monobloc chairs that were used in the meetings. Those chairs arrived alongside the number of followers the congregation had every Thursday—and amongst all the fantastical decorations and props, they were the only consistent objects in the space. I remember stacking them up high up to the ceiling and climbing them until my mother yelled that I should get off because 'that was expensive stuff.' But eventually, she would allow me to climb again, since at least I wasn't playing with my cousin's Barbies.

After a while, the Pentecostal congregation grew too large to continue using our party salon. My mother, tired of having a pastor in her living room telling my father that demons enter the family through the woman, decided we would not host any other religious gatherings. She was fine with her inner demons and besides, quinceañera

3   Bruno Baietto, *The Earliest Flowers to Bloom in Spring Are Those Who Stay at Home Forever*, 2020, detail, tapestry of melted plastic flowers.
4   Bruno Baietto, *The Earliest Flowers to Bloom in Spring Are Those Who Stay at Home Forever*, 2020.

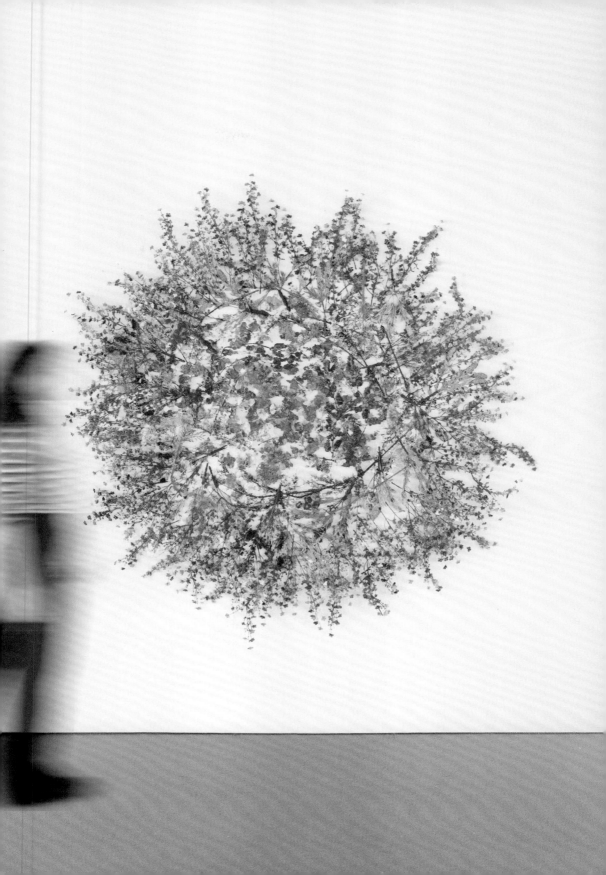

parties were more profitable for the bakery. Still, the impact of Pentecostal churches in Brazilian politics established a new wave of conservatism that continues to this day. Political issues became religious issues, replacing society's complexities with God's will. I remember that suddenly most of our bakery employees were attending Christian gatherings, using any opportunity they had with me to proselytize, reminding me that my Pokémon toys were Satan's work, or pronouncing homophobic claims in the name of God. But I could see through it—I was becoming a keen observer.

Now, more than twenty years after their start, Pentecostal churches have grown as big as multinationals and their influence in Brazilian politics is noticeable. Pastor-entrepreneurs became promising careers and religious organizations became profitable businesses supported by the State. Just as in the happy marriage between Protestantism and the entrepreneurial neoliberal lifestyle, Pentecostal churches grew alongside multinationals in a sort of contemporary crusade. Their temples, now ostentatious and monumental, resemble neoclassical shopping malls in the poorest areas of the country; meanwhile, their theatrical interpretations of Biblical precepts and renewed conservative morals seduce millions to support the alt-right agendas.

I have always been attracted to how the physical props and spaces used in the pageantry of ideology structures our convictions. And my perspective has remained as neither an insider or outsider; rather, I find myself in a unique position of observer—as a reluctant host to these uninvited guests (both as a child with them in our house and as a Brazilian hosting them in my country). In the process, I have experienced first hand their coming and going—the calm empty physical space before the morning set up and the depressing clutter after the service ends, with the facades and all the promises of spirituality swept up and dumped in big plastic bins. Having this vantage point from a young age has taught me much about the theatrics that occupy our

← 5

6

235

5   Bruno Baietto, *While We Dance and Spin in Our Mother's White Dress*, 2020, satin dress, 166 × 300 × 290 cm.

6   Bruno Baietto, *Glovase*, 2020, vase, 45 × 31 × 29 cm.

spaces and claim our hearts or minds. And that at the end of the day, what is left are its remains, which are not pretty.

Sometimes it's easier to be an observer than a designer. And for this reason, my current work explores the design of new forms of bearing witness with novel combinations of observation and critique: how design plays its role materializing ideology, acting as the mystical covering that interpellates our identity and defines our place in the structures we inhabit. For example, one of my recent projects takes shape as a trash bin: part robot, part puppet, it is a performative witness to design's ideologically infused pageantry, where through an illusion of autonomy it interacts with humans in public spaces, galleries, or design fairs. As part insider, part outsider, its role takes into account what is unsaid of the structures we inhabit as a lively reminder of the terms and conditions behind a given context, which in turn influence modes of behaviour. This bin is an extension of myself, a shadowy hybrid that directly reflects the theatricality of ideology—it is its own spectacle—while also reflecting upon it. I have sought to occupy this unique role of observer, making use of a perspective honed since childhood. In doing so, I explore the constructed nucleus of the systems that I inhabit.

As a designer, my work is situated between the grandiose bold aesthetics that promise a whole new world (the pageantry and props) and the actual agency of objects in shaping our relationship with each other and to the material world. This can be as elaborate as the aforementioned project or as simple as experiments of transforming props in different ways—such as playing with notions of beauty, taste, and class by melting, welding, and aesthetically reformulating garish plastic flowers.

The spaces we inhabit, the roles we take, and the positions forced upon us, inevitably shape how we decide to interact with the material and ideological world. To have my own home as a performative space for parties and religious events as well as the site for my family's own internally contested ideologies has left me with a deep sensitivity

236

7

7   Bruno Baietto, *Follow the Crumbs that Fall from Your Own*, 2021, detail, porcelain, 2021.

8   Bruno Baietto, *Follow the Crumbs that Fall from Your Own*, 2021, detail, piece of glass blown in bread, breadcrumbs, glass, 21 × 32 × 30 cm.

THE NOT-SO-PASSIVE OBSERVER

BRUNO BAIETTO

towards the relationship between the material realm and the ideological—how space and objects are so easily transformed, entangled, and discarded through the application of imaginaries, desires, hopes, or fears. As a designer, I tread carefully trying both to understand the materialized phenomena of ideology and how design is used to reinforce or reproduce this. My practice then becomes an embodiment of myself, a continuation of watching from the corner of our old party salon—except now I intend to explore how and what I observe, paying attention to the world outside and my own struggles and convictions.

← 9

10

9 Bruno Baietto, *Follow the Crumbs that Fall from Your Own*, 2021, detail, 'justin the dustbin', animatronic trashcan.
10 Bruno Baietto, *Follow the Crumbs that Fall from Your Own*, 2021, installation, ceramics, glass, plaster, wood, animatronic trashcan, 110 × 450 × 45 cm.

BRUNO BAIETTO (Montevideo, UY) is an artist and designer based in the Netherlands investigating the ideological frameworks that shape human perception. His work focuses on materiality, analyzing Western history, media culture, and everyday life in order to explore such ideological structures that shape design today. Baietto's work reaches from object design and material research, to sculpture and installations.

239

IDEAS   AND

DIALOGUES

The Self and the Other
A Psychoanalytical Reading of Auto-Ethnographic Design

Conversation with Ben Shai van der Wal

Michael Kaethler

MK You are a philosopher of design, with a particular interest in Lacan and psychoanalysis. Seeing as you work closely with designers, do you feel like a 'design psychoanalyst' and is such a role necessary in or for design?

BSVDW I love the notion of a design psychoanalyst. I'm not sure that's what I am, but I'm pretty certain that design could benefit from psychoanalysis. One of the things that psychoanalysis emphasizes is that we should never stop analyzing our choices—regardless of whether they're good or bad. Psychoanalysis is the pursuit of constantly mirroring oneself. And even though design is centred on culture and material—things that at first glance don't seem to have anything to do with psychoanalysis or the psyche—there's actually quite a lot there to unpack.

For instance, design and psychoanalysis both use their materials to shape and understand, and to reflect on ourselves. In design, those materials are usually tangible—things like plastic, wood, or clay. But the 'material' of psychoanalysis is language. According to Lacan, language contains a paradoxical quality: it's both the only way into our psyche as well as the material that stops us from ever really understanding ourselves. It can reveal our innermost thoughts and desires while at the same time inhibit and limit us.

243

Psychoanalysis is also much more concerned with the *process* of understanding ourselves than with 'arriving' at an understanding of ourselves—at some kind of fixed, definite identity. And when we try and grasp that process of understanding (i.e. when we try to understand *how* we understand things) that understanding changes as a direct result. You might ask yourself: who am I? But as you ask that question, your understanding of yourself is altered. Mirroring is the act of showing that alteration, of laying it bare, as it were.

MK What does it mean to mirror yourself and why is that important for designers?

BSVDW Mirroring entails a willingness to confront yourself by actively denying yourself, I would say, the possibility of being 'successful,' or of accomplishing anything meaningful. Designers in particular tend to finish projects, present projects, and imbue them with a sense of self, meaning and usefulness. I am much more interested in where designers fail, despite having finished their projects. Those are the fault lines that can offer us a glimpse into something more profound.

MK   Mirroring then is the act of distilling or boiling down our intentions, our desires—something in our subconscious or psyche—in order to understand what's behind the compulsion to make things, or to address things through making?

BSVDW   Yes, but without attempting to solve anything. Because once we understand that compulsion, or our subconscious desire, it changes. In fact, our subconscious can never be made conscious: we can never look directly at it. We can only see flashes of it from the corners of our eyes.

MK   From a psychoanalytical perspective, how do you interpret design? What is it: a desire, a compulsion, an exploration of the self through the world, an exploration of the world through the self, an attempt to make for others or to make 'others'?

244

BSVDW   First, I think that design could benefit very much from psychoanalysis as a critical practice. It has proved to be very useful in disciplines like literature, philosophy, politics, and anthropology. It's curiously, and conspicuously, absent in design. There are different schools of thought in psychoanalysis, and each of these schools might interpret design differently. I think Lacanian psychoanalysis would, to a certain degree, see design as a substitution of our need to manifest ourselves. If we see the self as an inherently fractured entity, we can see self-manifestation as our attempt to unify ourselves by creating an identity—a coherent image of who we are. Design is an attempt at self-manifestation, which is in itself an attempt at identity formation, and which as I mentioned before is doomed to fail. So design is only a stand-in for self-manifestation. Let's not believe that by manipulating materials we can do more than *attempt* to unify who we are.

MK This book frames auto-ethnographic design as a shift away from 'othering,' away from the creation of false distinctions between the self and the other, by re-orienting design from abstract notions of the other to more particular experiences of the self. Is there a false distinction between the designer and the intended user?

BSVDW Let's look at this distinction as a paradox: the idea that we have of ourselves being something distinct from the outside world—from the other—is primarily an attempt to cope with our own inherently fractured nature. We cope by projecting our fractured selves into the world. When a designer considers 'the consumer' (an 'other') as a separate being, as something outside of themselves—and our language is indeed structured that way with words like 'I' and 'you'—then we can only surmise that this is the way the designer wants things to be. That's the way we collectively want things to be. Even though a designer might, on a conscious level, believe that their design exists to benefit its users, the designer actually needs to construct those users in order to claim that their design is for the users' benefit. To think something like 'I am a designer and somewhere out there is a consumer separate from myself' is an act of phantasmatic desire; you need the consumer to be there so you can do the thing you want to do, which is design.

MK Are you saying that the designer denies the user part of their identity? We don't just design for the 'other' but also design the 'other'?

BSVDW The designer is diminishing the user's actual otherness by creating a symbolic otherness, one that can't do justice to the individuality and specificity of the other. It's always a simplified version of the other, one that the designer wants to envision. This is essential: you can't design without having an idea of what the other 'is,' or to be more precise, what you desire the other to be. In this sense, designers actually conjure their own users, they invoke them. And this is a necessary invocation: without it, one wouldn't be able to design.

BSVDW   No, it's not necessarily problematic, but it is inevitable. It could be problematic if a designer doesn't deepen their exploration of their own design practice—that is, if they don't engage in mirroring. Designers need to be aware that they're not designing for someone or something real, but for their ideas of what those things are. The designer invokes these others in order to influence them, to master them. The question is: What are you *actually* influencing? And more importantly: Why do you want to influence these things in particular?

It's difficult to find a good example to explain this idea, but perhaps we could start by taking a look at how NGOs operate. There's an issue in the world: poverty. To fight poverty, we come up with plans, strategies, etcetera. The end goal of an NGO is to abolish itself, to create a world where it is no longer needed. Of course, they never do. And before they know it, if they don't engage in mirroring, they actually start to believe that fighting poverty is the thing they're doing, without any consideration as to how they created this concept of poverty so they could be the ones to fight it. I don't mean to suggest that the intention is wrong; I'm merely arguing that a subject (a saviour of the poor and downtrodden, a designer or whatever) can only be formulated *because* the other is being invoked. It's a self-serving act of othering, but with a nice face.

MK   So you see the act of design primarily as a designer designing themselves, and only secondly as designing another world through the material?

BSVDW   Yes, that's true for design as well as other disciplines. It's crucial to understand that while your active engagement with materials does indeed shape the world, you're primarily shaping yourself—the designer.

MK   So then, design should be understood as an act of self-design, but not explicitly? In other words, do we design the other in order to design ourselves?

BSVDW   Yes, we only design the other in order to design ourselves.

BSVDW   When we address issues in the world, as we do, our
involvement with that issue shapes us into a specific
kind of subject: I see refugees as victims of a brutal war
(which they are), and therefore I become a benevolent
and generous subject. What's interesting is what happens
when we start to see ourselves as part of the issue; when
we look at the dynamic we create by engaging with
it. I mean, in the actual moment of recognizing others
as victims, what kind of subjectivity am I creating for
myself to inhabit? If I may invoke Nietzsche, the idea of
an ethical designer for me would not be someone who
designs 'well'—a designer who is either well received
or who has solved a problem—but rather someone who
bears the full weight of their design. An ethical designer
is someone who addresses issues beyond the self while
being fully aware that their lofty aspirations can never
transcend the self: the self will always be there, and it will
always need to be reckoned with.

MK   Given the nature of this book, which emphasizes design as a
means of knowing the self, do you feel that there's a greater affinity
between psychoanalysis and auto-ethnographic design than between
psychoanalysis and other design approaches?

BSVDW   Yes, but more designers need to understand how the self
is fractured, and learn ways to go about addressing this.
Auto-ethnography is a significant attempt to do just that,
as it can lead to critical self-reflection and acts of mirroring. If you don't engage in mirroring, you might end
up designing for what Lacanian psychoanalysis calls the
surplus: the by-product that we create by formulating the
world as a set of problems to be solved. A good way to
explain this might be to use the same issue I used before:
refugees. What if you were to approach this issue from the
other end of the political spectrum? You might believe
something like, 'Refugees are only here to steal from me,'
and as you try to provide reasonable explanations for
why you believe that, you are simultaneously creating an
identity, almost by accident. It's the thing that happens

to us while we engage with the world. As our identity is being created through our engagement with a particular issue, the issue itself just keeps moving away from us—it is deferred. What remains is the surplus, which in this instance would be our identity, or for designers, most likely the design.

What I really admire about auto-ethnographic designers is their ability to demonstrate this moment of deferral—to show it as it happens. And they don't show it by explaining it or by creating some kind of one-dimensional representation of it, but by allowing the design to be a living thing, and to act as a mirror for this process.

MK   What I hear from you is that design is a process of engaging with the material world to understand the fractured self and perhaps also to reassemble it (to use the language of design).

BSVDW   Yes, yes, yes, *except the last part*. The reassembling is the narrative we tell ourselves about what it is that we're trying to do. This is not real: the self always remains fractured. Perhaps it would be better to show how we fail at assembling it, which I think is what auto-ethnographic design aims to do.

248

MK   Can we design for our psyche?

BSVDW   Absolutely not.

MK   A psychoanalytical reading of design then is a process of coming to terms with who we are in the world through acts of making.

BSVDW   Yes, but more importantly it's about coming to terms with our constant failure to align who we are with who we think we are.

MK   Why are our failures important?

BSVDW   If we start to believe in the objects we make and their ability to shape the world, then we're back to this modernist idea of the creator as master of the universe. It's very clear that we are by no means masters of the universe—we're not even masters of our own desires. I'm not saying we should all start practicing some kind of wilful naivety; we actually need to practice the opposite of naivety, to the extent that this is possible.

Incidentally, when I talk about failure, I don't mean it in the sense of our expectations not being met. I mean it in the way Lacan describes sexuality, for instance. He argues that it is in the inability to successfully inhabit the other that we have different identities. It is because of the 'impossibility' of a sexual relationship—the failure inherent in the attempt to inhabit the other—that the people engaging in that relationship can define themselves as separate entities. By pointing out this impossibility, and by making the resulting identity formation process explicit, we don't solve the impossibility. This is existential. It is precisely *because* we are unable to truly solve anything that we design. Design is a practice that is predicated on failure.

MK   As one who is uninitiated in the world of psychoanalysis, I am intrigued and also a bit paralyzed in terms of reading design practice through a psychoanalytical lens. However, when I think of many of the works being shown in Section 2 of this book, I feel that there is something pure, non-explicit, and very much mirroring the self—I perceive a psychoanalytical character to them. Of course, there is intention (and thus surplus) but there is also plenty of raw, intuitive expression, which enables the designers to better understand themselves vis-à-vis giving shape to the material realm. How do you specifically interpret this auto-ethnographic turn in design?

BSVDW   I agree. I see it as a new attempt not to fail at becoming who we are. On another level, I also see it as design becoming more narcissistic. And again, I don't mean this as a psychological deviation, but rather that auto-ethnographic design sees itself as a mirror for those who design. Projects with an auto-ethnographic character are very interesting because they try to make explicit that design could be used to better understand yourself, and in doing so they create a new implicit space, one that can only be seen if you don't look right at it. And some of the projects described here indeed act as mirrors themselves. These are the problems I find most interesting, as you might imagine, because they exhibit a kind of paradox:

they show the subject in relation to the culture that *defined* it, speaking back to that culture. It's not simply a message expressed through a medium, but the act of mediating that is on display in these works. For me, the directness you mention is very much embedded in the act of mirroring.

MK   So in other words, the outcome ends up being the process?

BSVDW   Yes, but the process as it is taking place. If I simply present a process, or rather represent it, then all I'm doing is referring to it.

MK   You say you see auto-ethnographic design as narcissistic. But is it any less narcissistic than other forms of design that make bold claims about solving others' problems, but which must first invoke an 'other' to do so? In other words, the designer actively 'others' others in order for them to feel good about themselves?

250

BSVDW   On the one hand you have the classic notion of design as a practice that attempts to solve issues in the world (cultural or social issues) and now auto-ethnographic design has set out to solve this 'new' problem: the self. The dynamic is the same: they're both narcissistic. Every designer 'others' others, with the belief that they have good reason to do so; auto-ethnographic designers believe that they somehow 'other' to a lesser degree. But if your aim is to 'other' less, then my question would be: Which other are you invoking in order to do so?

MK   So design can't escape its own narcissism?

BSVDW   No, but why would we want it to? It's wonderful to see our attempts to escape our own narcissism, and to avoid the accusation of narcissism.

MK   This seems like a cat chasing its tail. Design shouldn't design for others because we can't truly know the other and in designing for them, we perpetuate false notions of the other (through invoking them). At the same time, we can't design for the self, at least explicitly, because that would involve 'othering' the self. The cat only resolves chasing its tail when it gives up out of fatigue, without results. Don't you feel that the perspective that you're elaborating on here renders design futile, a practice unable to engage within anything bigger than the self but also unable to engage with the self?

BSVDW   Nihilism is a great place to start. I love the image of a cat chasing its tail and giving up— all it has achieved is that it has tired itself out. When you keep asking yourself, 'What's the use of what I'm doing?' and when you keep getting mirrored at every turn, then I think you're on to something. You are always chasing something, after all. And there's no rhyme or reason to it, except to create rhyme and reason. What's interesting is that when you decide to give up—when you've grown tired of chasing your own tail—that's when the material takes over. That's when you get to understand how the world stands in for you. When I want to explore myself, I encounter only the other; when I want to learn about the other, I find only myself. I find this oscillation fascinating. Of course, we will continue to design and we will continue to speak, and we will endlessly speak about design, but at least if we keep looking at *how* we speak and *how* we design we might learn something, even if only about ourselves.

251

BEN SHAI VAN DER WAL is a writer, cultural critic, and philosopher. After completing his MA studies in Philosophy and Literary Science (cum laude), he has been researching, teaching, and tutoring in a variety of institutions (Design Academy Eindhoven, Vrije Universiteit, Sandberg Instituut, Akademie der Bildenden Künste in Nuremberg, Bezalel Academy of Arts and Design). His research project 'The (T)error of Existence' delves into the entanglements between existentialism, psychoanalysis, and semiotics.

Someone's in the Palace
'Turning' Design Towards the Self

Gabriel .A. Maher

Situated on the west side of Dam Square in the centre of Amsterdam, opposite the War Memorial and next to the Nieuwe Kerk, is the city's Royal Palace. Adjacent to the Palace's corner intersection is the former building of the printing and editorial office of the daily evening newspaper *NRC Handelsblad*. In 1977, the *NRC* was vacated and a year later squatted. The municipality bought the property in 1980; the squatters negotiated lease contracts. I (Gabriel) live here. I am one of six members of a queer/feminist woongroep [group home] that has been present in the building since it was squatted.

> This image captures a view of the palace from the *NRC*'s communal rooftop. The Palace, all 22,031 square meters of it, is supposedly empty—especially since the pandemic outbreak... Nevertheless, one of the roof air-vents to the right of the Palace is billowing steam. 'We' (the woongroep residents) interpret the rising steam as a sign of life and of potential occupancy; we imagine who might be there and comically exclaim: 'There's someone in the Palace again!' There is a strange domesticity to the steam rising, an intimacy—it's slightly secretive. Apart from the rising steam, which draws my attention, I never really notice the Palace despite its proximity... There's someone in the palace... Who?

This image (taken on 10.02.21 at 14:47) is locative: though simple, it is what prompted the reflective work of starting with where 'I' am.

> I stand in a thick layer of snow (Storm Darcy, February 2021), a gaze oriented towards the Palace. In the foreground: communal outdoor furniture—weatherworn Monobloc chairs stacked—a clear marker of the commons, a most common plastic chair. The Palace looms in the background, Atlas holds the celestial globe—a violent colonial marker symbolizing the 'entire universe' and the 'central' position Amsterdam was seen to occupy in the 'Golden Age.' What stark juxtaposition I witness here. A colossal materialization of power standing (empty), is viewed from the position of a resident who occupies a building with some of the last remaining rent controlled, shared spaces in the city centre... It represents a collision of worlds and narratives of lifestyle. The proximity is alarming and rare.

253

This image details a relationship and an experience—an aesthetic moment and an epiphany.

> Whether by epiphany, aesthetic moment, or intuition, we begin auto-ethnographic projects by starting where we are. From there, we begin to situate ourselves in story—our own story, the story told in existing writing and research on our topic or experience, and the stories told by others.[1]

As photographic 'sensitive data,' this image marks a moment of capture that prompted me to consider the premise of the auto-ethnographic turn in/towards design. I paid particular attention to the question of orientation—to directional qualities and subsequently to the question of positioning or positionality. More concretely, I look at the premise of an auto-ethnographic turn in design from a phenomenological perspective: one that centres structures of experience and systems of orientation. This perspective considers how we 'turn' towards or away from something (objects, people, spaces, ideas etc.) as pivotal, and as having meaning in terms of how we are directed and orient ourselves in the world. When thinking through the mechanisms and systems of design, a phenomenological perspective can support us in understanding how we (our subjectivities and our bodies respectively) are positioned through design and within/by the act of designing; a relational, causal (network) of affect is produced. In centring our lived experiences, we can both attempt to understand and deconstruct our relationship to design and the act of it—and, perhaps, question its very foundations.

> In saying this, I hope to use some of the key symbols and relationships captured in the image to structure and frame the ideas in this chapter, as well as share how this moment opened up a space to contemplate the central narratives that define the acts of designing in relation to culture ('ethno') and our personal lived experiences ('auto').

Palaces are, in their own way, places of contemplation, focused on power. They are functional/fictional buildings of the rich, and show to the 'ordinary' people what money can do: the aspect of wealth expressed in stone. The narratives of power inscribed in its material presence and symbology are connected to how

254

---

1   Tony E. Adams, Stacy Holman Jones, and Carolyn Ellis, *Autoethnography: Understanding Qualitative Research* (New York: Oxford University Press, 2015), p. 49.

I look towards/at 'design' and the narratives it has produced and continues to reproduce thus far—narratives I do not recognize or situate myself (or my stories) within. My view of the Palace sets up a collision of worlds: narrative distance against locative proximity.

But, let's talk about the 'turn' and the act(ion) of turning itself. Has the auto-ethnographic 'turned' towards design, or, has design turned towards the auto-ethnographic? What I like about thinking through 'turns' and the idea of 'turning' is the inherent symbolism and hinted physicality the act implies. The bringing together of fields and practices of design—auto-ethnography—within (&)—(the) (a)turn, outlines a mutually constitutive set of conditions.

What the auto-ethnographic turn in design implies is a turn towards self-reflexive and self-oriented praxis, leading from an 'I' position. What it also makes recognizable is a potential collapse in design's own 'self'-image and its long held position of 'neutrality.' Design discourse has been centred on an illusive 'we' position for quite some time—a generalizing, first person plural that tends to flatten a position or neutralize a subject. When design or designers say 'we' think, 'we' feel, 'we' ... the question should be asked: Who is this 'we,' and what does it signify?

Design, as a system of cultural production, holds a certain kind of power to foreground and uphold idealized, universal narratives of lifestyle under the guise of consumerism. Such a system sets up reliable yet fabricated constructions of reality, monopolized by representations of the comfortable, good, better life. Such a life has a particular structural orientation that privileges a white, heteronormative, cis-gendered, able-bodied, and middle-class narrative; it's along these lines that a universal narrative in design is established. Historically, this has appeased a universalizing 'we' that tends to loop back onto itself. Within this narrative, the politics of difference are omitted. As an underlying or subconscious orientation in design, these narratives do not begin with the 'auto' or the self, but instead, with a precept for what and how selves should be directed, positioned, organized, managed, and arranged.

As design theorist Bruce King Shey describes, the universalism of design is a 'self-referential, self-preserving, self-justifying narrative: better design, better products, better life for the universal citizen.'[2] By producing itself as the norm, the mechanism of design thinks of itself as representative, 'but produces a culture for a self-referential community of bodies.'

> We see how this materializes through standardizations, averages, ergonomics, or the mediation of bodies and objects.

Considering this, starting from the auto—'I'—position can reveal complex and de-stabilizing relationships towards universal narratives in design. This involves an act of self-positioning, which is particularly crucial to a shift in consciousness within the discipline.

So, what is it to turn towards 'I' in design? Looking at turning in relation to the 'auto' in auto-ethnography presents an intriguing link. If we consider, as Ahmed does, that 'turning' is crucial to subject formation, then:

> Life, after all, is full of turning points ... Depending on which way one turns, different worlds might come into view. If such turns are repeated over time, then bodies acquire the very shape of such direction. It is not, then, that bodies simply have a direction, or that they follow directions, in moving this way or that. Rather, in moving this way or that, and moving in this way again and again, the surfaces of bodies *in turn* acquire their shape. Bodies are 'directed' and they take the shape of this direction.[3]

How have we turned and been turned in and through the acts of design and designing, particularly in relation to design's dominant or universal narratives? Turning back to look at these subject formations centres ontological processes of unpacking and articulating the position(s) and privileges we occupy. It subsequently allows us to consider the personal in relation to the structural. While structures themselves are not personal, this is about whose identity or position benefits from dominant narratives and is therefore privileged. Within a design context, privilege translates as occupying a position that is seen as 'neutral'—or that is seen as not taking a position at all. Positionality troubles neutrality and prompts a position to be

2   Bruce King Shey, "Queering the Universal Rhetoric of Objects: Myth, Industrial Design and the Politics of Difference" (MA Thesis California College of the Arts, 2005), p. 29.

3   Sara Ahmed, *Queer Phenomenology, Objects, Orientations, Others* (Durham: Duke University Press, 2006), pp. 15–16.

256

taken within it or against it. In so doing, biases and blind spots can be interrogated and understood, shedding light on how this affects and influences the design process. With the universal narratives exposed, a space of questioning is opened up and 'we' must ask, 'Who' are we? And whom can we speak for?

> In this act of turning (again and again), our world unfolds and our position within it materializes and is enacted. We stand somewhere, perceiving and interpreting the world from this point of view. Our lived experiences are built, conditioned, and acted upon from this place. The concept of lived experience emerged from phenomenology and explores the ways in which the phenomena of our human experience appear as meaningful to us. Thinking through and working from lived experience validates a necessary shift in consciousness—one that acknowledges the multiplicity of ways in which the same physical world can be experienced depending on different individual, collective, and social factors.

The 'I' materializes in and through the act of making. In this 'I,' a vulnerability, a risk, is foregrounded. When our positions are not supported by the dominant narratives, what can result is that this position and experience be seen as an opinion, a statement that must be proven or evidenced before moving forward within the work. Setting such processes against the universalisms of design stretches and complexifies the narrative landscape while recognizing that not all positions are treated equally or have equal access within the dominant systems.

> Leading from lived experience(s) creates a certain type of auto-ethnographic authority—I have experienced this, I am positioned here, therefore, I can speak on it and make work based on it. A reflexive turning point and a learning point which foregrounds how our positionality and experiences affect the way we work and interact with each other.

Those plastic chairs ... and I'm sure someone's in there ...!

> 'There's someone in the Palace' makes a narrative or metaphoric link here—the Palace and the dominant narratives it has survived on—ones that have historically organized, ordered, and arranged bodies and subjectivities in particular ways, as well as assigned and taken away access and agency—I abstractly mirror in

the relationships between the universal narratives of design and narratives of self which collide in the auto-ethnographic turn. From my vantage point on the rooftop of the *NRC*, I can conjure an imaginary about the Palace being occupied, not by any royal subject, but by someone who has infiltrated and gained access somehow, someone who now claims a space within its narrative. This imaginary, for me, extends the narrative landscape of the Palace and decentres the narratives of power it is predicated on.

The discourse of design is ripe for questioning its power narratives. Because design is emergent (that is to say, something emerges from the process of designing) and because such emergence is being re-evaluated through auto-ethnographic turning points, in essence what comes about is a decentring of dominant narratives in design—a renewed appetite for self-reflection and self-criticism, captured in the practice of auto—narrative.

258

259

GABRIEL .A. MAHER (They/Them*) is a designer currently living and working in the Netherlands. With a practice established in Architecture and Social Design, Maher's work centres on critical and analytical approaches to design and design-led research. Within this sphere, they consider the effects of design and the act of designing on our bodies and the shaping of subjectivities and identities. Maher's investigations directly confront the conditions that frame concepts of gender, class privilege, and sexuality from a design as well as a power perspective. They traverse their practice as a queer and gender non-conforming person from a working class background; these intersections inform and frame their attitudes toward design and pedagogic practice. Maher teaches at Design Academy Eindhoven (NL) and at the Royal Academy of Art in The Hague (NL). Most recently, they were the recipient of the iphiGenia Gender Design Award (2019) and were shortlisted for the Hublot Design Prize (2018).

*They/Them/Their: gender-neutral pronoun, third person singular.

I Am the Matter of My Film
The Essay Film as Auto-Ethnographic Research Tool

Erik Viskil

I am involved in design education through the medium of film.[1] Years ago, this would have been an unusual construction, but since we now all have possibilities of expressing ourselves through moving images, this seems to be an obvious if not necessary combination. In my lectures and workshops, I approach filmmaking as a way of writing. The idea is older than the birth of the 'nouvelle vague,' but the consequences are still underestimated. I regularly show films of Jonas Mekas, the Lithuanian-American poet, journalist, collector, and filmmaker who succeeded in capturing his life in moving images over seven decades, from 1949 until his death in 2019. I also put emphasis on the possibility of film as essay. These topics crossed my mind when I began to think about an auto-ethnographical approach to design research. I wondered: does the way in which I approach teaching film perhaps amount to a type of auto-ethnography with moving images? In this chapter, I try to gain a better understanding of what such a filmic variant of auto-ethnography could be. In order to do so, I relate my experiences in teaching film and working on the essay film with accounts of auto-ethnography. Let's start with the latter.

Which Auto-Ethnography?

I am sitting at my computer with a pile of articles on my desk. It has become obvious to me that auto-ethnography is a plural, covering an abundance of approaches. I hesitate... do I just choose one approach in order to make clear what I am after, or shall I only indicate some ideas that enthused me? The first thing that comes to my mind is the way in which Arthur P. Bochner, one of the leading scholars in this field, characterized auto-ethnography as a genre of doubt. In his Mini-Manifesto, he describes it as a 'vehicle for exercising, embodying and enacting doubt.' 'Our discourse,' he writes, 'is not of order, stability, control, and destiny, but one of ambiguity, contradiction,

---

1   The term 'film' here stands for all forms and formats of moving images; nowadays film is usually digital video.

contingency, and chance.'[2] He calls it a genre of questioning, and it is clear that this questioning differs from the traditional academic way of critical inquiry. The doubt seems ubiquitous: it is explicitly and continuously expressed, referring to both the entire process of inquiry and writing, and to the state of mind of the 'vulnerable' researcher during this process. While writing these sentences it occurs to me that this chapter will unveil me as a writer with a scholarly background. I need literature, and apparently facts, in order to get words rolling. This is how I learned to deal with uncertainty. Bochner argues that research on human life should be oriented towards meanings, instead of only facts, and towards producing evocative, creative, and dialogic expressions of lived experiences. What stands out for me in his approach is not only the intimacy of what he expresses in his subjective and nuanced style, but also and especially his rare clarity of expression, which makes for an even rarer accessibility of his intimate stories. But there is something that hinders me: his sense of creativity seems far from experimental.

In auto-ethnography, there is both self-reference and reference to culture. It is a form of self-narrative, as the *Sage Dictionary* says, that places the self within a social context.[3] If I want to position my film lessons for students in design and the visual arts in relation to auto-ethnography, I need a conception of it that not only covers these aspects, but also gives room to experimentation without bothering too much about readability. The discourse of art and design differs from Bochner's discourse and probably from that of most auto-ethnographers, which must be aimed in one way or the other at the growth of knowledge and insight. However, these auto-ethnographers are not searching for generalized knowledge and their aims are broader: they also intend to provoke change in the reader in order to contribute to a better, more human, and liveable world.[4] That sounds familiar to me; it coincides with what art and design schools and many students and professionals currently find

262

2   Arthur P. Bochner, "Heart of the Matter: A Mini-Manifesto for Autoethnography," *International Review of Qualitative Research* 10, no. 1 (2017), pp. 67–80, p. 77.
3   Deborah Reed-Danahay, "Autoethnography," in *The Sage Dictionary of Social Research Methods* (London: Sage, 2011), pp. 15–16.
4   Carolyn Ellis, Tony E. Adams, and Arthur P. Bochner, "Autoethnography: An Overview," *Historical Social Research* 36, no. 4 (2011), pp. 273–290, p. 284.

important.[5] I again start wondering what approach to auto-ethnography would fit my purposes best. I grab an article from the pile on my writing desk.[6] I remember reading in it about an experimental branch of auto-ethnography, and start leafing through it.

What is called experimental in auto-ethnography seems to be experimental primarily for the social sciences. And what auto-ethnographers presented as experimental some ten or twenty years ago seems more conventional now.[7] I am slowly becoming aware that what I consider to be experimental from the viewpoint of design, art, and filmmaking, barely has a connection with what I am reading here. Even if a writer plays with 'directions and speeds of reflexivity' and 'shifts to and of genres,' and even when 'literary and narrative techniques' position 'authors as characters,' I am constantly aware of being engaged in reading scholarly work.[8] The inventiveness, creativity, and imagination involved do not, or hardly, relate to an artistic context. The function and setting of auto-ethnography within the social sciences and related academic fields of inquiry may prevent researchers and writers from exploring the possibilities of concepts, ambiguity, and layering in their work far beyond the undefined and unsettling.

Auto-ethnography should not be mistaken for art, though it touches upon contemporary practices in art and design and there are overlaps and similarities. These start with the highly personalized approach in which personal experience is key; emotions are included in the work. In both auto-ethnography and the arts (to use a broader denominator than art, design, and filmmaking), the researcher is positioned visibly in the work and can be the subject of inquiry as well as the author.

---

5 Art and design schools all over the globe have radically shifted their policies during the past decade (or even years) towards contributing to the future of society and transforming the world. We see this reflected in the missions and visions of, for instance, Parsons School of Design, part of The New School, and UAL's Central Saint Martins. Dutch art and design schools have included similar objectives, as seen in the institutional plans of Design Academy Eindhoven (Institutional Plan 2019–2024), Rietveld Academie and Sandberg Instituut (Institutional Plan 2020–2025), and the Royal Academy of Art The Hague (Institutional Plan 2019–2024).

6 Susanne Gannon, "Autoethnography," in *Oxford Research Encyclopedias: Education* (London: Sage, 2017). Accessed 3 January 2021.

7 Patricia Ticineto Clough, "Comments on Setting Criteria for Experimental Writing," *Qualitative Inquiry* 6, no. 2 (2000), pp. 278–291.

8 The quotations refer to Patricia Ticineto Clough, *The End(s) of Ethnography: From Realism to Social Criticism* (New York, NY: Peter Lang, 1998), p. 12, quoted in Gannon, "Autoethnography," see note 6.

In both contexts, we find combinations of the imaginative and what is often carelessly called 'the documentary,' a mixture of facts and fiction. Moreover, in the past decades we have seen in both contexts the rise of a strong focus on performative aspects of expression. One of the representatives of such an approach in auto-ethnography is Stacy Holman Jones. In her writings, I come across many statements that are also true for a range of contemporary practices within the arts, and which therefore shed a light on a possible common ground.[9] Holman Jones regards auto-ethnography as radical democratic politics. It is, for her, 'making the personal political' through intimate provocation. She calls it 'a critical ekphrasis' that must both incorporate theory and praxis, and that is oriented towards the world and committed to changing it. Of course, there are artists and designers—and probably auto-ethnographers as well—who will reject this, but that does not detract from the observation that tendencies in the diverse contexts are pointing in the same direction. Although Holman Jones does not present her approach as experimental, her conception of auto-ethnography still borders on more experimental, contextually oriented practices in art and design.

The Essay as a Personal Process of Discovery

In 1957, Chris Marker made the film *Letter from Siberia*. The title indicates that it was a personal account, but it is also an ethnographical report of his travels in the eastern Soviet Union. The film includes a remarkable sequence in which workmen are equalizing a road. We see exactly the same images three times, but with a different voice-over. Each voice-over introduces a different perspective on the men's labour. In the end, it is obvious that the different interpretations can both be true and untrue at the same time. Through repetition, the sequence questions political ideologies from a personal perspective—a postmodern

9   Stacy Holman Jones, "Auto-ethnography: Making the Personal Political," in *Handbook of Qualitative Research*, eds. Norman K. Denzin and Yvonna S. Licoln (Thousand Oaks, CA: Sage, 2005), pp. 763–791.

critique *avant la lettre* on how we read situations and images, and what can be held for true or just. It is from here that an argument unfolds, a rare incident in the history of filmmaking. When critic André Bazin saw Marker's film, he described it as 'an essay documented by film.'[10] Essays have much in common with auto-ethnographies.

They are also centred around the *self* of the subjectively writing author and they are reflective.[11] Michel de Montaigne, who coined the term *essais* (essays) at the beginning of the sixteenth century, had been writing his 'attempts' for years assuming that he was working on philosophical texts on a wide variety of topics. At the end, he discovered that in fact they

Chris Marker, *Letter from Siberia*, 1957, film still.

were all about himself. 'I am myself the matter of my book,' he wrote.[12] Bazin recognized the subjective and reflective character of *Letter from Siberia*, and was aware that what Marker was overtly doing was a kind of trying, attempting, essaying: four steps ahead, one step back, two to the left, one to the right, trying to come to grips with the alienating culture and the overwhelming nature of Siberia from his personal, often changing perspective.

265

When I first read that the discourse of auto-ethnographers is not of order, stability, control, and destiny, but of ambiguity, contradiction, contingency, and chance, images of the essay films of Chris Marker crossed my mind, as did the *Essais* of Montaigne. With *Letter from Siberia*, Marker made a film like crazy quilt, with engravings, photos, and even animated cartoons interfering long 'documentary' takes of natural sceneries. Montaigne wrote as if associations and side roads were

10   André Bazin, "Bazin on Marker," *Film Comment* 39, no. 4 (2003), pp. 44–45, p. 44. Translation from French by David Kehr. Originally published in *France-Observateur*, 30 October 1958.
11   According to Rascaroli, subjectivity and reflectivity are the main characteristics of the essay and the essay film. Laura Rascaroli, "The Essay Film: Problems, Definitions, Textual Commitments," *Framework* 49, no. 2 (2008), pp. 24–47, p. 25.
12   Michel de Montaigne, *Essays*, transl. Charles Cotton, ed. William Carew Hazlitt (Auckland: The Floating Press, 2009).

more important than arriving at conclusions. What is intriguing about these two Frenchmen who lived in completely different times but seem to have had a similar deviant sense of 'order' and a comparable curiosity for the unknown and unrelated, is that they were masters in preserving elements of their process of inquiry— their thinking and making processes—in their works. What they are showing is a modest and vulnerable process of trying to discover, not of justifying, what is found. What they are doing in their texts and films is research through writing and through filmmaking. They carry out this research extremely reflectively, and it is as much about themselves as it is about their subjects, and their time and culture.

This is exactly my starting point when I teach film.

Diaries beyond the Personal

Auto-ethnography comes close to autobiography. I write this rather quickly and then pause to think. Of course, it should be the other way around. I know what I want with this paragraph, and that I want to move to the diary film, but I need to fill a gap. When searching for additional literature on auto-ethnography and film, I stumbled upon Catherine Russell's 1999 book *Experimental Ethnography*. It was a kind of shock experience. At the end of the book, she devotes a whole chapter to the topic, paying tribute to both Chris Marker and Jonas Mekas. I realize that what I am working on has already been prepared more than twenty years ago. Of course, it is no secret for me that diary films are subsumed under the heading of essay films. I even considered that an entire bookshelf could have been written on film and auto-ethnography, but to read precisely the two names I am highlighting here gives me an awkward feeling. Russell writes: 'Autobiography becomes ethnographic at the point where the film or videomaker understands his or her personal history to be implicated in larger social formations and historical

processes.'[13]
I think this 'point'
is crucial for
the rest of this
chapter. How to
connect?

Jonas Mekas, *As I Was Moving Ahead Occasionally I Saw Brief Glimpses of Beauty*, 2000, film still.

'This is a political film.'
The words are on the
screen for no more than
a few seconds. It is an
intertitle from Mekas's
diary film *As I Was
Moving Ahead Occasionally
I Saw Brief Glimpses Of Beauty*, a five-hour long montage of
sixteen mm fragments from the life of the protagonist among
his family and friends. The intertitles—title cards like in silent
movies—are part of a variety of means he uses to stage himself.
Others are melancholic voice-overs, seemingly distorted frame-
by-frame recordings, rhythmic editing, and images shot by him
and others showing him sitting, walking, dancing. Especially
through the voice-overs and intertitles, but also with the help
of other communicative means, Mekas transgresses the bubble
of the self and connects his 'home movies' almost implicitly to
broader social, cultural, and historical contexts. Mekas's diary
films, which stage a vulnerable, displaced, and doubting 'I,'
make the personal political—just as Stacy Holman Jones expects
from performative auto-ethnography.

267

Essaying Film, from the Personal to the Contextual

When I teach film, I often start with showing examples
from Jonas Mekas's diary films. I emphasize that he was
recording his own life; though in principle anyone could

13   Catherine Russell, *Experimental Ethnography: The Work of Film in the Age of Video*, (Durham, NC: Duke
      University Press, 1999), p. 276, book collections on Project MUSE.

do this, for an artist or a designer there is a potential hidden in it, especially if one dares to go beyond the domestic. Why would a designer or an artist who excels in visual thinking and whose means are visual primarily use written language in doing research? What I am after is to stimulate the students to document their research through moving images. We watch essay films and so called 'documentaries' in order to gain a better understanding of how the medium can be used; they start working on their films, which at first we do not regard as products to realize but as processes to learn from and to extract information from, that can serve as input for the design process. Often students forget the importance of the process and turn filmmaking into a result-driven 'design project,' with interesting outcomes. In some cases, students produce not only design research through filmmaking, but films that provide insight into research and design. They succeed in reflecting through moving images, and deliver a modest essay film that can be surprisingly rich in visual information and in analysis and storytelling. I think it will not be long until such films will be accepted and promoted as an equivalent of written theses and dissertations.

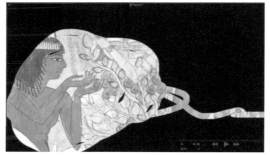

Lorraine Legrand, Design Academy Eindhoven, *Where do figs come from?* 2020, video still.

A crucial point—I now return to the idea that in auto-ethnography the researcher relates their personal history to larger social processes—is that the filmmaker connects to a broader social and cultural context. This sounds easier than it is. The step from the personal to the contextual or the more general, perhaps even universal, is a difficult one to take. The opposite is sometimes even harder. What can we learn from auto-ethnography in this respect? Firstly, that the filmmaker not only instantiates themself or their own situation in the film as the subject of inquiry, but also finds out how to employ the various cinematographic means available in order to generalize findings to a larger group or culture. Secondly, that the filmmaker makes sure that they are a member of this broader setting, so that the film is not only about others. Thirdly, that the filmmaker generates input by engaging in dialogue with other group members beyond the self and by reading, watching, and listening to accounts of others.[14] The most important lesson that auto-ethnography carries within is that from the outset, self-analysis and self-narration are intended to reflect on, provide insight into, and have an influence on the world that we live in. We want to grasp the world through grasping ourselves.

The Value of Self

After having written the last paragraphs, I realize that the way I represent my teaching practice here is not untrue, but probably a bit too neat. I wonder if I am not presenting things more sophisticated and well thought-out than they actually are. Why is the last paragraph as it is? I did not use these 'lessons' myself. Why did I not write about thinking through moving images? Is it on purpose that I refer to Orson Welles's artificial film *F for Fake* only now, or am I in a way forced to mention it at this point? I feel doubt rising within me about this chapter, and about the whole idea of self-narrating and its wider use. How much are authors in control of their stories? How much grip do filmmakers have on what they produce? What agency do texts, films, and designs have as they are developing, and what role does this play in their construction? The only thing that I can be sure of is that I have been writing about myself. It is like something I read in a modest but illuminating article from 2006: 'So much of what I want to say about auto-ethnography is about me (...).'[15]

269

ERIK VISKIL studied Museology at the Reinwardt Academy in Leiden (NL) and Speech Communication, Argumentation Theory, and Rhetoric at the University of Amsterdam (NL). He is currently professor of Research and Discourse in Artistic Practice and academic director of the Academy of Creative and Performing Arts at Leiden University (NL). Viskil runs a yearly film lecture programme at Design Academy Eindhoven's (NL) Master's programmes, and teaches film intermittently in its Master's of Contextual Design. His research focuses on moving image discourse and discursive practices in the visual arts.

---

14   These three suggestions are loosely based on requirements Leon Anderson has formulated for analytic auto-ethnography, a more rigid form of qualitative research; see Gannon, "Autoethnography," see note 6, pp. 8–9.

15   Sarah Wall, "An Autoethnography on Learning About Autoethnography," *International Journal of Qualitative Methods* 5, no. 2 (2006), pp. 146–160, p. 146.

All Knowledge is Biased
Different Readings of Reality

Conversation with Barbara Visser

Louise Schouwenberg

You are heading a Master's at the Sandberg Instituut in Amsterdam with the remarkable name: *F for Fact*.[1]

BV   It's an experimental programme where we work with students from different professional backgrounds on the relationship between knowledge and imagination, to create new narratives, para-fictions.

I think it's important to see how knowledge is re-shaped when it is communicated, and important to develop a sensitivity to ask the right questions. We cannot simply assume that in opposition to for example fake news, there's something like objective truth. All knowledge is unstable, biased, coloured by obvious as well as hidden agendas. But why is that a problem? Accepting that idea can lead to another perspective on what information is. Scientists may attempt to research the world as objectively as they can, and they should never refrain from that ambition, but they are as locked in their own world as the next person. To fully admit that neutrality is a fiction makes room for different readings of reality and its representations.

LS   When I studied history in the seventies, students all around the world protested against the biased images of scientific truth that were still prevalent. What had landed in the official history books presented a one-sided, if not distorted, view of the world. In recent years, several activists' groups have brought to light more historical biases. What's your distinct focus in this debate?

BV   What's different is our idea of how subjective or personal views can contribute to knowledge production by not pretending they are something else. We've moved beyond the post-modern idea of multiple truths and the nihilist conclusion that knowledge thus has no real significance. The cynicism has gone. What you call the auto-ethnographic approach links very well to the objectives of our department. We accept the subjectivity of choices and make a plea for being upfront about this.

F for Fact focuses on how knowledge is represented. It's not about producing more knowledge per se, but about working

---

1   The department's name 'F for Fact' refers to the 1973 docudrama/film essay *F for Fake*, co-written, directed by, and starring Orson Welles. *F for Fake* investigates notions of trickery, authorship, authenticity, and the value of art through the biography of an art forger.

with existing knowledge and making it accessible in new ways. For instance, taking a personal focus as an alternative perspective for developing a narrative.

LS   Does this questioning of knowledge align with you on a personal level?

BV   Totally. In my view, nothing was ever obvious—there was no such thing as normality. Growing up, I was always observing the situation I was in, and wondering about the weirdness of it all. Who are we, how did we get here? The biggest question of all was: Why is everyone behaving as if it's completely normal? From a young age, I used a camera to try to make sense of it. Photography gave me the feeling that not everything was elusive after all. When I entered the Gerrit Rietveld Academie, I was not inclined to become an artist, as I merely intended to continue what I had been doing before. When working in photography there's always the 'real world,' but we should know by now that the real world can never be depicted as it is. Taking a picture is to make choices, to frame and leave out the context that created the situation. These rather obvious views on photography's inherent biases in depicting the world were surprisingly unpopular with my photography tutors at the time, and at some point I decided to change departments. Although I didn't care about labelling my work as art, I was wholeheartedly welcomed in the art department, which is now named 'VAV– moving image.' So you could say that I was never attracted to art, but art became attracted to me. Photography remained part of my practice until the seriality of my photographic work was naturally overtaken by film as my medium of choice.

272

LS   What was the prevailing view in art when you studied?

BV   In the eighties, in the context of the Gerrit Rietveld Academie, it all needed to come from an unknown place, perhaps called intuition, as a materialized expression of one's personality. Bellybutton-art. The fact that something like ratio or intellect is inherently part of a person's make-up did not fall on fertile ground. References to other artists or popular culture were supposedly undermining 'authenticity.' That term puzzled me;

Barbara Visser, *Detitled/ EGG19992811/FT/L/c*, 2000, detail from a series.

I hated it, I don't agree with that reductive idea of art. A sometimes-conceptual approach of topics does not exclude being very personal in my work. In fact, the whole idea of originality was lost on me. I saw 'authentic' as a term that ignored the fact that we are all the product of endless influences.

The demand to be original was also paired with the false idea that we should not pollute our unspoiled imagination by too much knowledge. Possibly *F for Fact* is my ultimate revenge on those ideas! One cannot be spoiled by too much knowledge. Regardless of whether you're an artist, photographer, or designer, you're the author of choices, and you better make them consciously. I've always thought there should be a school on that: 'C for Choice.'

Barbara Visser, *Last Lecture*, 2007, video still.

Can you elaborate on how you teach your students that knowledge production is always informed by subjective choices?

BV   During the first year students are, among other things, subjected to various archives and collections, as those are the conventional loci for what we call 'knowledge.' These archives can range from very personal, tiny collections, to scientific archives; the city as a living archive full of references, the body as a living archive. Gradually they develop an awareness of the perspectives in these collections, the methods used to form them, how the research is represented, and what it means to re-imagine the information.

We stimulate the immersive as well as the critical distance when looking at a body of knowledge and ask them to carve out a personal narrative in that knowledge. Yet they should also question these narratives: Why are some stories dominant while others stay hidden or are blatantly ignored?

One exercise to open the eyes of students to these narratives is based on a book called *On Looking: Eleven Walks with Expert Eyes*.[2] One of the tutors, Bart Haensel, organizes a series of walks through Amsterdam. The walk follows the same route every week, but each time the tour is guided by a different 'expert,' showing how looking at the same part of the city through a different lens can totally change your perception of the surroundings: what you see depends on what you're looking for. The first route is guided by a smell expert who tells the students about the repugnant smell of Amsterdam in the seventeenth century, thanks to the canals serving as its sewage and garbage systems. Reminders can be found on paintings of the time that depict women wearing so-called 'pomanders' that exuded a spicy aroma of ambergris from the whale's intestines, or musk and herbs to combat the stench. So, what does the city smell of today? Another tour provides a Black Heritage lens, showing the omnipresent traces of the Dutch colonial past throughout the route. Yet when the group passes the famous De Bazel building on the Vijzelgracht, the carved-out figures on the

275

2   Alexandra Horowitz, *On Looking: Eleven Walks with Expert Eyes* (New York: Simon and Schuster, 2013).

front door depicting two Indonesian women are hardly mentioned: apparently they are not the lens through which the tour is designed. So even a Black Heritage Tour organization sees what it is looking for, while having a blind spot for other geographical aspects of colonialism. A third tour looks at what can be found under the pavement, the archaeology, and so on—the variations are potentially endless.

LS   How would you describe what students learn from such exercises?

BV   First of all, it's about the common experience. Then it's about the training of perception, discovering, and exchanging new insights on the bigger picture or in the details one might easily overlook. Apart from such experiences, the programme tries to create a sensibility to recognize pre-formed assumptions—which I hope all art education does, by the way. It's as basic as: How do you pose a question? What *is* a question? Who decides what's a good or a bad question? It forms an awareness of the difficulty, if not the impossibility, of filtering oneself totally out of research. Instead of ignoring this, students can turn subjectivity into a tool for shedding new light on things, which is the main focus of the second year where each student is embedded in a knowledge institute and chooses a specific, personal focus on the institute and archive. We advise them to filter knowledge through their personal experiences and make a clear distinction between hard facts and imagination, but to use both.

There are many ways to translate knowledge into a personal or subjective narrative. Writing is one way, and we present the requirement to write a thesis not as a dreaded academic hurdle, but as an invitation to engage with text in a way that suits the individual need of the student. The joy of reading and writing is central. The theses tutor starts on day one of the first year, not, as is usually the case, in the second year, just to make sure they manage. Visually, we focus a lot on film—the cinematographic essay is an excellent medium for investigation.

276

LS   Of the auto-ethnographic turn in design we claim that starting from personal experience ensures true engagement with the world.

Barbara Visser, *Manual/2*, 2015, installation, video still.

BV This turn in design deals with the fundamental question of owning the narratives one creates. It's a good question, I think, especially now, as it challenges creatives to deal with the implications and consequences of what we do. It has always been my biggest frustration with art that the extreme personal offers room to say and do everything you want, but at the same time, once the label art is attached to it, there's a detachment from the world. Artists do comment on reality and they do so from a distance. Don't get me wrong: one needs to keep a distance from a system to be able to question it. But being outside of the system also creates this paradox of not actually becoming part of it and thus not being able to have a profound influence on it.

When tutoring artists, I tend to limit the options, I try to create focus. Tutoring designers, I usually show them the opposite: how much broader they can go, and I try to enhance them to take a distanced position every now and then, step out of the system, and move beyond the conventions of their field. Design has a more direct relation to the world, enabling direct measures and comments.

278

Apart from this reflection, I find it exciting to lend terms from other fields, such as 'authorship' or 'auto-ethnography,' to help explain things within a domain. For artists the term 'author' does not feel alien, but for design, the term still seems to contain a friction.

Barbara Visser, *Detitled/ EGG19992811/FT/L/c*, 2000, detail from a series.

Barbara Visser, *Detitled/ EGG19992811/FT/L/c*, 2000, detail from a series.

LS   In design, stressing 'authorship' is part of a marketing strategy to accomplish more attention and financial gain.

BV   Auto-ethnography seems to be about taking personal responsibility for one's actions, rather than just pursuing credit as a (star-) designer. It's interesting how the quality of the individual position can manifest itself in different ways. By using the term auto-ethnography, we somehow shed the ego of the designer, and keep the advantage of a very personal way of making sense of the world.

BARBARA VISSER (Haarlem, NL, 1966) is a visual artist, filmmaker, and educator with a broad experience in education and policy making, living in Amsterdam (NL). Her work is driven by wonder and a productive discontent, but the driving force—ultimately—is curiosity. She tells stories through different media: photography, film, text, installation, print, performance. Visser's work focuses on cultural and historical narratives: how they are 'written,' how they are 'read,' and how time and context influence our perception of information. By questioning our memory and belief systems, Visser aims to provoke a new perception of what normality has rendered invisible.

ALL KNOWLEDGE IS BIASED

An Architecture of Criminality
Photographing Collective Wounds

Adelaide Di Nunzio

It is an early morning in Naples. I am in my neighbourhood, San Lorenzo-Vicaria, in the square next to my favourite bar. The old square has been completely abandoned and is now degraded. More than a neighbourhood square, it's an open space. For years, it was known for its clothing markets—in particular, the famous Mercato delle pezze americane (American rags market), a legacy of the post-war period. Unfortunately, this space is now only a meeting place for pigeons and mice, garbage, dog shit, and poor alcoholics. Every now and then, a few football matches between African immigrants from the neighbourhood take place in the space.

> Walking in this empty yet crowded space (overflowing with waste—glass, paper, plastic...), I see a dead pigeon on the ground.

I puzzle over how this poor pigeon died. I start speculating: it ate a piece of glass; had a heart attack; fell in flight; was kicked; was beaten; stoned? Perhaps the pigeon got in the way of a firecracker used in neighbourhood festivities. Perhaps it was shot in Camorra-related crossfire. Finally, I decide that we simply cannot know why this poor pigeon died.

> My grandfather told me that during the war, pigeons were seen as a meal. Misery, hunger, and the simple act of survival make everyone equal... just like when pigeons battle it out for a few breadcrumbs.

I walk away wondering if or when the dead pigeon will be removed. In the meantime, I look around and see an old courthouse—alluring in its state of abandonment. Next to it is a Renaissance church boasting a shiny silver-grey dome above its faded and decrepit walls.

I am now in the old hamlet of Sant'Antonio Abate: jolting sounds, market stalls, smells of pizza and coffee. This is the backdrop of what was the ancient city's main entrance, Porta Capuana, where the Sebeto River used to flow. Residents remember this river because of its fountain, erected to commemorate the premature death of a young woman whose passion for the neighbourhood's history ran deep.

> We Neapolitans have a strong bond with our city—a bond that I feel. I often find myself observing abandoned structures in my city: villas, buildings under construction, unfinished roads... Sometimes I try (and succeed) to

Author: Adelaide Di Nunzio
Location: Statale 106, Reggio Calabria
Description: Unfinished structure, photographs taken from the book *Criminal Architectures*
(Crowdbooks Publishers, IT, 2020).

Author: Adelaide Di Nunzio
Location: Statale 106, Reggio Calabria
Description: Fire in Campo Rom, Ponticelli Naples, photographs taken from the book *Criminal Architectures* (Crowdbooks Publishers, IT, 2020).

forget all of this and am drawn in by the beauty of the
sea, mountains, and sun. But the degradation is like an
invisible cancer... though it can be ignored, it can't be
cured: it spreads lethally.

Driven by a desire to 'freeze' these abandoned structures in time,
and drawing from my work as a journalist, I decided to photo-
document these spaces in my publication *Architetture Criminali*
(*Criminal Architectures*).

 283

These abandoned structures are carcasses scattered throughout the city: rotting out just like the putrid pigeon on
the ground, but seemingly sublime in their outlines and
shapes. Sometimes they remind me of ancient ruins.

The sun shines on me as I walk past the shadows of these ruins;
it warms my face, the faces of passers-by, the pigeon rotting on
the ground.

I go back to my musings: Who will remove the pigeon's
corpse? Who is to blame for the pigeon's death? And who
is responsible for the pigeon, be it alive or dead?

Someone just absent-mindedly stepped on the dead pigeon;
he swears profusely at no one in particular. We aren't meant
to know anything about this pigeon (circumstances of death,
removal, final destination etc.); our only choice is to be indiffer-
ent to it, enjoy the landscape, and move on.

Imagine something absurd: imagine I make a phone call
to an administrative office and communicate the death of

the pigeon as well as its position in the city. I am told that this is not their responsibility, but that they are willing to check the situation and look for a solution. Imagine that they come, and resolve to build a fence around the carcass.

Anyone living in this city knows the scenario far too well. We see fences everywhere: around construction projects immobilized for multiple reasons, around houses, around confiscated buildings, around dead people. These are not just sore spots to the eye... they make our hearts literally ache. *My* heart aches.

After a few days, the pigeon is still there—but now it lies within a fence and is so decrepit that it is almost unrecognizable. It reminds me of a scene in Curzio Malaparte's *La pelle*: the body of a man on the ground, crushed by an American tank on the ancient Roman road of the Appia. Malaparte compares the man's body to the Italian flag at the end of the Second World War: a people physically crushed and morally brutalized ... the filthy soles of shoes.

I take refuge in the blue sky and in the ancient piperno stone, slowly trying to eliminate all the degradation from my sight. I have a coffee; the sun illuminates the ancient gate of Naples from afar and all its majestic antiquity. In the meantime, in one stark leap, a cat eats the pigeon. Nature finds solutions, be they a brutal/messy ones.

I tell the story of this pigeon because it represents everything that is left to itself, irrespective of its surrounding beauty, which so easily distracts. The story of the pigeon also conveys the idea that crime, and not only the actions of the mafia, is collective. Responsibility for crime also falls in the hands of a public who does not intervene promptly, of a flawed and overly complicated institutional system, a sense of indifference, or the prioritization of the private domain. The pigeon story is also my act of auto-ethnographic storying, using both narration and speculation to articulate deeply personal knowledge about a complex and multifaceted topic. Ultimately, I tell this story to come to terms with being Neapolitan, belonging to this city, and seeking to understand what this means. To tell these stories of pigeons and monuments is to indirectly tell my own story. However, my true auto-ethnographic medium is not writing but photography, where I can elaborate visually on the tensions of what it means to live in a city that has been dominated by corruption.

This book is about the auto-ethnographic practice of design. I am not a designer, I am a photographer. However, I have spent the last years photographing a type of design that is particularly close to me—criminal architectures. An auto-ethnographic practice for me has implied taking a certain posture towards the objects of my camera. These are not objects to be studied coldly, like foreign artefacts. My work attempts to avoid 'othering' these buildings and making them alien, but rather to help understand how they are part of us, part of me, and part of my own story. These structures and the stories they tell are painful for me; whether I like it or not, they are part of my identity, part of what constitutes my experiences of being from Naples. Taking this approach has implied a closer assimilation with what I am documenting, leading to images that combine a desire to document the reality of these buildings with an artistic framing, situating architecture within light and shadow, giving life to buildings that are dead and showing the fateful mortality in the buildings that are still inhabited. My work emphasizes both the design of the buildings and how the buildings further design the lives around them. In my photobook *Architetture Criminali*, my work has expanded beyond just architecture photos to include images of those whose lives are intertwined with these buildings: street workers, prostitutes, farmers, entrepreneurs and even photos of 'heroes,' men and women fighting against the mafia. Despite being behind the lens, not for a second do I consider myself outside the thematic frame of the topic. This is also my story.

285

ADELAIDE DI NUNZIO holds an MFA from the Naples Academy of Fine Arts (IT) and studied photography at the 'Richard Bauer' School of Milan (IT). Her photography covers different genres, from fine art to reportage.. She teaches graphics and fine-art photography. Her reportages have been widely published in international newspapers and she has worked with many international photo agencies. Di Nunzio's solo exhibitions include the photography exhibitions 'Criminal Architecture' at La Mediterranea gallery (Naples, 2016), and 'La pelle' at the Galerie 21 (Cologne, 2019) and at the International Foundation Casa Morra (Naples, 2019). In 2020 she published the photo book *Architetture Criminali* (Crowdsbooks Publishers, crowdsbooks.com).

It's About the How, not the What
Discover and Accept Your Personal Talent

Conversation with Gijs Assmann

Louise Schouwenberg

LS   What does this object want to be? What does the material want to be? Many of your former students remember you posing these questions, time and again. You are also remembered, and praised, for being an excellent tutor. What do these questions reveal about your approach?

GA   Students should lose the idea of making a good work. Instead, they should learn to trust their impulses and artistic imagination, and let the dynamics of the process lead the way. What else can one do in education? It's all about strengthening the guts to follow what students already know by heart.

LS   You're an artist yourself. Does your approach to education mirror your artistic work?

GA   It does. Let me first take you on a detour. I was trained in the eighties in a department (at AKI Academy of Art & Design in Enschede, NL), which was then known for its conceptual approach. Materials were considered subservient to the overruling concept. It all revolved around positioning and how to legitimate a work within the prevailing art discourse. Already in those days, this approach of what I consider an overvaluing of artistic criticality and an overestimation of the presumed ideas behind artworks, clashed with my intuition. A focus on concepts, which has persistently defined art, mostly leads to visually poor works, triggering only a few senses. And mind you, not many artists are capable of producing something surprisingly clever and can thus rightfully call themselves conceptual artists.

Apart from these considerations, I think conceptual art produces a false conception of what art is. Even if you and I would start from a similar idea, our translations would differ completely. Not the *what* informs what a work communicates, but the *how*. What matters is how ideas and intentions have been materialized and translated into images.

Let me give an example from the past. Gijs Frieling, a friend of mine, told me about the preserved original contract for one of the iconic altarpieces by El Greco. Before the painter had ventured his first brush stroke, he knew exactly what was expected because the commissioner had meticulously described the whole piece: from the hues of the costumes to the number of figures to be depicted. Imagine somebody dictating a painting to a contemporary artist. They would certainly exclaim 'Make it yourself!' I agree with Frieling that El Greco could show his highly personal and distinctive style because he could focus on the *how*, and did not need to bother about the *what*.

LS   Did conceptual education do anything positive for you?

GA   What I took from it is the need to understand the context in which you operate. As an artist you need to be able to formulate in which tradition your work fits. Partly through my training, I've become sufficiently acquainted with the language that enables access to a work, both my own and that of others.

What disturbs me most about conceptual art is taking art as the subject. Positioning becoming the theme, and no longer one of the elements of the practice to be dealt with. For me the topic of art is being a human being. How does one live? How does one cope and make sense of the world by way of art? Art is a tool, not the subject. To make a jump to education: it starts with the artist, the designer, the student. Whatever a work expresses or what it does, it all boils down to it being informed by something else, and this 'else' is not the concept of what art is, but resides both in the personal experience of the maker *and* their capacity to produce images. As for me, my personal expertise resides in visual intelligence.

LS   Your work is very accessible. Is that important considering your views on art?

GA   I relate as a fellow human being to other human beings with my work. Not as an artist vis-à-vis an art audience. In life, there are only a few themes that are timeless and worthwhile dealing with, such as hope, love, religion, death, and more importantly the fear of death. These loaded topics appear in many guises and hide in the most mundane situations of each person's life. With my work, I dive into the complexity of a topic, and try to make it

Gijs Assmann, *The world has lost me*, 2018, ceramics, 89 x 47 x 35 cm, photo Friso Keuris, 2018.

289

Gijs Assmann, *Deer and Hunter*, 2007, bronze, 340 × 270 × 134 cm, Beekpark Apeldoorn (NL).

bearable, attractive even. Given my aim at directly relating to the viewer as a fellow human being, a work must be inviting. Therefore, I don't merely take inspiration from how I personally cope with the world, but also use a variety of methods to pull the spectator into a work. Once you zoom in, you discover that behind the often light-hearted first impression hide uncomfortable layers of meanings.

LS   Does this insight on the large themes that matter in life, and how you take inspiration from your personal experiences, inform your tutoring?

GA   Absolutely, it's all connected. I teach my students the insights I have learned in life, which all revolve around the words 'courage' and 'compassion.' Not to think in terms of solutions, but to know the importance of a sincere attempt to relate to these issues; the importance of trying and daring to fail—that's the most powerful weapon one has. Whether you succeed is not so important. At least in education, the notion of success should not have a prominent place. So next to criticality, one needs compassion, the capacity to forgive oneself, be kind. For a main part education is about teaching people how to embrace the personal lenses through which they observe and cope with the world.

LS   Apart from these psychological insights, do you also acquaint students with the more practical methods you use to visualize and materialize a theme, as well as the methods for making your work accessible?

GA   In my own work I use multiple methods, such as consciously employing an amateur style in certain parts of my installations or, seemingly opposite, showing the traces and love for craftsmanship in the details. I often refer to classical sculptures and offer the comfort of recognition—for instance, by referring to personal experiences and passionately felt beliefs. I don't aim at creating a kind of diary, but recognition brings me closer to the spectator. Even though people don't know me personally, they do know the private situations I address. But this is my toolkit, my methods, which don't

291

necessarily work for a student. Students should get acquainted with their own user manuals, and as a tutor, I help them find these. To make a comparison to soccer: as a tutor I don't play ball myself, but ensure there are circumstances for the ball to be played. Morality needs to be taken out of the process. I will never ask the question 'Why?,' which in itself is a legitimate question, but it destroys more than it produces.

LS   What changes if you guide a design student?

GA   Nothing. In my tutoring I don't differentiate between art and design students, I react to what they present me. I look at a student's work and try to judge it according to its inherent merits. Naturally, I'm not ignorant because yes, absolutely, there are differences. The contexts in which works usually land are different, the discourses are different, and I know that in the cultural field there seems to be a continued need to differentiate between art, applied art, and design. But I often wonder how valuable it is for the work itself to make such a distinction. Once you place a vase outside of the design department, the tradition of the discipline vanishes, or the references of that same tradition add an extra layer of meaning. Just look at Grayson Perry's work.

LS   Design is linked to use and functionality, art to autonomy, total freedom.

GA   The excessive and now anachronistic attention to the autonomy of both the artist and the work of art are part of the cliché conceptions of fields. What interests me is how something works in the world and what it says about how we cope with that world.

LS   Artists creating design are more easily accepted by the design world than designers making art by the art world. The art world is a closed bastion, which is rather strange, given the fact that many contemporary artists speak of multidisciplinary art practices. The old opposition of high and low is preserved even in our times. What are artists afraid of?

Gijs Assmann, *for H*, 2018, Stedelijk Museum Schiedam, photo: Tom Haartsen.

293

For the past twelve years, Gijs Assmann has been sending his beloved a card or collage by post every day: an A4-size picture that he has cut, pasted, and written a message on the back of. It is his way of telling her over and over again that he loves her and why. These more than a thousand expressions of love were shown in chronological order in the Stedelijk Museum Schiedam from 13 October to 3 February 2019. *for H.* is an intimate and at the same time megalomaniac project. It has to do with the time in which many people share their daily lives through social media.

GA   Artists are right in being scared of a blurring of disciplines. Designers can point to usefulness as a legitimization of their craft, but artists merely have autonomy to defend the raison d'être of their discipline. That possibly explains why art has withdrawn in autonomy and has turned its back to society, and it explains why artists defend their free zone against possible intruders who would kill the idea of autonomy.

LS   At the same time, one cannot deny the fact that design is less useful and more personal than is often claimed, and art is less autonomous than it seems.

GA   It's also simply about producing commodities for a market and figuring out how to reach an audience. In the first lesson I give, I tell my students: 'I'm not here to teach you the content of your work. I try to make you discover and accept your personal talent and make it flourish. Only thus will you be able to use your creativity to make a better world, and mind you, it does not matter which discipline you use to make that happen.'
I advise both my art and design students to rely on personal experiences as a handhold. To come back to your initial question: no, I don't see a difference in teaching artists or designers. What I see in many students, also my design students, is that they are not dealing with functionality, but that they deal with the motives of design, which are the daily objects we are surrounded with. That's the language by which students express how they cope with the world.

LS   How about the practical level of tutoring art students versus design students?

GA   At the art department in Arnhem, I usually say 'just go ahead, make it, go for it.' But at Design Academy Eindhoven, there's less need to make students *do* something. You can talk about content and what's on the table, which usually is a lot. In Arnhem, there are mainly local students, in Eindhoven they have travelled a long stretch, have paid a lot, know nobody, and that all comes with a different urgency. Another difference: designers come in with some innate inferiority complex when I compare them with artists. I also had a kind of arrogance when I started as an art student at the AKI in Enschede, though I was not an excellent student. In general, designers have a much more natural curiosity for materials, contexts, collaborations, and the world they live in; whereas artists are loners. Remarkably, teaching designers is more fun for me.

LS The demand of autonomy can be experienced as a burden by art students, as it hinders them from taking personal experiences beyond the private. For design students it's the other way round.

GA Indeed, once design students feel the relief of not having to obey to some commissioner's brief and not having to make something functional per se, they are very agile in translating personal experiences into works that communicate something valuable about the world at large. And, as said, *how* they do this determines the final value of their works.

295

GIJS ASSMANN ventures with his works into an enigmatic universe of drama and comedy, farce and destruction. In his works he juggles with folk art, caricature, and fine art. Assmann has made many many sculptures for public spaces and exhibits in past years with solo exhibitions, among others, in Schloss Ahaus (DE), the Stedelijk Museum Schiedam, and Museum Jan Cunen in Oss, and recently in a group presentation at Kunstmuseum Den Haag. Assmann studied at the AKI Academy of Art & Design in Enschede (NL) and the Rijksakademie van beeldende kunsten in Amsterdam (NL).

Social—Critical—Speculative
Auto-Ethnography as a Working Method

Conversation with Jan Boelen

Louise Schouwenberg

JBo   It helps to link a name to this approach to design. Though I haven't referred to it explicitly as such, I'm aware of it having been part of my teaching approach at the MA Social Design of Design Academy Eindhoven. Time and again, I used to tell my students that they should depart from their own experiences, their personal inspirations, and fascinations. In their personal context, they can find the right energy, needs, and motivation.

JBo   There was always a point in time when we challenged students, asking them about the relevance of their ideas and plans. A project should not stay self-referential. Something can start with a small and weird anecdote, a personal story, something that happened in a specific time. As a tutor, you try to bring the student back to that moment, because you sense an energy and a fascination that you don't see in the other things on the table. You then try to enlarge that peculiar story, and stimulate the student to embrace it as an excellent starting point for a project.

297

If I look at the bigger picture, it started with the participatory turn, which opposed the old practice of marketing deciding what a product should look like. Via the participatory approach, other people could take part in the design process; gradually, this moving away from the designer has developed into the current situation in which algorithms increasingly define the design of things.

As a natural response to this, we now witness a growing awareness of the importance of personal fascinations, of staying close to the body, and thus staying also close to haptic experiences. In this process of revaluing bodily experiences, auto-ethnography and its focus on personal experiences marks an important turn.

Most design schools are constructed around the demand to fit the *Dezeens* of the world, focusing on publicity and thus on media-genic works. They don't care how a designer reached that end result. But in my view, designers only have a right to speak about something if their projects stem from genuine and authentic interest. Every project needs to start with an intuitive, sensorial exploration of the self. At the same time, it's paramount that a project does not stay within the confined world of personal experiences, but communicates in such a way that others can relate to it.

At Social Design we advised students to build references around their personal experiences to ensure they would have a better grip on how to position themselves in the world. Such a widening of horizons can for instance happen by collecting facts and figures. It's not enough to feel your own heartbeat; it only becomes interesting and relevant when you start to measure your personal heartbeat, then immediately measure the heartbeats of others, and let the notion of difference come in.

LS   By reflecting on the self, do you also reflect on the other?

JBo   Absolutely. If you speak of the self, that always includes speaking of difference, i.e. the other. It's not about merging with others, but about being different from others and being aware of that difference.
It's the same with terms like 'autonomy' and 'freedom.' Autonomy starts when you relate to the rest of the world and freedom starts where you reach the other's border. Otherwise, the 'auto' in auto-ethnography merely stays self-referential.

I always tried to provoke the students by saying that true social design starts with 'me, myself, and I,' which is the most antisocial attitude one can have, and must have, for that matter. If you don't succeed in relating a research topic to yourself, it won't grant you any authority in speaking about it. But subsequently the project needs to move beyond the personal.

LS   Do you have an example that shows how personal experiences grant one authority?

JBo   If a student wants to make a project on sex workers, which one of our students did, then they only have authority if they come from that world or are willing to

298

step into that world, thus avoiding the danger of treating sex workers as exotic others. In the case of this particular student's project, its success depended on her knowing the work from the inside. As with the other students, there was a moment in which we started to drop the question of 'Why?' and asked for the wider relevance of the project—which she was very capable of answering. I don't think anyone without personal experience could have created this project.

LS   In the department of Contextual Design, which I headed while you headed Social Design, we posed the question 'Why?' and asked for the relevance of a project that has started from personal experiences probably in a less rigorous manner. Or we would ask for it later on in the process. In my department, most tutors were artists, so I expected from them a natural inclination to trigger the students' imagination and intuition. They would seldom ask 'Why?' Instead, they would accept whatever students came with. The 'why' usually needed to come from the theory tutors and me. Maybe you and I had different timings before we would ask for a larger legitimization of projects, but quite often the resulting projects carried many similarities.

JBo   True. And mind you, I often defended students in Social Design who could not answer that question. Sometimes I even said the question should not be posed, so the project could stay poetic, beautiful. Asking for relevance is not always necessary or productive.

LS   The *raison d'être* can reside within a project, no external justification needed. At your department, some students started from social issues, others from their own experiences. Were the latter more successful?

JBo   If the students succeeded in going beyond fear, yes. Quite often, this entailed that they start unlearning what they had previously learned. We have all been confronted with strict educational models in previous schools, with certain ways of upbringing, with specific cultural contexts. These protective contexts encapsulate you, and they also cause you to no longer listen carefully to your real feelings and ambitions. Because of that, it's inevitable you become alienated from reality. The realities we live in, and the systems that reign in those realities, continue to alienate us every day. To me, this explains why there's so much frustration in society. Life was never as good as in our times; nevertheless, we fight with discomfort because we've lost ourselves, became disconnected from our roots. This has happened in all areas of our lives, including how we relate to food and food production, how we relate to our bodies, to ideas, how we've accepted being reduced to mere consumers, have accepted that decisions on our lives are taken by others. We've outsourced so many things, while keeping the illusion of being in control of our lives. We know so much more, while having fewer possibilities to make decisions. These paradoxes continuously cause new frustrations. That's why it's so important in education to help students accept their personal intuition and find their own voices.

LS   How about professional designers who have made their way in the world: should they also stay in tune with their personal experiences?

JBo   For me, Konstantin Grcic is one of the best examples. We had many talks about sitting. If I recall well, he said: 'There are so many postures and so many behaviours, and they keep on changing.' In our times, we've become accustomed to sitting motionless in front of a screen, staring at a thing that offers a window to the world outside. Due to the COVID-19 pandemic, this sitting in front of a screen and communicating with others via the screen has become even more important. These changed behaviours do not merely comprise the act of sitting, and how the body relates to the composition of seat, table, and computer, but also how one positions oneself in front of the camera. Grcic says our bodies have acquired different postures due to changed circumstances, and that these new postures should define different designs from what we know.

LS   Grcic's form language does not seem very personal.

JBo   In fact, his language is very personal. I have not told this to many yet, but I consider him a great intellect, on all levels. Even with a straightforward industrial commission, he succeeds in translating his very personal experiences and intuitions into forms, materials, colours—which communicate something beyond the personal, something universal about our humanity here and now. He's an all-rounder, intelligent, and capable of observing relations and power structures, and translating these into statements and designs that evoke reflection; at the same time, the other part of his brain can accomplish the engineering.

LS   Let's try and zoom out. You're a director of a school. I've spoken with another school director, who told me, 'Whatever I do in my studio merges with how I live, and is thus fully based on personal experiences. But in my role as director, I need to make other choices and look at what the world needs.'

You were trained as a designer, you worked as director at Z33 (House for Contemporary Art, Design & Architecture in Hasselt), you curated many exhibitions worldwide, you were head of the MA Social Design of Design Academy Eindhoven, and now you are director of HfG, the University of Arts and Design in Karlsruhe. Does this new role require you to zoom out and think of what's needed in art and design at this moment in time? More specifically: How do your views on education relate to the topics you address within your organization, with the choice of tutors and lecturers, the departments you set up?

301

JBo   I made a plea to rely on personal experiences in Eindhoven, and I continue to advocate this belief. Autoethnography is a working method, which makes it very interesting because it offers room for many focuses and also for a combination of focuses.

I now show you a transversal scheme I'm currently working on, which I intend to develop in the years to come.

In the left quadrant, on the 'pragmatic solutions' axis, 'products' refers to the traditional, industrial conception of design (which contrasts with the scenarios of speculative narratives). On the other axis is the 'social' (Papanek, and his plea for a more socially engaged design, which eventually developed into the term 'relational design'), in which the focus is no longer products but systems and networks. On the opposite end of this axis is the 'critical' in design, which is much more political, causing debate. Naturally, there are also in-between areas, such as the one-off objects between product and critical design.

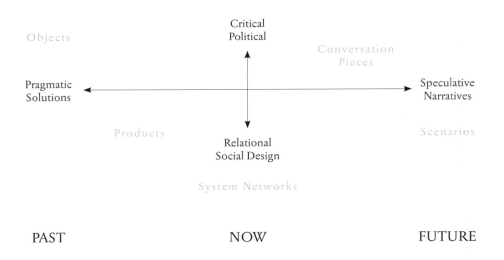

DESIGN

Objects

Critical
Political

Conversation
Pieces

Pragmatic
Solutions

Speculative
Narratives

Products

Scenarios

Relational
Social Design

System Networks

PAST   NOW   FUTURE

302   LS   Here I would differentiate between critical objects that are meant to entice debate and reflection, and the so-called design-art pieces of the turn of the century, which merely mimicked the sculptural forms of artworks. These were usually created by way of labour intensive craft methods and thus became very expensive, non-functional commodities for an overheated art market—far remote from both design and art, uninteresting. What you speak of seems to point to designs as conversation pieces, whose working resembles art as a subversive practice, aimed at criticizing institutes and outdated value systems.

       JBo   There's a whole range of projects one can place in this area of criticality, ranging from objects as conversation pieces to strategies. To me, Forensic Architecture is a good representative. Possibly, also the early work by Dunne & Raby. But most of their work falls into the fourth category of my scheme: 'speculative narratives.' Many projects by Dunne & Raby revolve around futuristic and 'what if' scenarios and stories.

Mind you, I have nothing against the field of product design because, naturally, we need good solutions for daily problems and thus we also need good products. In fact, I believe that the new directions in design will eventually change and innovate the field of product design. To come back to your question on the choices I make as director of HfG: I position my school on the right side of this scheme, and would like to focus on the critical, social, and speculative, while promoting an auto-ethnography approach within all of these fields. The approach of any topic needs to start from a personal vantage point and a personal fascination, but at the same time there are larger issues that no designer can avoid dealing with. Bruno Latour says, 'We don't seem to live on the same planet.'[1] There's one question everyone in the broader design world simply has to pose: For which planet are we designing?

JAN BOELEN (1967, BE) is a curator of design, architecture, and contemporary art. He is rector at the Karlsruhe University of Art and Design, and artistic director of Atelier LUMA in Arles, France. Boelen is the founder and former artistic director of Z33, House for Contemporary Art in Hasselt (BE). He was curator of the 4th Istanbul Design Biennial (2018) and initiated Manifesta 9 in Belgium (2012). Boelen recently edited *Social Matter, Social Design: For Good or Bad, all Design is Social* (Valiz, 2020). His writing addresses the implications of design in everyday life, and how artistic practices shape the discipline.

303

1   Bruno Latour, "'We don't seem to live on the same planet...'—a fictional planetarium," in *Philadelphia: Beyond the Horizon: Designs for Different Futures–Catalog of an Exhibition* (Philadelphia Museum of Art, 2019).

Shooting a Satellite into Space
Creating Enticing Circumstances

Conversation with Jurgen Bey

Louise Schouwenberg

JBe   It often feels like I'm in a submarine, under water, surrounded by a very loud noise, because so many people are continuously banging on its steel hull. But each time I go up and look around above water, I regain a sense of 'Wow, we've accomplished so much!'

LS   These are your last years as director of the Sandberg Instituut in Amsterdam. I imagine that you will probably not remember them as your easiest years. Currently, all art schools in the Netherlands battle with many forces, both from inside and outside. Governmental regulations increase, bureaucracy is on the rise, whereas the schools' communities have become very articulate in their ever-growing demands.

JBe   I'm tired, true; I don't always feel supported and I'm not sure whether I'm a good fighter. But at the same time, I wholeheartedly embrace recent developments in the world, which have strengthened our community. Racism, inequality, me-too—all these issues that our generation and the ones before us did not solve are finally being addressed. I'm very positive about this. But when criticisms are directed at me personally, or seem to be, it's not always easy to take a distanced look and recognize what went well and at which points I needed to compromise.

305

LS   Isn't compromising part of life? You have accomplished a lot, and you've gained quite some recognition for it, including prestigious awards. Your ongoing research on alternative ways of (co-)living and working has led to a wide variety of conceptual, semi-functional objects as conversation pieces, innovative products, proposals for alternative urban planning, and experimental landscape architecture. Apart from your own work, you gained a reputation for how you lead the Sandberg Instituut. In particular, the idea of organizing temporary MA programmes testifies to innovative thinking in education.

JBe   It was partly born out of some practical considerations, but the main idea was being able to let programmes focus on urgent themes of their time. It's paramount for education to link to important societal issues. Fixed programmes also address them, but are less flexible to react on the most recent developments in the world.

LS   Before we dive into the school, I would like to first discuss your way of working as a designer and how that relates to the topic of this publication, the auto-ethnographic turn in design. If I look at the projects of Studio Makkink & Bey led by yourself and architect Rianne Makkink, and if I look at how you've set up your multidisciplinary studio both at the Rotterdam location and in the countryside of the North-East Polder, I can easily recognize the auto-ethnographic turn in your resolve to create a hub of like-minded creatives for whom lived experiences are paramount for how they approach their work.

JBe   I always wanted to interweave life and work with a small community. So yes, the auto-ethnographic is a normal way of working for me, regardless of where I am. I live in a certain place and it's there that I experience things, develop my knowledge, and use the materials I find around me, together with the people we collaborate with (consisting of theorists, architects, artists, fashion designers and product designers). All of our work results from being a community in a specific place.

It would be my ideal for such communities to become circular entities, in which all is connected, socially, culturally, and also economically. By now, I'm well aware that the industry has not been changed by our way of working, which was my ambition when I started. You could say that our projects present model worlds, but don't reach the real world on a large scale like only industry can.

LS   In 2010, you became the director of the Sandberg Instituut (which offers MA programmes, whereas the connected Gerrit Rietveld Academie offers BA programmes) and could thus embrace a larger project. Can you explain how your vision on the interweaving of life and work has influenced your directorship?

JBe   A school is different from a studio. Whereas the latter belongs to my private life, allowing me to do whatever I want and invite whoever I want to work with, the first belongs to the public domain. In the public context of a school, it's no longer about me. If in daily life I believe in a merging of living and working, and basing all designs on how I personally experience things, once I'm in the context of a school I need to see the bigger picture. Many

306

positions are needed; the one I choose in my personal life is merely one of them.

I didn't have a fixed image of the Sandberg in mind, which merely waited to be realized. It was more like sensing something and then trying to create the right circumstances for it. In fact, I intended to create opportunities for others to realize *their* dreams and visions, those others being the heads of programmes and their teams of tutors. From the onset, I ensured that there were few rules, few boundaries in what they could do, hoping for an interesting diversity to grow.

LS   Didn't your personal views define which heads you would offer the freedom to do whatever they wanted? In 2010 you were quoted in a Dutch newspaper: 'The changing world asks for critical artists and designers who are able to collaborate and make themselves subservient to a larger goal.' So you *did* have an idea you wanted to realize?

JBe   I hoped the programmes would influence each other, not as some predefined mission, but as a possibility. I like the metaphor of shooting a satellite into space, steering it along a range of celestial bodies. They don't touch, but slowly start to have an effect on each other's trajectories.   307
People will not even notice the subtle change of direction or the speeding up of pace. It's not about pushing people into specific directions, deciding for others, but creating the circumstances in which subtle change and mutual influencing can occur.

Indeed, I *did* have ideals. One of them was shaping a collective, creating a parallel universe of people who, from various positions, would develop something individually but at the same time, work on something communal. People who could create something larger then themselves. This ideal of the collective required small-scale education; one that could not go beyond twenty people within a programme, with at most ten graduates. Only if the groups would be small could people get to know each other and weave strong personal ties. Once they would have graduated, the same people could possibly continue as a collective.

LS   How did you choose?

JBe When I came, some programmes stayed as they were and when it came to making small changes and choosing new programme heads, I chose heads with clear visions and gave them the freedom to develop distinct educational models. I had some guidelines in mind, especially in my first years at the Instituut. The design programmes should for instance not compete with a large design school like Design Academy Eindhoven (DAE), where I studied in the eighties. DAE has many departments, all of which focus on design. For the Sandberg Instituut I intended to create distinctive voices that would have strong ties with the context in which we operate, being an art academy. In various ways, all programmes should serve the arts, taking the arts in the broad sense of encompassing both fine arts and applied arts.

As I'm not an artist myself, when it came to choosing a head for the Fine Art programme, I let myself be informed by people who had more knowledge about this field. The only mission I had was to give more societal impact to the projects that would be created in this programme: not as in demanding such importance, but ensuring the arts would get it. It's similar to welcoming small children and giants. They should not have to demand the right to be somewhere, but by placing a small and a large chair in a room, lowering the toilet and adding a high toilet, you show both the child and the giant that they are wanted. It should also work that way with art. One of my objectives was ensuring society would become more receptive to art, and this could for instance happen by letting artists work side by side with designers. Both can learn from each other's language.

For the applied programmes, I kind of searched for the opposite, moving them towards the arts. I searched for heads that were educated in their respective applied fields (such as architecture and design) but that, content-wise, would work from an artistic heart. It was a combination of making room for topics I deemed relevant at the time and choosing the right persons for the jobs. I considered the topic of spatiality and materiality as very important, for instance, and because I liked the experimental way Anne Holtrop addressed these topics, I asked him to become head of the Studio for Immediate Spaces. At the time, Anne worked mainly with models and approached his topics as artistic challenges, and so he fit perfectly into the context of an art academy. Something similar happened with the Product Design programme. I considered it paramount for designers to be able to collaborate with the industry, but also be able to work within the field of autonomous art, *and* I considered a commitment to group projects important. I thus asked Jerszy Seymour, who combined these three areas. He immediately changed the programme's name from 'Vrije Vormgeving' (Free Design) to 'Dirty Art.'

LS How about the urgent topics for which you set up various temporary programmes. How did you choose from all the ideas you had in your head?

JBe As with the fixed programmes, I chose what I considered to be relevant. One such topic was 'vacancy,' which was a big problem in the Netherlands at that time. The topic was addressed at the 2010 Venice Biennale by the Rietveld brothers of studio RAAAF. So the topic existed, the project existed, a book was made about it, *and* the team existed. I merely had to ask Ronald and Erik Rietveld to head the temporary programme of Vacant NL (2011–2013). Something similar happened with Cure Master (2014–2016), which was headed by Martijn Engelbregt and Theo Tegelaers. I had seen an exhibition by Martijn in which he addressed the notion of fake pills and questioned what health and sickness are in our current society—topics that are still very important. When I asked him to develop a Master's programme, I actually asked him to redo the project, but this time with students. Various temporary programmes were set up like this. I encountered projects that I thought addressed something important in society, and I asked people to set up temporary programmes around those topics.

LS You succeeded?

JBe Not all went well, and within the organization we had to battle with many things. I had anticipated the temporary Master's programmes would become an investigation into the future of education. One of the plans foresaw

309

that they would attract money and energy from the outside world, for instance by connecting to companies, workplaces, and other parties. But the times were not favourable for this. Some programmes succeeded in attracting external funding, such as Designing Democracy, and Fashion Matters, but most were less successful in attracting funding, as companies had no extra resources. By the way, this did not hinder them from building excellent programmes. I'm proud we have at least experimented with the urgent question of 'What's next in education?'

LS   As I recall from my time at the Sandberg Instituut (heading Material Utopias, 2013–2015), there has always been opposition from inside the Instituut.

JBe   The fixed programmes never embraced the temporary programmes, and they thought I totally overplayed my hand with the Underground University (2017–2019), which caused quite a stir in the communities as some students got exempted from paying tuition fees, others not. It was an effort in trying to find extra resources, but I had not anticipated the downsides. At that point, a growing number of students wanted to have a say in choosing the temporary programmes—which has happened, and mind you, I wholeheartedly embrace this development. For the upcoming years, the 'Research' and 'Unsettling' committees of the school can come up with proposals for temporary programmes. Instead of assuming the departments find external funding, the focus is now on research and diversity within the domains of Artificial Intelligence, the City, and Materiality. We have developed non-hierarchical cell structures, in which it's not per se the Lector who decides, but also Senior Researchers and Research Fellows, consisting of tutors and alumni, who decide.

LS   Aren't these cell structures close to how you operate in your own design studio, where you connect lived experiences and research?

310

JBe   They are: both when it comes to allowing all people to
        have a say during the process, and when it comes to
        interweaving research and practice. In contrast to other
        schools, which usually have separate Lectorates with
        their own agendas that drain money and energy from the
        overall organization, research at the Sandberg Instituut is
        closely connected to the programmes. Usually, students
        don't get to see how their tutors conduct research in
        their studios, and the tutors stay dependent on the
        coincidental projects students come up with. By having a
        range of researchers within the programmes that conduct
        their research within the school's building, the notion of
        what we call 'Window Education' is born: you can see it,
        you can take part in it, and most importantly, all elements
        of education become integrated. Research immediately
        feeds back into educaton.

LS   At the beginning of our conversation, you said that there is a big gap
     between your personal ideals and what the industry might accomplish
     on a larger scale. Isn't it easy to accept this gap and abide with
     presenting speculative scenarios for the world? Hardcore industrial
     design has borders in understanding complex contexts.   311

JBe   Naturally. But still, someone like Joep van Lieshout
        proves that moving to a larger scale is not some faraway
        impossible idea. Just look at how he has become a devel-
        oper, developing real estate, but from the perspective of
        culture. He was educated in the Arts, started his living
        and working community within that cultural field, and
        gradually succeeded in expanding it. Currently he's a
        main player in developing the harbour of Rotterdam!
        Usually the artworld looks down on economics, but that's
        a reality we also need to cope with, and Joep does it.
        Many more people should work like that. I am jealous...
        But not to worry, I'm jealous in a healthy way!

LS   How about your career from now onwards? You said it currently
     feels like you're in a submarine, surrounded by noise. But you also
     mentioned that going up every now and then, looking around and
     getting an overview, you sense again the enthusiasm about what you
     have accomplished.

What this Instituut has accomplished! Yes, I don't look back with regret. I've learned a lot. I will definitely take many things with me on whatever next journey I embark on. To start with, at the Studio we have some exciting new plans. Apart from this, I hope I will resume a place within an institute after leaving the Sandberg Instituut. One can do so much more! As for me personally, I don't need a luxurious life, I'm very good at spending money on labour for projects I believe in. We've always done so with our Studio, investing every earning in new plans, time and again, and in ensuring the team could go on, even in COVID-19 times. We are a caring community and a community needs labour to develop. Labour is the driving force. However, if you want to change something on a larger scale, you need the resources of an institute, its network, its collection, its archive, and its knowledge. My ideal is making an inclusive society, and what I mean is a genuine inclusive society—inclusivity not coming from a predefined moralistic view, but from developments that organically occur once you create the right circumstances. I see my role as the one who can influence, but not the one who will decide, dictate, and impose things on others. That's very important for me. I envision something like this, the Sandberg Instituut, a learning institute to address the culture of change in behaviour and language. In my ideal world, it's all about creating communal living within a cultural landscape. I like to live my life public.

312

JURGEN BEY has been one of the most influential Dutch designers of the last three decades with his designs such as the Tree TrunkBench, Kokon furniture, and Ear chair, now icons within the world of design. Besides his creative work, he is also the director of the Sandberg Instituut (NL) and the Master Programmes of Art and Design at the Rietveld Academie in Amsterdam (NL). In his approach to design education, he aims to pass on his design strategy and focus on expanding the role of the designer-architect to the most strategic function possible.

313

Towards Intrinsic Value
The Production of the 'Self' in Relation to the Other

Conversation with Hicham Khalidi

Michael Kaethler

HK   Recently I've been doing a lot of reflecting and thinking about the 'perceived' universality and superiority of Western knowledge, which continues to act as a foundation for a persistent form of colonialism and Western imperialism. It has led me to question the structures that exacerbate certain inequalities and hierarchies that we want to overcome. As a curator, I engage with these questions through the lens of art and design—exploring how art and design are related to ongoing crises and alternative avenues for thinking about art and design, and how they provide capabilities to work with these crises.

What I read into auto-ethnographic design is the idea of self-building in relation to the other, which seeks to overcome the forces of systematic hierarchies and externalities and instead conceives of design according to its intrinsic value. The act of producing and the production of oneself in relation to the other raises questions of how, and more importantly *why,* we produce; it also raises the question of what this production means for others, the environment, society, human and non-humans etc. As relational beings, we are fundamentally responsible for what we produce. Such questions of the how and why are fundamental when rethinking art and design in an age of crisis; these are questions that we so crucially need right now.

315

HK   If we denounce the market, we need new models that allow or support people to create from intrinsic values. By an intrinsic value, I mean that everyone can and has the right to create regardless of market or cultural hierarchies (autonomy). This goes against the idea of a universal / modernist idea of quality, and proposes a pluriversal idea as laid out by Arturo Escobar. Such a notion of quality, at the same time, adjusts itself from the given colonial and neo-liberal Western hierarchies and gives precedence to personal and individual sovereignty in relation to the other (without falling into the trap of individuality which is a neo-liberal concept—things such as liberty and freedom). There is no autonomy without the other and vice versa.

An intrinsic design calls for an awareness of the connection between the self and the other. It should be able to take into account the 'other' in all aspects, human and non-human. It should go beyond extractivism—using the means of production to create hierarchical narratives—and should instead seize control of the means of production to create value for all and everything. This of course is difficult. Let's say someone doing a residency at the Jan van Eyck Academie is spending a year doing research in their own studio. Is this experience of doing a residency extracting from someone else's need and want? Yes and no. If one is not aware of one's privilege and the inequality inherent in the control of the means of production, then it would be extractivist; if one is aware of this privilege, then I would say it is not extractivist because the production would then take into account the conditions under which the production has taken place and would account for the inherent inequalities present in production. So, basically what I am saying is that this notion of the intrinsic goes beyond the idea of autonomy in the arts, which has always been seen independent from social or societal structures/responsibility.

What I'm emphasizing here is a type of autonomy in the arts that takes into account the inherent inequalities present in the means of production and in so doing, goes beyond these inherent inequalities. What does this mean for art and design practice? It means that one needs to think about how and in what kind of context production takes place, as well as in what way context affects the means of production and the production itself. One needs to think about material use/resources, organizational structure etc.; in other words, one needs to think of every form of energy put into the system and every form of energy taken out of the system.

MK   How do we support a system that sustains an intrinsic value in design— one that supersedes the limits of the 'colonial/modernist/Western' design values? And what do we need to put in place to foster a change in attitudes and systems?

HK More and more often, I think about the disconnect
between production and presentation. Presentation,
to some extent, determines what we produce since it
is an essential part of 'creating value' through being
viewed and/or used. But what if the current COVID-
19 crisis were to be extended into the future (a future
with restricted travel, limits to resources, and an entirely
different world dominated by the online)—how would
this affect how we produce design? What would this
mean for the systems of value that surround design? To
what extent can designers disconnect their production
from presentation and be present (being out in the
world) and still produce? What kind of design schools
would we have then—schools more concerned with
the production of oneself (perhaps personhood/
subjecthood) than with the production of products
(externalities)? The solution for me is to connect the act
of production to the act of living, so that we account
for being able to produce oneself. In that way, one
does not have to externalize oneself but only produce
oneself. Presentation is a form of externalization creating
hierarchies and extracting resources. 317
We need institutions that take into account several key aspects:
overcoming quality and excellence (universal narratives); a
structure for people to be able to create/produce, disconnecting
production from presentation or the valuing of production;
a discourse on how production takes place, the context of
production, adjusting for the inherent inequalities that come
with the control of the means of production; producing people
instead of products.

MK Can you give me an example of what this might look like?

HK At the Jan van Eyck Academie right now, we don't focus
on the 'quality' of the object but rather on the human
being, who the artist or designer is as a human. This
resonates a lot with what you're proposing in this book,
which sees design as a practice of life, about self-building.
We add to that, proposing that you cannot build yourself
without being in relation with the other. So, we take into
account how the production of the self is constituted.

It's about that spot between the practice of art and the art of living (together). This is a totally different approach than making products aimed at market expectations and universal values. This idea of the art and living resonates well with what an art residency can be.

MK How do you gauge the quality of designing the self rather than designing objects?

HK You don't, *you don't*; it's fluid and it's plural. You can't.

MK Should we do away with terms like excellence?

HK We should move away from universalist notions of what constitutes excellence. Art residencies can be exclusive to begin with—the fees to participate, the language gap, and the selection procedure etc. Institutions have been re-producing an exclusive and narrow notion of 'excellence' for years. 'Excellence' is just furthering these power relations.

318 MK I hate to sound repetitive but what do you strive for then in design if it's not excellence?

HK Design then becomes a conversation, an act of practicing ourselves through our senses. You look at the stories, the experiences, and the changes that are part of interacting with the (material) world—shaping it and being shaped by it. We strive towards designing better selves.

MK This could seem extremely self-oriented.

HK Art and design are the practices of changing yourself. And changing yourself is to change the world. Whatever you produce is an extension of yourself. It's an attempt to speak and communicate through the self. There is no self without the other and no other without the self. Communication is in fact an approximation of the changes undergoing in yourself; it's an attempt to understand the world, to be with the world, to understand your desires, fears, or hopes.

MK　How is this connected to something bigger than ourselves or our understanding of the world?

HK　Behind all of these big changes, whether it's climate or questions of justice, there are personal aspirations and desires. This requires work that is sincere and intimate. If you can foster this, then you are able to exact considerable change. In this way, transformative design is not about explicitly addressing externalities but about connecting oneself with others.

MK　You make a compelling case. So what now?

HK　We must learn to practice the art and design of living—no results, no objectives, just allowing yourself to become who you are through an exploration of the material world.

HICHAM KHALIDI (1972, MA) is the director of the Jan van Eyck Academie in Maastricht (NL), which offers residencies to international artists, designers, writers, curators, and architects, and is committed to exploring the agency and roles of art, design, and other creative practices in relation to the climate crisis and its manifold effects. Khalidi previously worked as an associate curator of Lafayette Anticipations in Paris, curated the ACT II group exhibition in the Beirut Sharjah Biennial in 2017, served as a cultural attaché to the Biennale of Sydney in 2016, and was chief curator of the Marrakech Biennale in 2014. He programmed exhibitions and festivals for STUK, Leuven (BE) and was the director of TAG, institute for contemporary art and music in The Hague (NL).

Acknowledgements

We would like to thank all those who directly or indirectly contributed to this book, those who challenged us with their ideas on design, who pushed us to think differently, and who joined us on this journey in one form or another. In particular, we want to thank the many authors who contributed to this book, for sharing their bright minds and inspired practices.

Louise's work, which has been a central inspiration for this book, is rooted in decades of design education. She feels a deep gratitude to the (guest) tutors who were influential in shaping so many of the chapters in this book, in particular: Gijs Assmann, Jan Konings, Gabriel .A. Maher, Tjyying Liu, Jan Konings, Ben Shai van der Wal, Sjeng Scheijen, Erik Viskil, Jesse Howard, Karel Martens, Jennifer Tee, Laura Herman, Noam Toran, Marianne Theunissen, Barbara Visser, Dries Verbruggen, Yvonne Dröge Wendel, Mikel van Gelderen, Hewald Jongenelis, Nadine Botha, Frans Bevers, Maarten Baas, Tamar Shafrir, Guus Beumer, Bogomir Doringer, Jing He, Alexandre Humbert, Martina Muzi, Vincent de Rijk, Ted Noten, Esther de Vries, David Mulder, Barend Koolhaas, Irene Stracuzzi, Anne Hoogewoning, Hans Venhuizen. Thanks are also in place for the people who took care of the indispensable logistics in education, including Hilde Talstra, Ilse Meulendijks, and Judith Konz. On a personal note, Louise would like to thank Rob Schwitters, Vita Sophie Köster, Jan Boelen, Gijs Bakker, Mikel van Gelderen, and Hella Jongerius for their endless support, friendship, critical reflections, and good advice. And last but certainly not least, Louise would like to thank all those fantastic, intelligent, weird, overly sensitive, extremely original students she worked with in various schools, over the course of many years. Not all of their works have landed in these pages, but that doesn't mean they did not contribute to enabling an auto-ethnographic turn in design.

Michael would like to thank the many anthropologists with whom he dialogued in the making of this book, in particular Andrea Gaspar, as well as the design students who pushed him into the uncomfortable fringes of creative production, Peter Lastwin for his troubling intellectual confrontations, Florian Schubert and Elena Suarez who continue to shape his ideas on art, culture, and 'buen vivir,' and finally his friend and mentor Frank Moulaert for imparting the plurality of knowledge, research, and epistemology.

We are extremely grateful to Astrid Vorstermans from Valiz, whose enduring support and guidance has fostered this book from the start, to Liana Simmons for the intensive copy-editing and endless patience, and Irene Stracuzzi for the beautiful visual identity and graphic design. Finally, we thank the Creative Industries Fund NL and we thank Joseph Grima and Raf De Keninck, the directors of Design Academy Eindhoven, for their generous financial contributions to the book.

322

Index of Names

A

B

C

Colophon

EDITORS
Louise Schouwenberg
Michael Kaethler

CONTRIBUTORS
Anna Aagaard Jensen
Gijs Assmann
Bruno Baietto
Jurgen Bey
Joel Blanco
Théophile Blandet
Jan Boelen
Hsin Min Chan
Chongjin Chen
Meghan Clarke
Adelaide Di Nunzio
Billy Ernst
Hi Kyung Eun
Teresa Fernández-Pello
Andrea Gaspar
Konstantin Grcic
Metincan Güzel
Jing He
Aurelie Hoegy
Michael Kaethler
Hicham Khalidi
Žan Kobal
Lorraine Legrand
Gabriel .A. Maher
Micheline Nahra
Thomas Nathan
Miguel Parrrra
Timo de Rijk
Marie Rime
Sjeng Scheijen
Bianca Schick
Louise Schouwenberg
Carlos Sfeir Vottero
Weixiao Shen / 申薇笑
Matilde Stolfa
Irene Stracuzzi
Oli Stratford
Marianne Theunissen
Goda Verikaitė
Erik Viskil
Barbara Visser
Ben Shai van der Wal

EDITING
Liana Simmons

PROOFREADING
Elke Stevens

INDEX
Nic de Jong
Elke Stevens

IMAGE EDITING
the contributors
Louise Schouwenberg
Irene Stracuzzi
Rosie Haward

GRAPHIC DESIGN
Irene Stracuzzi

TYPEFACES
Jannon 10 Pro
Diatype Programm

LITHOGRAPHY
Mariska Bijl, Wilco Art Books

Graphic designer — IRENE STRACUZZI (1992) is a designer and researcher based in Amsterdam, NL. Specializing in graphic design, art direction and information design, she works for and with clients in the fields of art and culture. Her research practice aims at translating complex findings into accessible visual formats, reflecting on the role of design as a critical tool to share knowledge.
www.irenestracuzzi.com

PAPER
Inside: Fedrigoni X-Per 100 gr
Cover: Fedrigoni X-Per 250 gr

PRINTING AND BINDING
Wilco Art Books, Amersfoort

PUBLISHER
Valiz, Amsterdam, 2021
Astrid Vorstermans & Pia Pol
www.valiz.nl

This publication has been printed
on FSC-certified paper by an FSC-
certified printer. The FSC, Forest
Stewardship Council promotes
environmentally appropriate, socially
beneficial, and economically viable
management of the world's forests.
www.fsc.org

334